I FORESEE MY LIFE

I Foresee My Life

My Life

The Ritual Performance
of Autobiography
in an Amazonian Community

Suzanne Oakdale

UNIVERSITY OF NEBRASKA PRESS

LINCOLN AND LONDON

Acknowledgments for the use of
previously published material appear on
page 197, which constitute an extension of the copyright page.

Publication of this book was
assisted by a grant from the
University of New Mexico
College of Arts and Sciences

Library of Congress
Cataloging-in-Publication Data
Oakdale, Suzanne.
I foresee my life : the ritual
performance of autobiography in an
Amazonian community / Suzanne Oakdale.
p. cm.
Includes bibliographical references
and index.
ISBN 0-8032-3578-X (cloth : alk. paper)—
ISBN 0-8032-0513-9 (electronic)
1. Kayabi Indians—Social life and customs.
2. Kayabi Indians—Rites and ceremonies.
3. Kayabi Indians—Biography.   4. Auto-
biography—Brazil—Parque Indígena do
Xingu.   5. Shamans—Brazil—Parque
Indígena do Xingu.   6. Discourse analysis,
Narrative—Brazil—Parque Indígena
do Xingu.   7. Parque Indígena do Xingu
(Brazil)—Social life and customs.   I. Title
F2520.1.K45035 2005
323.1196′073′009046–dc22
2004019554

Set in Quadraat by Kim Essman.
Designed by R. W. Boeche.
Printed by Thomson-Shore, Inc.

For my parents

CONTENTS

ILLUSTRATIONS AND MAP

Photos

Map

PREFACE AND ACKNOWLEDGMENTS

In March 1992 I disembarked from a small plane at one of the posts in the Xingu Indigenous Park, a Brazilian Indian reservation located in the state of Mato Grosso. I had hired the plane and pilot to drop me off in the park, since during the wet season travel by bus to the park over unpaved roads is extremely timely and difficult. I was a student conducting research for my doctoral dissertation in sociocultural anthropology and had arranged by letter and radio contact from the capital city of Brasília to live in a Kayabi village in the Xingu Park, where I would study Kayabi rituals.

The post where we landed, called Diauarum, is the park's northern administrative headquarters. It consists of a small group of wood-and-thatch houses with a few more permanent structures made from cement, all ringed by grass. A group of people—men dressed in shorts and T-shirts, women dressed in homemade dresses, and children each wearing an article of clothing or two—stood in a ring around the plane as we stopped. As I jumped from the plane, a light rain began to fall. While I looked around, wondering who these people were, a tall man, Marcos, accompanied by a smiling woman, his wife, Vera, and a few small children came up and greeted me in Portuguese. "Suzanne, You've come. We've been waiting for you."

They quickly ushered me to one of the houses and fed me a meal of roast fish and *farinha*, a manioc cereal ubiquitous in Brazil. Resting in one of the hammocks as chickens pecked the dirt floor beneath me, I could not take my eyes off of a bright neon blue and purple clock with a silhouette of a palm tree on its face that was hanging on one of the stick walls. Try as I might to focus on my hosts, the clock drew my eyes like a magnet. It so sharply contrasted with its earth-tone surroundings. I followed its black cord down the wall as it disappeared between two of the sticks. Was it plugged in? I watched the hands. Were they moving?

"Are you finished eating?" Marco's voice broke my meditation on the electric cord. "Oh yes, yes," I snapped back to attention. "Let's go then. It's getting late. I don't want to spend one more night here," he said as he packed up with lightening speed, leaving the house in practically a sprint. I and his family ran to catch up. I took one last furtive look at the clock. No, I decided, the hands were most definitely not moving.

As we all boarded the small motorboat for the village, I learned that the family had been waiting for me at the post for several days. I had had to delay my trip and had radioed the Xingu that I would be arriving a few days late. Marcos and Vera had, however, not received the message until after they arrived at Diauarum and were therefore stuck there until I finally appeared, growing ever more uncomfortable as the days passed.

After several more hours of travel on the river, we finally arrived at their village, here called Kapinu'a, the locale where I was going to reside. From the water, the rooftops and semicircular plaza were just barely visible behind the palm and cashew trees standing near the shore. A group of people, turkeys, and dogs was standing on the gentle dirt slope leading into the water in front of the trees. Marcos and Vera informed me, as we traveled on the water, that the village chief, João, would approach the boat and say, "*ere ko ra'e*" (you have arrived), when we pulled to shore. I was to respond, "*jere ko wei*" (I have arrived), before disembarking. After I repeated my lines to Chief João, as I had practiced them, the group on shore responded with a few giggles. As I stepped out of the boat, Chief João shook my hand and greeted me in Portuguese a second time.

Because I have come to know the residents of Kapinu'a best, their lives are the focus of this book. Residents of other villages and hamlets from downriver, such as the "great shaman" Monkey-Leg, are also important in the lives of many living in Kapinu'a, and they are included as well.

It is to the residents of Kapinu'a that I owe the most gratitude for treating me with kindness, generosity, and, above all, humor. Chief João and his wife, Pretty, hosted me in a partitioned corner of their house for my stay in 1992. When I came back for a few months in 1993, they let me live in their empty house while they were away from the village. Much of the time, João also operated as a sort of research advisor. When he thought my research was lagging a bit, he announced, "I want you to do a census." Drawing on his experience with other anthropologists in the park, he took me to each of the households in the village and requested that I write down each person's name and how they were related to each other. I owe João and Pretty many thanks for their hospitality and guidance.

As soon as I arrived in the village, João arranged for the Kayabi men who taught in the Brazilian-style school to teach me Kayabi for several hours each day. In exchange I was to teach them arithmetic. I am above all thankful to these teachers, Bird and Fire-of-the-Gods, for dedicating so much of their time to this arduous task and for sitting through many hours of arithmetic lessons. After about six months of these lessons, it was revealed to me that the lessons where mainly intended to help *me* feel as though I had something to offer *them*. Bird and Fire-of-the-Gods helped me transcribe many tapes, explained the many aspects of Kayabi life to me, and, above all, were good

x

friends. My understanding of Kayabi life and ritual would not have been the same without their instruction. I also owe a special thanks to Stone-Arm and his family (including his son and daughter-in-law, Marcos and Vera) for their care and concern during my stay in their village. I hope all Kayabi people will understand and excuse me for giving them and their village pseudonyms, for translating their names into English, or for referring to them by names that they long ago gave away.

Because I spent long hours in the schoolhouse transcribing tapes, I never really participated in the quotidian rhythm of the day for any stretch of time. As a result, some villagers had a hard time figuring out how I fit within familiar categories. While I was taught to use the female versions of third-person pronounces and the appropriate vocatives used by women, I also spoke Portuguese the majority of the time. Given that mostly only men speak Portuguese, this meant that I conversed with men much more than with women. Because I have blond hair, many of the people I knew less well also seemed to find my age a bit of a mystery. More than once I was addressed as "old woman." When I arrived in the Xingu I was twenty-nine years old.

It was as a graduate student at the University of Chicago that I first became interested in anthropology and the Amazon. An undergraduate class with Mackim Marriott first opened my eyes to the fact that other peoples had other ways of conceptualizing what "a self" or "a person" might be. It was Terry Turner's research on the Kayapó, who live just to the north of the Kayabi, that finally helped me decide to go to Brazil when I enrolled as a graduate student a few years later. I am especially thankful for his support and guidance over the course of many years as my dissertation advisor.

In my third year of graduate school I had the chance to work as a graduate assistant on a project headed by Waud Kracke of the University of Illinois at Chicago Circle and José Carlos Levinho of the Fundação Nacional dos Índios among the Kagwahiv in Amazonas, Brazil. Eager to find out just how one "did fieldwork," I quickly signed on. Although I did not know it at the time, my parents, who lived in the Chicago suburbs, wanted to meet with Waud before I trooped off into the jungles with him. Not mentioning a word to me, they arranged a lunch with him and read his book. Luckily for all of us, they liked his sensitivity and psychological training.

The shock of fieldwork in the Amazon was softened for me by Waud. I learned practical things such as the kinds of foods to take and the need to always have a mosquito net. I also learned more subtle interactional queues that only someone trained in psychoanalysis, like Waud, could have taught me. Participating in research in a Kagwahiv community and talking with Waud and

Levinho in many wonderful conversations upon returning from the field also directed my interest to research on Tupian-speaking peoples.

As luck would have it, a Brazilian Tupian specialist, Eduardo Viveiros de Castro of the Museu Nacional in Rio, came to the University of Chicago the year I came back to graduate school. Eduardo became my Brazilian sponsor and gave me a general intellectual orientation to things Tupian. For both I am grateful. Elsewhere in Brazil a special thanks goes to Helga Weiss of the Summer Institute of Linguistics (SIL) in Brasília for her generosity and instruction in the Kayabi language. I am grateful also to the staff at the Fundação Nacional do Índio (FUNAI) and Centro Ecumênico de Documentação e Informação (CEDI) libraries in Brasília and at the Museu do Índio in Rio.

I am grateful to several institutions for funding my research. During 1991–92 my fieldwork was funded by a predoctoral grant from the Fulbright Institute of International Education (IIE) Commission and during 1992–93 by a predoctoral grant from the Wenner-Gren Foundation (no. 5372). A travel grant from the Center for Latin-American Studies at the University of Chicago also contributed to my 1993 fieldwork. A Scholar Award from the P.E.O. Sisterhood aided my dissertation writing. Archival research in Brasília and Rio in 2001 was funded by a Research Allocations Committee Grant and a Latin American and Iberian Institute Field Research Grant from the University of New Mexico.

This book, in its various forms, has benefited from the comments and suggestions of many. In addition to those previously mentioned, other faculty at the University of Chicago, in particular Ray Fogelson, Michael Silverstein, Manuela Carneiro da Cunha, and Nancy Munn, were influential in shaping my thinking and offered comments on this work in previous forms. Conversations with my colleagues in the Anthropology Department at the University of New Mexico have also helped shape this book. Special thanks, however, go to Marta Weigle and Keith Basso for reading drafts of this manuscript. Thanks also go to two student research assistants, Miya King and Joseph Feurstein, for their contributions. My thinking on the material presented here has been shaped in immeasurable ways by the formal and informal comments of friends and colleagues, such as Richard Bauman, Thomas Biolsi, Michael Brown, Judy Boruchoff, Beth Conklin, Ray DeMallie, Marco Antonio Gonçalves, Laura Graham, Carol Greenhouse, Ken Kensinger, Patricia Lyon, Robert Moore, Dale Pesmen, Michael Scott, and Stanton Wortham, as well as by anonymous reviewers for the University of Nebraska Press. I am also grateful to the participants in the 1996 Annual South American Indian Conference at Bennington College and the 2002 and 2004 meetings of the Society of the Anthropology of Lowland South America.

To my family I owe the most thanks. My parents and sister in particular have been unfailingly supportive. I am especially grateful to my husband, David Dinwoodie, for numerous readings of my work and unending philosophical conversation. Finally, I thank our two daughters for giving me new perspectives on the world.

NOTE ON TRANSLATION,
TRANSCRIPTION, AND ORTHOGRAPHY

I recorded all the narratives featured in this book. I then replayed the tapes for either one or sometimes two of the men who were assigned by the village chief to teach me Kayabi. One of them then repeated the Kayabi for me very slowly so that I could write it down. Next, either one or both of them gave me a line-by-line translation into Portuguese. A few hours of tape would therefore take many days to transcribe and translate, especially if, as often happened, they took time to explain references to Kayabi cosmology, kinship, myth, ritual, and so forth. From memory, we would all try to reconstruct the gestures of the narrator as we listened to the tapes. In most cases I was also able to go back and ask narrators about aspects of their performances. Much later, only after I left the field, I was able to work closely with the linguistic material produced by SIL (Dobson 1988) on Kayabi to better understand the transcripts. Finally, I translated the texts that appear in this book into English. I have tried to maintain some of the stylistic features of these narratives, given the constraint of also trying to make the texts readable and engaging. I have, for example, preserved repetitions (Tedlock 1981) or, at least in some of the longer songs, indicted which lines were repeated or where a choral refrain was sung. Key gestures, pauses, and changes in volume are also noted—though each of these features is not signaled in every narrative. Rather, I only represent these features when they are important for making a larger point about how the narrator is relating to his audience (see Sammons and Sherzer 2000, xvi; Sherzer and Urban 1986, 11–12). Because I make different points about each ritual genre, the texts in the three genres I discuss here are each presented in very different ways.

In transcribing the Kayabi language I adopted the orthography developed by the SIL missionary-linguists who worked in Kayabi communities. This system is used by some Kayabi, including education monitors residing in the village where most of my research took place. According to SIL orthography, a tilde (~) denotes a nasalized vowel or consonant. A single apostrophe denotes a glottal stop. A y is used for i, a sound that can be approximated by English speakers by making the vowel sound found in the word look while pulling one's lips back into a partial smiling position. A is pronounced as the a in the word park; e as the e in the word egg; i as the vowel sound in the word feet; o approximately as the o in the word north; and u as the ue in the word pursue. SIL also uses j to represent both j and dj—sounds similar to the y in the word yes or, in the case of dj, similar to how an English speaker would pronounce the y of *yes* if preceded by the *d* of *dog*. The consonants *f*, *k*, *m*, *n*, *p*, *r*, *s*, *t*, and *w* are pronounced as they are in English.

I have made a few slight changes in SIL orthography to simplify the process of presenting texts and to maintain certain consistencies in the literature. For example, I use *ng* where SIL orthography uses *g* to stand for *ñ*. This is pronounced as the *ng* in the word *sing*. I also use the spelling "Kayabi" rather than "Kajabi" or "Kaiabi." Although, according to the orthography I use here, the spelling should be either "Kajabi" or "Kaiabi" (depending on the pronunciation), I use "Kayabi" to be consistent with the spelling usually found in the ethnographic literature (including that produced by SIL).

I FORESEE MY LIFE

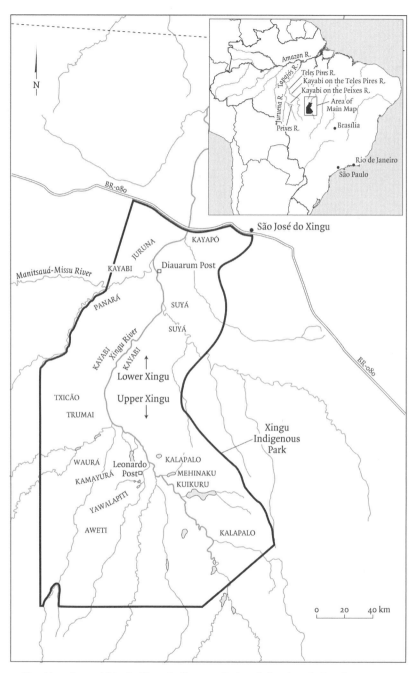

Kayabi territory within the Xingu Indigenous Park and elsewhere in Brazil, ca. 1992

INTRODUCTION

Late in the afternoon of March 5, 1992, the day after I first arrived in the village of Kapinu'a, one of the most renowned shamans among the Xinguan Kayabi, called Stone-Arm, began to sing, accompanied by a chorus of the village men. The Kayabi are a Tupi-speaking indigenous people, many of whom have moved into the multiethnic Xingu Indigenous Park reserve from other locales. Stone-Arm, others told me, was singing about his dreams. They said his song was a signal that he was beginning to perform a cure for a patient—his young grandson, who had gone with his mother and father, Marcos and Vera, to the park's northern administrative post to greet and accompany me back to the village. While at the post, Stone-Arm's grandson had fallen ill. Posts have large numbers of goods from Brazilians, such as machines, radios, clothes, and salt, all of which carry a debilitating smell. While I was thinking about how my arrival had contributed to the boy's sickness, my hosts urged me to go to his house to listen to and record the cure. Seeing many other people walk over to his thatch-roofed house, I took their advice, gathered my tape recorder and microphone, and made my way there. I tried to make myself look as inconspicuous as possible with my equipment by sitting on the dirt floor against a stick wall next to several others who were there to listen to the cure. Not long after I had arranged myself, however, a wooden bench was brought in, and, much to my chagrin, Stone-Arm beckoned me to sit in the very center of the group, just a few feet away from him, his chorus, and his patient. After a few minutes, Stone-Arm stopped singing and began to tell a story in Kayabi about his career as a shaman. With great dramatic flair he pointed out small scars on his arms and thighs as proof of how he had fought with different malevolent spirits in the past.

One of the most striking aspects of Stone-Arm's performance (which I learned later, after my tapes of his performance were translated into Portuguese) was how he made reference to vastly different kinds of powers and relationships over the course of his autobiographical narrative. He spoke about how to address ancient Kayabi spirit beings, understood to have been created during previous cosmological epochs, as well as how to interact with me, the newly arrived foreign researcher.[1] Through his narrative about himself as a shaman, Stone-Arm encouraged others to feel a connection to me, to become my teachers, and to explain aspects of Kayabi belief to me. This was, of course, after he issued a diagnosis of his grandson's illness that called attention to just how dangerous the world from which I came could be.

1. Stone-Arm showing the tattoos that correspond to some of his names.

Stone-Arm created a connection between myself and others through a masterful use of quoted speech that framed and commented on his autobiographical account. His quoted speech gave the impression that he had taken on the subjective perspective of different kinds of audience members. For example, after describing how he first became a shaman and began to dream about various spirits that inhabit the Kayabi cosmos, he commented on his own performance from the perspective of different types of audience members. Assuming the position of those skeptical of shamanism, he said, " 'He lied about his life,' you all say among yourselves." Then, looking at me, he said, " 'After writing and recording sitting down, I'll bring this to my country to show,' she is saying." Next he reported the future speech of people who would (or should) be casually talking about the performance with me, " 'Like this the shaman sings music. After this shaman dies there will be no one as powerful for us,' you all say to her." He then paraphrased his own story about how he became shamanically empowered from the point of view of the two men whom the village chief, João, had just appointed to teach me the Kayabi language. Turning to these two men he suggested exactly how they should explain his performance. " 'He is seeing one of the spirits called Mait because the sloth spirit pierced a hole in his thigh. There is an eagle spirit underwater in the deep, but the Mait are things that come from the sky above us. His deceased grandfather showed this to him, enabled him to see the Mait,' you all say to her." As he spoke we all became subjectively aligned through our orientation to his autobiographical account. In conclusion he announced, "Thus, I foresee my life."

This book is about the ritual performances of the Kayabi living in the Xingu Indigenous Park in the early 1990s. These performances show leaders' foresight, confidence, and ability to enlist support for their community at a time when aspects of their lives are changing rapidly. I focus on the autobiographical performances, such as that of Stone-Arm, that are embedded within these events. I examine autobiographical performances in the context of political oratory, shamanic cures, and mortuary rites.

This study fits within a general trend in anthropology to connect ritual to history. As the authors of a recent review of the study of ritual have pointed out, while much scholarship has treated rituals only as "*types* of events," "[i]t is the possibility that rituals are historical events that now intrigues many anthropologists," with Michael Taussig (1980) and David Lan (1985) being two examples among others (Kelly and Kaplan 1990, 120). The tension between ritual as a type of event and ritual as a historical event is particularly apparent in the autobiographical portions of Kayabi rituals. Leaders use well-established ritual forms for talking about their own historical, lived experiences such as their relocation to a national reservation, their experiences with government policies, or the growing consumption of commodities. Moreover, the events that leaders narrate also involve scenarios that others use in thinking about how to behave with respect to other contemporary situations. While not all individuals who aspire to leadership positions are skilled narrators, the most successful are able to intuit how parts of their autobiographies apply to contemporary circumstances; to create believable personas within the context of specific ritual genres; and to tie the roles, identities, and values of characters in their narratives to the roles, identities, and values of people in the ongoing ritual event. Their autobiographical narratives work together with the standard formal dimensions of the rituals to encourage various participants to identify with the narrator as well as others over the course of the event. These kinds of identifications, in turn, encourage ritual participants to evaluate contemporary issues in their own lives in various ways. These performances illustrate the historicity of ritual or, in other words, the "cultural schema and subjective attitudes" that make other times and places currently meaningful for Kayabi (Whitehead 2003, xi, xii).

A focus on the autobiographic narratives embedded in ritual events suggests a new way of doing life historical research. Using specific ritual events as starting points rather than eliciting life histories in the context of ethnographic interviews leads to an appreciation of culturally specific forms of autobiographical narrative. Indigenous genres then become privileged windows on culturally specific notions of self and person. I am interested in the nature of how (or the extent to which) the human being is conceptualized by Kayabi as a center of experience (a self) and as "a somebody" who authors conduct (a person) (Harris 1989).[2]

Much conventional life history research assumes, following modern Western notions of self and person, that the experiences narrated in a legitimate life history are unique to the narrator. Kayabi-specific forms of autobiography embedded in ritual events, however, give a glimpse of how, in this cultural tradition, accounts of experiences also circulate among people. Eduardo Viveiros de Castro (1992, 2001) has formulated an Amazonian structure of the person that is marked by a continual process of "Other-becoming" rather than "being." In the events I focus on in this study, accounts of experiences, and the experiences themselves in some senses, circulate in a way that is consistent with his formulation. Narrators (and audience members) are involved in a process of identification with the experiences of others, including members of other ethnic groups, spirits, and deceased individuals. For example, in some cases narrators frame their accounts as repetitions of what others have experienced. At other times, while not framing them as such, the stories are a repetition of another's account.

Bakhtin's observations about language in general that it "lies on the borderline between oneself and the other" and that the word "is half someone else's" (1987, 293) apply nicely to these autobiographical accounts. The narratives performed in these events all emphasize the extent to which they are dialogic. As narrators talk about their own experiences, they very self-consciously orchestrate others' conversations, songs, and inner speech, many of which provide radically "other" perspectives and points of view. As a result—much as Ellen Basso has described for the biographical narratives told by the Kayabi's

Carib-speaking neighbors, the Kalapalo—these narratives do not provide a picture of the self as a coherent, unified entity (1995, 294).

Looking closely at how autobiographical accounts are situated within ritual events also provides a glimpse of the role these kinds of narrative performances play in ongoing social life or, in other words, of what these kinds of accounts "do" for ritual participants. [3] In a general way, the Kayabi rituals discussed here are vehicles for leaders to direct their followers on how to live. At some level what they "do" is give participants a sense of power or ability to face life's challenges, a sense of "agency" in the language of those influenced by practice theory. [4] From a Kayabi perspective, oratory generally involves counseling followers on the correct or most empowering way to behave; cures involve moving from a state of sickness to health; and mortuary rituals involve moving from the debilitating sadness of mourning to a sense of strength and well-being. The particular ritual events I discuss accomplish these general tasks by addressing the changes and issues characteristic of the 1990s. A focus on these events leads away from conceptualizing agency as strictly a property of an individual who can disassociate himself or herself from others and toward a more Amazonian (see Pollock 1996) understanding that the ability to act comes from certain kinds of interpersonal involvements.

Approach to Ritual

Some of the events I focus on, such as Stone-Arm's performance, fit easily with the kinds of happenings anthropologists usually treat as rituals, but other events I write about are less set off from everyday life, are less stylized, and produce less profound transformations. These events have what could be called ritualized dimensions. [5] Following several others, I understand ritualization to be present to some degree in any event but also that some events are more ritualized than others. [6] Kayabi shamanic cures and festivals to end mourning, called Jawosi, fit most easily with stereotypical notions of ritual. [7] Almost everyone in a local group interrupts their daily routine to participate in these events. Shamanic cures and Jawosi also both involve several days of singing. Music, as Ellen Basso (2001) points out, is generally associated with a powerful type of communication and creative transformation in Amazonia. [8] Kayabi oratorical practices are, on the other hand, less set apart from everyday activities. Kayabi individuals do, however, talk about all these kinds of events as different from other moments, as times of intense perceptions or concentration, and as moments that do effect changes for those involved.

All three of these kinds of events are currently a vital part of the Xinguan Kayabis' lives. While individuals may criticize how these events are performed or question whether a practitioner has the appropriate authority to undertake the event, these types of events are understood in general to be efficacious by both young and old. In fact, while some Kayabi rituals have ceased to be performed, shamanic cures and Jawosi are performed to a greater extent in the Xingu now than they were in past decades outside the park (Grünberg n.d. [1970]; Travassos 1984). The park context has increased ritual participation for several reasons. In the park, practices understood to be "traditional" are encouraged rather than discouraged, as they were outside of the park. Population is also on the rise, and local groups possess enough economic and emotional resources to devote their energy to these kinds of activities. Whether this kind of intense ritual participation will continue, especially if the Xinguan Kayabi's situation were to change, is unforeseeable. The kind of ritual life that I am describing is, therefore, historically and locally specific.

Following a "performative approach" to ritual, I ask the audience members what they understand each ritual performance to be doing and look at the semiotic means by which the performances (particularly the verbal portions) get these tasks accomplished (Tambiah 1985). [9] I am attentive to both the more fixed meanings of ritual symbolism as well as the ways in which rituals are linked to the status claims and problems of particular participants. As I understand these kinds of performances to orient people toward their present circumstances, each ritual event is understood as sensitive to the contemporary political economic changes the Xinguan Kayabi face. [10]

While autobiographical accounts might be considered "personal" or a subjective aspect of rituals, "the personal" and ritual are combined in a way that is distinct from the way these two topics have been brought together in more psychologically oriented discussions of ritual, such as those focusing on the personal significance of ritual symbols or on the interpretation of rituals through the lens of an individual's own predicaments. [11] I am interested in questioning the way ritual processes provide "models of and for" Kayabi persons and selves as well as generate and circulate perspectives on contemporary issues (Geertz 1973). How, for example, does the autobiography of the narrator become a model or way to organize other participants' autobiographic details in the face of contemporary challenges? How does the narrator give his audience access to new kinds of experiences or social relationships through his performance? How does the narrator incorporate others' concerns, aspirations, or experiences into his performance?

In these Kayabi rituals, personal experience is not expressed only to be purged or normalized, as in African traditions of confession, for example (Turner [1967] 1982, 50). Rather, leaders' first-person accounts offer a series

6

of relational identities, roles, interests, and moralities that are mapped onto and come to be inhabited by other participants. When leaders narrate their experiences, people at the storytelling events become aligned in shifting ways with the characters featured in the narrated events. [12] Kenneth Burke's use of the term *identification* to describe the way speakers or writers involve their audience members in a kind of "consubstantiality" or the sharing of "common sensations, concepts, images, ideas, [and] attitudes" (1953, 21) with the characters they present is suggestive of the dimension of performances with which I am concerned. [13] The dual presence of the narrators in the storytelling event and the story itself offers the possibility of encouraging listeners to feel a very powerful sense of engagement with the characters, even those who inhabit a very different world from their own, such as, in the case of shamanic narratives, the world of spirits or the newly arrived anthropologist. Leaders use these alignments to persuade and move people in various ways.

By focusing on the moments of identification between different subjects, this work builds upon research concerning the social construction of self and person that highlights the ways identities shift or are differentially deployed in various contexts rather than research that focuses on identity in the sense of a continuity of self over time. [14] I do not, however, make any claims that a sense of identity or continuity over the lifetime for Kayabi individuals is lacking—that, for example, they necessarily live a postmodern existence. Rather, I focus on how interpersonal identifications play a part in the creation of persons who feel they have the strength to act in the world.

Because Kayabi people do not all have exactly the same ideas about how to have power and strength in the present, I emphasize the distinct perspectives expressed by different types of leaders in different ritual contexts. For example, I focus on the accounts of a young, new-style village chief and a senior, traditional family headman in moments of political oratory. I also look at how a senior religious leader narrates his life in a shamanic cure as well as how senior family headmen sing about their experiences in Jawosi. Elderly shamans, young reservation village chiefs, and older family headmen all encourage different types of interpersonal involvement or alignment in the different ritual events they control. Through their autobiographical performances, they present distinct perspectives about how strength is achieved. While shamans, in cures, stress identification across generations, both living and deceased, leaders, in their political oratory, encourage a break from past generations, and senior family headmen, in mortuary rituals, encourage an identification among the living but a distance from the dead.

By highlighting the differences between leaders' performances, this ethnography is an attempt to portray the texture of intracultural variability and contradiction. In this respect, it follows recent calls for attention to heterogeneity in the representation of cultural worlds. [15] To avoid presenting homogeneity all over again at a lower level by creating such homogeneous subsets as "shamans," "seniors," or "youths," I have tried to show how people can also shift perspectives in different contexts. Because the Kayabi leaders featured in large-scale community ritual events are male, I have been limited to focusing on how men inhabit these different perspectives. Yet women play important roles in these ritual events as well and are key characters in the narratives that male leaders tell. They are, therefore, a significant, if more silent, presence in this book.

Approach to Autobiographical Narration

One way to clarify the approach I take to Kayabi leaders' autobiographical accounts is to contrast it with the different ways that similar types of material, which are called more generally "personal documents," have been treated in anthropology. [16] Narratives concerning personal experiences have long been used as a means of obtaining or presenting data on a variety of subjects. [17] Since the early years of anthropology, personal documents have been seen as the means through which an anthropologist can get an "inside view" or a "direct experience" of a culture (Radin 1920, 1, 2). They have also been used to find or present generalizations about a culture (Dollard 1935; Shostak 1981), personality in a cultural context (DuBois 1944), cultural transmission (Kluckhohn 1939), culture change (Mintz 1960), and a view of postmodern society (Fischer 1986). The approach followed here shifts the focus from the usefulness of autobiographical narratives as a medium of gathering and presenting data to an emphasis on the construction and circulation of autobiographical narratives.

In keeping with my focus on the performance of these accounts, I have also steered away from issues of accuracy—for example, questioning the extent to which leaders' accounts faithfully represent the past or the extent to which leaders are typical Kayabi and accurately represent Kayabi culture, unless of course this is a concern for other Kayabi audience members. [18] Rather than worrying about the extent to which individual leaders' accounts are accurate representations of events or a culture, I link their accounts to the nonnarrative or "real world" in a different way and ask how these accounts encourage a sense of agency and a course of action for people at the moment in which they are narrated.

The accounts presented here are neither elicited nor edited to create a unique life story. I therefore use the term *autobiographical narrative* to refer to the kind of personal documents discussed here rather than the term *life history*. Much as elsewhere in the lowlands (Basso 1995; Hendricks 1993) these kinds of narratives have an episodic quality. They do not necessarily refer to the "whole life" of the narrator. A focus on when and how Kayabi leaders give accounts of their experiences addresses one of the most frequent criticisms of "life history" research—that it artificially projects a Western consciousness onto other cultural forms. Arnold Krupat (1985, 1992, 1994) and David Brumble (1988) make this point when they call attention to the influence of Western literary genres in the telling, editing, and reading of Native American autobiographies. Pierre Bourdieu (1987) explicitly expresses this criticism when he argues that one of the main problems with life history research is that it assumes that life is a history with a coherent linear development that is the expression of a subjective intention and project. [19] By looking at self-representation in context, as part of ritual events, this study avoids some of these problems.

Several recent works have insightfully focused on the forms in which Native Americans have traditionally presented experiences, such as coup tales, vision stories, and pictographs, as well as pointing to the traces of these indigenous genres in elicited life histories and autobiographies produced collaboratively with others. [20] Generally speaking, these works have been concerned with genre in the formal sense, as a set of themes, features, or a structure characterizing a text. Following performance-oriented or discourse-centered approaches, I use a Bakhtinian sense of genre. [21] I am interested in speech that is connected to social life, oriented to specific audiences, and associated with social groups defined by features such as age, gender, and occupation—in other words, language that "takes a position between people organized in some way" (Bakhtin and Medvedev 1978, 131). [22]

Several recent works, in a variety of disciplines, that focus on discourse have looked specifically at autobiographical practices as they are connected to the sociology of their performance contexts. Recent research in child development, education, and sociolinguistics has concentrated on narrative self-representation as it emerges within moments of everyday discourse, such as that found in interactions between children and caregivers, in the classroom, and around the dinner table. [23] Ethnographic research in lowland South America has also been attentive to some of the ways similar kinds of self-representation are linked to the social interaction of particular kinds of events. For example, Ellen Basso looks at how new attributes of Kalapalo selves are asserted in storytelling (1985) and how a leader's testimony is a commentary on contemporary leadership (1995); Laura Graham (1995) examines how an elder's dreams, performed by a Xavante community, link those involved with mythic characters; Janet Hendricks (1993) looks at how a Shuar warrior's autobiographical narrative is used to perpetuate his legend; and Greg Urban (1989) looks at the management of selves in Shokleng mythic discourse. All these works emphasize the importance of the formal dimensions of language, aspects such as parallelism, repetition, volume, gesture, and the structures of participation, including the co-construction of autobiographical narratives. Building on this research, this study is attentive to many of these dimensions. They are, however, taken into consideration only to the extent that they contribute to an understanding of how interpersonal identifications take place in ritual events.

Works that explicitly focus on how an autobiographical narrative is linked to the shifting relationship between an interviewer and a narrator, such as Vincent Crapanzano's Tuhami (1980), have been some of the first to point out that the anthropologist needs to be recognized as a participant in these kinds of encounters. While I did not elicit the accounts that follow, nor were the rituals explicitly staged solely for my benefit, I was, of course, a part of the event in each case. In some rituals, such as Stone-Arm's cure that coincided with my arrival, I was directly addressed as a researcher and ushered into the center of the action with my tape recorder in hand. In these situations my identity as an anthropologist was pronounced. At other times, particularly as time passed, other identities were more significant. Throughout, I have tried to be attentive to how narrators situate me with respect to various identities and identifications over the course of their performances.

Works on autobiographical narrative often focus on one individual narrator. Just as they have been used to gather data on culture, autobiographical narratives have also been used throughout twentieth-century anthropology to gain access to the individual. Clyde Kluckhohn, for example, views life histories as offering a picture of "the individual as an idiosyncratic member" of a group (1945, 138). Lawrence Watson and Maria-Barbara Watson-Franke (1985), drawing on existentialism and phenomenology, see them as revealing a unique individual subjectivity and consciousness within a sociocultural context. More recently, in lowland South America the life history format has been used to reveal an "individual's subjective point of view" through a focus on the artistry and formal dimensions of the language in which it was told (Hendricks 1993, 28) and the struggle of an individual within his own and a nationally dominant culture (Rubenstein 2002). In my own reading of life histories and autobiographies, I have always found the strong sense of particular personalities to be engaging, and I hope that some of this texture is apparent here despite the fact that I do not focus on one narrator. Following others' insights about Amazonian conceptualizations of the person, I am interested in not only how these kinds of accounts are connected to specific narrators but how they are linked to other people as well, in both their construction and their circulation.[24]

Outline of Chapters

The chapters that follow are divided into three parts. Part 1 presents the historical background necessary for understanding the Xinguan Kayabi's situation in the 1990s. I focus on significant changes in their lives and the problems and issues they currently face. Part 2 is devoted to particular autobiographical performances in political addresses, cures, and Jawosi rituals. Part 3 addresses the ways in which the autobiographical genres are related to each other and explores their dialogic nature, specifically, how they orchestrate "others'" voices.

Contemporary Issues and Changes in Kayabi Life

THE PERILS OF LIVING IN THE
XINGU INDIGENOUS PARK

Here in the Xingu, we are fostering culture.

CHIEF JOÃO, 1992

In the afternoon heat one day in April 1992, men and women began to prepare to sing in Jawosi style in Kapinu'a village—the men were being painted with charcoal and red *annatto* body paint and the women with black *genipap* dye. Jawosi singing can be done for many reasons, including to greet a visitor, to celebrate a hunting party's return, or to help mourners forget their grief. It has also become a preferred way to display what is distinctively Kayabi, what some more cosmopolitan park residents would label "Kayabi culture." On this afternoon, people were gathered near the largest and only traditional-style (that is, rectangular) wood-and-thatch house in the village. This house was owned by Chest, the young village chief's father, and was the location where most of the singing would later take place. As I approached the house I could hear the young chief, João, and a few other young men discussing in Portuguese whether the Kayabi still had their culture, or *cultura*. As someone interested in the concept of culture I was curious to hear what they might say. Having established a routine of tape-recording and photographing events such as this one, I was outfitted with my camera and tape recorder. When they saw me approach, several of the adult men whose songs are featured during Jawosi immediately asked me to take their pictures. One was Zé, a man who had recently relocated to the park from the state of Pará. Clad in a T-shirt and shorts, he was holding one of his arrows, beautifully fletched in a distinctive Kayabi style. (Arrows are often used metaphorically to stand for one's relatives in the texts of Jawosi songs.) As I focused my camera on Zé, Stone-Arm's back and curly hair suddenly appeared directly in front of my lens. After issuing directives in Kayabi, he explained in Portuguese that this event was to be "pure Indian" and that if people were to have their pictures taken during this festival they would have to take off their Western clothing. He explained that if they wore clothing they would not look like Indians. Stone-Arm insisted that Zé in particular take off his T-shirt, though he finally conceded that Zé could keep his shorts on. Zé, standing patiently in front of my camera, dutifully took his shirt off and hid it behind his back for the photo, tucking it into the waist of his shorts.

Thankful that the situation had been resolved so quickly and eager to return to the discussion about culture, I snapped Zé's photo as well as those of several others. Much to my dismay, however, the group discussing culture had disappeared. With some time remaining before the singing started, I decided to take a bath in the river to cool off. Returning to Chief João's house for my soap and towel I realized that the action had shifted from Chest's house to João's. Upon entering I saw that several women and men were gathered there talking. Senior women were painting designs on some of the younger women's faces and upper bodies with black *genipap* dye, which stains the skin for several months. After a few moments, one woman suggested that I too should be painted for the festival. Fire-of-the-Gods, one of the young men who was working as a teacher in the Brazilian-style school run by the residents of Kapinu'a and who was helping me transcribe my tapes, added that I should not be allowed to wear Western clothing either. After some negotiation, it was decided that I would be painted, but that I could wear as much (or as little) clothing as the other women participating. On this decision, Fire-of-the-Gods humorously commented that other anthropologists who studied in other communities in the Xingu Park all went without clothing and that if I too were "studying culture" I could at least do what other researchers had done. As all Kayabi adults wore some form of Western clothing during this Jawosi, I could not help but think to myself that, if I really did attend wearing only body paint, I would have been one of the most "cultured" people present.

The Xingu Indigenous Park, where many Kayabi live, is a celebrated national reservation. It is a location where talk about culture and concern about cultural distinctiveness have been present for many decades. Officially petitioned in 1952 and legally declared in 1961, the park was set up to protect its residents from the harmful effects of the national society (Davis 1980, 50, 52). It is the home of several indigenous groups who have been living in an interethnic community for many centuries as well as of peoples who have recently relocated to the area. Most of the groups who are indigenous to the area live in the southern part of the park, in an area called the Upper Xingu.[1] Upper Xinguans have long had the reputation of practicing their traditional ways of life in relatively unchanged fashion. Those who live in the northern part of the park, the Lower Xingu, such as the Kayabi, are outsiders to this community. Many were, in fact, traditionally enemies of the Upper Xinguans.[2]

With the exception of the Eastern Suyá and the Juruna, many of these people are also newcomers. In the early 1990s the recently relocated groups included the Kayabi, the Western Suyá, the Panará (Kren Akróre), and a portion of the Northern Kayapó.[3]

Kayabi families have been moving into the Lower Xingu since the early 1950s from territories located to the west of the park. In these areas they lived and worked with rubber tappers, ranchers, and miners. In these locales the assimilation of native peoples was, and to some extent still is, encouraged in contrast to the protection of and emphasis on cultural difference present in the Xingu Park. The majority of Xinguan Kayabi adults have, therefore, resided in two very different kinds of national spaces and have had to deal with very different facets of Brazilian Indian identity. Outside the park Indian identity has had a pejorative connotation: it implied being outside the progress shared by the rest of the national society. Kayabi ways of life and dress were something to hide or ideally to shed. Within the park, while still having the connotations of being outside of time, Indianness has the positive associations with purity. Cultural distinctiveness and talk about "culture" are rewarded and encouraged. In the park it is nonindigenous customs, such as Zé's T-shirt, that are to be hid or shed.

Both outside as well as within the park, Kayabi people have shown a pattern of engaging with their neighbors and of openness to other customs. This orientation toward various others in combination with their move from areas where assimilation was encouraged places Kayabi people residing in the park in an unusual position. Much as the comments of Stone-Arm and others show, many have a concern with the extent to which they have "culture" in the park. Negotiating where the Kayabi fit with respect to Xinguan "Indian identity" and "having culture" are problems that all Kayabi, but especially Xinguan Kayabi political leaders, must address and negotiate.

The Xinguan Kayabi

At the time of my research, the majority of the Kayabi (536 persons) lived within the Xingu Indigenous Park.[4] Most families lived and continue to live along the Xingu River and one of its tributaries, the Manitsauá-Missu. Entering the park from the most northernly guard post, located where Highway BR-080 cuts through the park, and taking a motorboat up the Xingu, a traveler can see Kayabi hamlets and villages along the shore. After passing a large Juruna settlement, one sees the thatched roofs of a few independent Kayabi homesteads behind the vegetation along the bank. Hours later, one of the largest Kayabi villages appears. It is a square cluster of wood-and-thatch houses around a clean and expansive plaza. Next, the park post of Diauarum is visible. Residents from the northern part of the park staff the post. In the 1990s, Kayabi men as well as men from the two groups who have resided in the Lower Xingu for centuries, the Suyá and Juruna, occupied these positions. In the 1990s post personnel, their families, and one nonindigenous nurse lived year-round in the post's wood-and-thatch houses. Planes, like the one that initially brought me to the Xingu, can land on the dirt airstrip at this post.

After leaving the post and passing more small hamlets, one arrives at the village of Kapinu'a, which is populated mainly by people who came from the lower and upper Teles Pires River areas (located to the west of the park). They came to the Xingu with other Kayabi families in response to pressure from rubber tappers, ranchers, loggers, and miners in their areas with the help and urging of the park's founders, Orlando, Cláudio, and Leonardo Villas Boas. While not all Kayabi families chose to move, the majority did in fact relocate. The first Kayabi families came in the 1950s from the upper Teles Pires River area in the state of Mato Grosso. [5] Later, in 1966, more families came from the Peixes River area—a tributary of the Arinos River situated to the west of the Teles Pires. In 1966, the 1970s, and the early 1990s, other families and individuals, such as Zé, came from a third area: the lower Teles Pires in the state of Pará. [6]

From Assimilation to Protection

The park sharply contrasts with the areas where the Xinguan Kayabi previously lived, areas in which the standard government policy of assimilation was promoted. While the park's founders, the Villas Boas brothers, sought to provide a space where indigenous peoples could be protected from the national society and could enter the nation as distinct ethnic groups several generations into the future (Cowell 1974, 17; Davis 1980, 47), the standard policy outside the park of the Brazilian government's department in charge of the protection of indigenous peoples—now called Fundação Nacional do Índio (FUNAI) but previously called Serviço de Proteção aos Índios (SPI)—was, and to some extent still is, to encourage Indian peoples to merge or assimilate quickly with the national population (Ramos 1998, 82). In places such as government Indian posts set up for the Kayabi and others along the Teles Pires and Peixes Rivers, this was explicitly attempted by turning them into "national workers" (Souza Lima 1992, 254).

The first step in this assimilation process was to attract indigenous people through "pacification" or, as it has been more recently relabeled, "attraction" (Ramos 1984, 90). This stage involved offering industrially manufactured goods—such as axes, knives, beads, and pots—to "uncontacted" peoples.

This procedure was to be nonaggressive, as the motto of the SPI suggests: "Morrer se preciso fôr, matar nunca" [Die if necessary, never kill]. After a hostile (bravo) group was attracted through these goods, they were to become tame (manso) and settle at posts, where ideally they would learn skills so they could obtain wage work and buy these goods for themselves (Souza Lima 1992, 253–54; see also Maybury-Lewis 1991; Ramos 1998).

The rhetoric of SPI "pacification" depicts the indigenous groups as relatively devoid of agency throughout this process. According to this model they are "attracted to" or "contacted by" the national society and then prodded by their new needs into labor (Ramos 1998, 147). Several Kayabi men, however, commented that in their opinion the whites did not "contact" Kayabi but rather their relatives went out to meet the whites. In Kayabi areas the first SPI pacification post was set up on the Verde River in 1922 (Grünberg n.d. [1970], 45).[7] Kayabi elders remember the interest in posts as stemming in part from the goods they distributed, but there also is a sense that the Kayabi were "pacifying" the whites as well by going to meet them (see Graham 1995 for a similar view among the Xavante). With respect to the Kayabi in the Teles Pires area, one senior man, Jacaré, told me his uncle's story about how his uncle, grandfather, and two other men had traveled to make their first acquaintance with non-Indians. While his uncle is described as initiating the encounter only to obtain knives, his grandfather is remembered as being more intent on making peace. Upon arriving at the post, he is described as having shouted to the whites from across the river, "Don't be hostile toward us."

Some Kayabi clearly gave goods to the Brazilians during their first contacts as a gesture of hospitality. In Antonio Pyrineus de Sousa's account of his 1915 expedition on the Teles Pires, he describes how Kayabi individuals brought gifts to the whites in the following manner: "In the Kayabi bay we met two Indians who from the bank asked for apinacó and apinin and offered us a cake of polvilho [a delicacy, the starch from the manioc tuber] carefully wrapped in a banana leaf. But, on disembarking with the asked for objects, they laid the cake on the ground and ran, disappearing in the jungle" (Pyrineus de Sousa 1916, 75; my translation from Portuguese).

Pyrineus de Sousa mistakes api'nako and api'ni, the respectful forms of address used when speaking to a male who is senior to the speaker, for the Kayabi terms for "ax" and "knife." Changing the translation of these terms significantly alters the tone conveyed in this passage, as well as others, in his journal. The Kayabi seem to be as concerned with making the whites peaceful as much as the whites are concerned with "pacifying" the Kayabi.

Several accounts of the initial encounters with Kayabi also describe how Kayabi people offered food to explorers. Eating together as well as being fed are key parts of sociable encounters from a Kayabi perspective. Pyrineus de Sousa writes that at one location on the Teles Pires, where Kayabi helped his party cross some waterfalls, two girls hand-fed them peanuts (1916, 80). Similarly, Max Schmidt describes a Kayabi visit to a post in 1927 involving a type of ritualized food sharing: "[On] April 21 some Indians appeared again, there were two men—one of which was treated as a captain—his wife, a boy and a girl. . . . They let themselves be convinced to visit me inside my lodgings, where I got acquainted with the very disagreeable ceremony of the first visit, practiced by the Kayabi Indians. The Indian woman went up to each stranger, one after the other, putting her finger with honey on it in each one's mouth. This honey was taken out of the gourd with the same finger each time. Happily I was the first to be subjected to such treatment" (Schmidt 1942a, 246; my translation from Portuguese).

After initial encounters and often a period of hostilities, many Kayabi families relocated to the vicinity of posts largely to take advantage of the goods distributed there. For example, ninety individuals appeared in 1941 at Kayabi Post on the Tele Pires River, and forty-two more came to the same post in 1942 (Nimuendajú 1948, 308). According to Kayabi accounts, many other families, however, moved further into the forest expressly to avoid the influence of the posts.

Contrary to their supposed intent, posts in the Teles Pires River area, like posts in other indigenous areas, did not offer much education other than instruction in various sorts of manual labor and some Brazilian agricultural techniques, which for long-time cultivators like the Kayabi were usually much less suited to their environment than those they already possessed.[8] As a result of living at posts, a few Kayabi did seek out employment at Brazilian farms and ranches. The most significant sort of labor that government posts on the Teles Pires River encouraged, however, was rubber tapping. Stone-Arm remembers the fervor to collect rubber at José Bezerra Post in the 1940s. He interpreted it as the result of the order issued by Marshal Rondon (founder of the SPI) that all indigenous posts should collect rubber.

Induction into the work force was accelerated in the 1950s and 1960s when posts began to implement the renda indígena (indigenous income), a policy under which the posts were to pay for themselves through the selling of indigenous labor, crafts, or resources on indigenous lands. After a period during which this policy was criticized, the renda indígena was reinstated in the 1970s (Davis 1980, 57). At this time, the president of FUNAI, General Bandeira de

Mello, echoing the notion that indigenous people should enter the national society through their labor, is quoted as having said that indigenous people "must be oriented to a well defined planning process, taking into account their participation in national progress and integration as producers of goods" (Davis 1980, 56–57).

In 1959 and 1960 the researcher Roberto Décio de Las Casas visited a government post on the São Manuel River serving the Kayabi. According to de Las Casas, the poorly funded post and the nearby Franciscan mission serving the Mundurucu had become either extensions or rivals of the commercial rubber plantations in the area (1964). Las Casas notes that, in addition to the lack of funds and the poor preparation of personnel, the post treated indigenous people as *aviados* (debtors) rather than *protegidos* (people who are protected) (12). The posts were, in effect, fulfilling the ideal of the renda indígena and surviving on the labor of the Indians whom they were "helping" to enter the nation. The effect of turning posts into centers for rubber collection, according to Las Casas, was that the heads of the posts became businessmen who had an interest in keeping the people who were supplying rubber to them, that is, the Indians, under their control (14). The chief of this particular government post was reported to have used both his authority and physical force to keep indigenous people at his post (14).

As a result of the oppression at government posts, Kayabi individuals often switched to commercial rubber-tapping companies, where they hoped conditions would be better (Las Casas 1964, 14). At these companies, however, they became even further enmeshed in debt. According to the system of *aviamento*, rubber tappers could buy consumer goods (at very high prices) at the company store and then work off their debt by collecting rubber. This usually resulted in the tappers becoming debt peons. The aviamento system was particularly dangerous following the period in which SPI freely gave out goods to "uncontacted" indigenous people. Intervention on the part of SPI or, later, the Villas Boas brothers seemed to be the only way indigenous people could be freed of their debt at these institutions. Stone-Arm, for example, said that he had to work for a rubber company for approximately eight years, working off a debt he could not pay. According to Stone-Arm, Marshal Rondon, or his proxy, intervened and freed him of his debt.

The negative connotations that indigenous traditions carried at posts, rubber companies, and farms encouraged many Kayabi, like so many other indigenous peoples, to begin to dress like other Brazilians living in the interior. Much as Eduardo Viveiros de Castro has observed for indigenous Amazonians in general, Kayabi conceptions of acculturation focused on the "incorporation and embodiment of Western bodily practices" (1998, 485). Most Kayabi, for example, stopped tattooing their faces. Currently, only a few of the very oldest people have face tattoos, though many Kayabi continue to tattoo parts of their bodies in ways that correspond to their personal names. Like the majority of indigenous people in Brazil, Kayabi also wear Western clothing of some sort, though women frequently go topless.

Eating habits were also an issue for indigenous peoples while working with non-Indians. Stone-Arm remembered an instance while working with a crew of Brazilians when there was no other meat to eat except a recently killed snake. Not willing to eat snake because of its spiritual power, he requested only rice. He said the leader of the work crew refused him any food at all because he would not eat the only available meat like the rest of the workers. As Darcy Ribeiro writes about stereotypes in intensely colonized frontier areas, the indigenous individuals who received the most respect from Brazilians were those "obedient ones" who didn't "seem like an Indian" (1970, 362).

The Xingu Park was organized as a contrast to this type of assimilation through wage work and the consumption of industrially manufactured goods. The founders and first directors of the park, the Villas Boas brothers, first traveled into the Upper Xingu in 1946 to build military airstrips as members of the Roncador-Xingu expedition.[9] As they tell the story, they were struck by the isolation of the Upper Xinguan peoples they met in the area and felt the need to protect them from the social disorganization and epidemics that were sure to ensue if the area were opened up to the usual sort of colonization found in frontier areas (Villas Boas and Villas Boas 1973, 3). As a result of this experience, they designed a reservation that would be closed to any outside development, such as ranching, farming, mining, or tourism. Missionaries were also prohibited. As a result, the park has had a history of being relatively well protected from interests that freely operate in other frontier areas (Davis 1980, 50, 52). Eduardo Viveiros de Castro has pointed out that the park, which receives an unusual amount of media coverage, functions as a kind of "smoke-screen," hiding the majority of other indigenous areas where indigenous people live much less well (1979).

There have always been exceptions to the park's isolation, however. In 1971, for example, a highway was built directly through the park, cutting off its northern portion (Davis 1980, 58). Dignitaries have come to the park for short but celebrated visits as well (see *Veja*, December 5, 1990, for one of President Collor's visits, after his "jungle training course"). When the Villas Boas brothers ran the park, short trips by private financial supporters were also common (Serra 1979, 60). Currently, representatives from nongovernment organizations (NGOs) come through the park to monitor the effects of their support. Missionaries have also been allowed in at certain times, in certain capacities, though never explicitly to give religious instruction.

Other visitors are regulars within the park. The São Paulo Medical School provides a dedicated team of doctors and nurses, some of whom live in the park and some of whom visit it for several months a year. A group of medical students also spends time in the park each year. Excluding medical teams from São Paulo, the most frequent visitors to the Xingu Park are, in fact, anthropologists. The park has been one of the most celebrated areas for anthropological research in Brazil. In Stephen Schwartzman's estimation, between 1950 and 1988, anthropologists have spent approximately "twenty person years" in the Xingu (Schwartzman 1988, 348). Research within the Xingu is, however, very well controlled. Only those with permits can enter the park, and obtaining a research permit for the Xingu often requires waiting, as I did, for a year or more.

Attempts to reduce the amount of traffic into the Xingu have been successful, yet Xinguans are still able to travel outside of the park to some extent. The NGOs now active in the park and the indigenous administrations are less isolationist than the Villas Boas were when they ran the park (until 1974). During my stay, one NGO financed a boat to travel up and down the Xingu. Kayabi used this ferry to transport their crops to sell in the towns on the periphery of the park. They also had a plan to furnish a truck to transport crops to a larger, more distant town, São Felix do Araguaia, where better prices could be obtained. In addition to selling crops, Kayabi leave the Xingu for a variety of other reasons. During 1992 several people rode the ferry to the nearby town of São José do Xingu to participate in the mayoral elections.[10] Men and women of all ages have spent extended periods of time in São Paulo or other urban centers for extensive medical treatment for themselves or their relatives.

Travel has become more common for some as a result of the takeover of park administration by the Xinguans themselves. This transformation occurred in 1984 as a result of the activism of those living in the north, particularly the Kayapó (Veja, May 16, 1984). Since 1984 Kayabi men have worked in the administration of the park at Diauarum Post, at guard posts, and in the Brasília offices. At least three Kayabi men who worked in the park administration in Brasília in the 1980s and 1990s, for example, maintained houses in Brasília with their families. Chiefs of posts and village chiefs also have frequent opportunities to travel to Brasília and other major urban centers to visit both government (FUNAI) headquarters as well as NGO offices.

Extensive or frequent travel is not, however, a possibility for the vast majority of Kayabi people. The most significant deterrent is the cost. Kayabi individuals rarely have money for transportation or for living expenses en route to their destination. As a result, many Kayabi cannot travel to the distant places where some of their families continue to live outside the park.[11] One family who moved to Kapinu'a in the early 1990s, for example, was discouraged from moving back to Pará because of the cost of traveling. According to the Brazilian anthropologist Elizabeth Travassos, between 1966 and 1982 there had only been two visits between the Xinguan and Peixes River Kayabi (1984, 25).

In addition to physically separating the park as much as possible from the surrounding area, indigenous peoples in the Xingu are also encouraged to keep a distance from Brazilian customs. Residents were encouraged by the Villas Boas and other park directors after them, such as Olympio Serra, to maintain their traditional ways of life. This included holding their ceremonies, speaking their languages, and maintaining their values, with the exception of warfare. As a result of this separation, the availability of instruction in such subjects as Portuguese and mathematics has historically been very limited within the park.[12]

Managing Indian Identities

Under the various indigenous policies operating outside and within the park, Indian identity has had very different connotations. Nonetheless, in both cases it has implied that those who possess it are outside of time. Frontier areas, for example, were considered to be just beginning the "march toward progress." Many believed that the indigenous inhabitants needed to be brought into the flow of time and harnessed for national development. The park is also understood to be outside the flow of time, but it is ideally to remain that way. In both cases indigenous residents in these territories are understood to be in similar positions with respect to history. Timelessness is, however, evaluated differently within and outside the park. Outside the park, Indian timelessness is viewed pejoratively and implies being undeveloped. Within the park, it has positive connotations of purity and of being untainted by the negative effects of "civilization."[13]

According to the logic that guided the assimilationist policies of SPI and later FUNAI, indigenous people had come to participate only very recently and minimally in the development and progress of the human race. Laboring for wages and goods was conceptualized as the crucial means to help them enter into the flow of history or "progress" shared by others in the nation (Souza Lima 1992, 253).

In contrast to frontier areas, the Xingu Park was set up explicitly as an anachronism, a place that would supposedly represent a contrast to the "progress" of the rest of the nation.[14] It was to be, to some extent, a measure of progress in Brazil as compared to some original time still located in the Xingu. In the words of the Villas Boas brothers, the park was set up to preserve "a natural reservation where fauna and flora would be safeguarded for the distant future of the country, as evidence of Brazil at the time of its discovery" (Villas Boas and Villas Boas 1973, 3).

In the media, the Xingu is frequently presented as an untouched, primitive space deep in the heart of Brazil. In the Brazilian press, the Xingu has been described (in some of its more sensational coverage) as a "place where Indians still live an existence . . . like their forefathers before the discovery of America" (translation of a notice for the film *Aspectos do Alto Xingu* in *Journal de São Paulo*, September 6, 1949, quoted in Ferreira 1983, 66) or as a place where tribes "live as in the times of Cabral" (from *Manchete* ca. 1981, quoted in Schwartzman 1988, 331). Olympio Serra, on being dismissed as the director of the Xingu Park by the Villas Boas in 1979, wrote with hopes of dispelling this aspect of the park's identity that "utopia and myopia occasionally mingle" and that the illusion that has come about for the public is that "the Xingu National Park, in its original form, constitutes a prototype of Brazil" (1979, 59).

The park has been described in similar fashion for the international audience: a precontact utopia standing in contrast to the world's industrialized countries. The Xingu has been presented as a place where "the perfect image of pre-conquest America" can be encountered (Hanbury-Tenison 1973, 62). The founder of the Rain Forest Foundation, rock star Sting, wrote the following about his trip to the Xingu: "We are paying homage to our primeval history. We have stepped back to the Stone Age. . . . In some ways Western man is in reverse evolution, we've forgotten our real potential. The Xingu can remind us of what we really are" (Sting and Dutilleux 1989, 39).

The coverage for the 1992 Earth Summit represented the Xingu as a sort of paradise of the end times, in which the best of all epochs is combined. A special English-language issue of the Brazilian magazine *Manchete* features, for example, the Yualapitis of the Upper Xingu in an article entitled "Heading toward the Third Millennium." This piece begins with a two-page photo spread of Yualapiti men from the Upper Xingu working on a solar energy panel, barefoot but with colorful swimming shorts. Part of the text reads, "[They are] modernists without losing their culture . . . high-tech Indians without abandoning their bows and arrows" (*Manchete* 1992b, 85). A millennial theme surrounded the coverage of the 1992 Earth Summit in general. The marriage of high-tech (such as images from satellites and genetic testing) with a concern for the natural environment is represented throughout this particular issue of *Manchete* as the combination necessary to recover "the paradise we lost" (*Manchete* 1992a, 33). The Earth Summit coverage replaced the earlier representations of the Xingu as a locale where history has not yet begun or is still in the Stone Age with another sort of timelessness—that which is characteristic of the utopian end times.

The challenge for the Kayabi living in the park has been to adapt to these particular versions of Brazilian Indian identity. Leaders, particularly young village chiefs but also senior men like Stone-Arm, help others negotiate the sort of self-presentation called for within the Xingu with considerable acumen (for other examples in Brazil see Conklin 1997, 2002; Conklin and Graham 1995; Ramos 1998). They are aware of the benefits of conforming to the identity of "pure Indians" just as they were aware of the benefits of adopting certain Brazilian traits when assimilation was the dominant policy outside the park. Chief João, for example, told his community that they should not mention that they kill animals or eat meat when representatives of an international NGO came to visit. Much like Stone-Arm, who was concerned about the presence of T-shirts in my photos, João was concerned that animal-killing, meat-eating Indians would not fit the image of purity that has been mapped onto the park and that the Kayabi would be seen as already too impure, too fully inserted into the process of history to merit foreign aid. His wariness was likely a result of the criticism Mario Juruna, a formerly prominent indigenous (Xavante) politician, received after he supposedly spoke out at the Earth Summit against ecologists who defend animal rights at the expense of human rights. João mentioned that he and others who participated in the Earth Summit had gotten into an argument over Juruna's statements. The preservation of endangered species was one of the main topics of concern at the conference.[15]

In more general terms, Chief João showed that he was at least practically aware of what Alcida Ramos calls the "hyperreal Indian." The "hyperreal Indian" is a fabrication or model Indian that she sees operating for non-Indians in the indigenist circuit. It is a "perfect Indian whose virtues, sufferings, and untried stoicism have won him the right to be defended by the professionals of indigenous rights" (Ramos 1998, 276). These simulacra of Indians are, among other things, "unaware of bourgeois evils," such as, in the example from the Earth Summit, the excessive use of animal products (277).

The park's identity as a place outside of time where one is likely to find the "hyperreal Indian" has also shaped the system of exchanges that has developed between indigenous and nonindigenous peoples in the park. The

Villas Boas were famous for supplying park residents with copious amounts of "presents." Schwartzman has written that they modeled the Xingu Park community on the Upper Xinguan peoples' culture in which generosity along with nonaggressiveness is a paramount value (1988, 325–61). Perpetual gifting, in effect, made the first phase of the pacification process a permanent condition within the park. After a "hostile" group was attracted and made "tame" through industrially manufactured goods, in most posts outside the park, the distribution of goods was curtailed (see Maybury-Lewis 1988; Ramos 1998; Turner 1991). The curtailment was explained in large part by shortages in SPI's funding. It also likely took place in order to bring about the next phase, that of encouraging Indians to work for goods. Under the Villas Boas' directorship, the first moments of contact (of unending presents) were frozen in time, in keeping with the identity of the Xingu as a place out of time or a place perpetually at the origin of history.

Gift giving continues to be an important aspect of life in the Xingu. As many have pointed out, it has become a routine between Xinguans and researchers. At least in Kayabi communities, researchers do not pay Kayabi an hourly wage for their help in research, nor are myths and ceremonies paid for directly. The absence of these methods of payment is not the result of unfamiliarity. Many Kayabi have worked for missionary-linguists from the Summer Institute of Linguistics (SIL) according to the hourly wage system, so they are familiar with it in the context of research. Leaders instead organize payment for research in terms of gifts. Before I left Brasília for Kapinu'a, Chief João communicated with me by short-wave radio at the FUNAI headquarters and gave me a lengthy list of items that I was to bring for gifts, including boxes of ammunition, knives, fishhooks, about twenty pairs of sandals, cloth, blankets, hammocks, and flashlights. The quantity of goods was thankfully negotiable, and my obligations were met in part by my teaching them arithmetic.

Gift giving on a more personal level seems to have become routinized on both sides as well. The following story illustrates this aspect of exchange in the Xingu. On one of my trips to Brasília, I saw a postcard collection of Xinguan Indians in traditional dress in a bookstore. One of the cards pictured Stone-Arm, as a much younger man, in a shamanic costume (with paint and feathers), playing a flute. Unsure if he knew about this picture, I brought the collection back for him as a gift. He graciously accepted it with what I thought was a hint of weariness. Only later did I realize as we looked through his dusty suitcase of photographs how many of these card collections he already owned or, better, had owned. Many were missing, but the thin carton in which they were sold remained stored away amid his other photos. As a renowned shaman and fluent speaker of Portuguese, Stone-Arm was one of the best-known residents of the park. Every researcher and medical worker must have brought one of these collections back for him.

In the Upper Xingu, each group has a craft in which they specialize, such as pottery, shell necklaces, or cotton weaving. The so-called craft specialization of non-Indian researchers in the Xingu Park as a whole could be said to be their objectifications of indigenous culture that are given back to the residents. This sort of objectification has not had entirely negative or dehumanizing effects in the Xingu (see Turner 1991 for the relationship between ethnography and political consciousness). I nevertheless remained somewhat chagrined about the ordinariness of my gift to Stone-Arm until I read the following passage about Hanbury-Tenison's 1971 visit to Stone-Arm's homestead. "In [Stone-Arm's] hut there was a very fine hat made out of sloth skin which looked rather like a badger but was much softer. 'Ear-ings' made out of red feathers hung on either side and he put it on, indicating to me that it was his ceremonial chief's hat. . . . After talking for a time, and visiting the rest of the village which seemed to be relatively prosperous, the rain stopped and we all went back down to the boat again. Just as we were pushing off from the bank, [Stone-Arm] impulsively took off his hat and gave it to me which pleased me very much" (Hanbury-Tenison 1973, 79). Stone-Arm also spontaneously gave me a sloth-skin hat on my departure in much the same manner.

"Having Culture" in the Xingu

As well as being examples of the Xinguan routine of gift giving, these three incidents from 1971 and 1992 recall the negotiations over wardrobe (including mine) at the Jawosi festival I attended in April 1992. Much like Stone-Arm's sloth-skin hats and his shamanic costume depicted on the postcard I gave to him, this Jawosi was an example of how residents of the Xingu are expected to, and do in fact, present representations of indigenous culture in some form to nonindigenous visitors. These events show the complex relationship that exists between how Xinguan peoples are represented by others to have culture and to be Indians, how they represent themselves with respect to these issues, and how they momentarily include others within this display. We outsiders are crowned with sloth-skin hats (or more usually, elsewhere in the park, feather diadems) and are painted for rituals: for a fleeting instance we partake in an indigenous culture, not only as the audience but as a part of the play.

Although many Kayabi individuals are not conscious of this "cultural display," leaders and other well-traveled individuals have thought and worried explicitly about "having culture" for a long time. As early as 1979, for example, Berta Ribeiro reported that Stone-Arm explained to her in the course of discussing the Xingu Park that "[y]oung Indians need to know how to make baskets [and] dance. . . . if not, the culture is over" (Ribeiro 1979, 100; my translation). More recently, I have heard several discussions among young men about whether the Kayabi "have as much culture" as other groups in the park, such as the Upper Xinguans. The Xingu is, in this respect, much like other areas in Latin America where culture is discussed in the contexts of schools, medical care, workshops, indigenous rights organizations, and interethnic festivals (see Jackson (1989, 1991, 1995a, 1995b, and Gow and Rappaport 2002 with respect to Colombia; see Briggs 1996 with respect to Venezuela, among others).

Collective rituals are one kind of event in which those Kayabi concerned with "culture" have the sense that it is being displayed or encouraged. Jawosi singing and shamanic cures are most frequently singled out as examples. It is with reference to these kinds of events that Chief João commented, "Here in the park we are fostering culture." (Several people wanted me to take pictures of these events so foreigners would see that they were still "Indians" and would be moved to send the Kayabi aid.) Other sorts of practices that are signs of "culture" in various contexts include speaking the Kayabi language, undergoing puberty seclusion, following food taboos after childbirth, as well as making Kayabi-specific styles of tucum nut necklaces, cotton baby slings, hammocks, feather diadems, arrows, and baskets. In addition to being termed "culture" in Portuguese, these practices are also called "our law" in Portuguese as well as in Kayabi.

Echoing numerous other examples in Amazonian ethnographies (Conklin 1997), nakedness is clearly linked to "having culture" in the Xingu, and the Kayabi consequentially debate the appropriateness of using Western clothing. I heard men discuss whether the use of clothing meant a "loss of their culture." In one conversation a few men mused with Chief João about whether they could go back to living without any clothing at all. This particular discussion ended with jokes about how so-and-so would get thorns in his feet and be reduced to tears or how so-and-so would get too cold at night. This preoccupation with clothing is, however, a serious one. While to some extent it is encouraged by nonnative photographers who want people to look "Indian," it is also a response that has roots in Amazonian cosmologies (Viveiros de Castro 1998, 482). Putting on a mask or clothing is understood not so much to cover or conceal a person's body but to encourage transformation, "to actuate the powers of a different body" (482). Changing the body or the surfaces of the body is the native Amazonian counterpart to the European theme of spiritual conversion (481).

The indigenous inhabitants of the Upper Xingu have historically been upheld by the park administration as examples par excellence of traditional indigenous culture. The Upper Xinguans, therefore, provide a sort of measuring stick for the Kayabi with respect to the extent to which they have "maintained their culture." These were the peoples reported by the Villas Boas in the 1940s to be living exactly as they had been in 1884 when von den Steinen traveled through the Xingu (Villas Boas and Villas Boas 1973, 13). In 1884 von den Steinen described them as "the true Stone Age tribes" (1942, 376). As a result of their reputation, the Upper Xinguans have historically received some of the most celebrated visits from outsiders who come bearing gifts. During the Villas Boas administration, government officials and dignitaries were invited to intertribal rituals in the Upper Xingu, such as the kwarúp (mortuary ceremony for chiefs) (Schwartzman 1988, 353). The Upper Xingu was also the site for the filming of a television serial in 1978 and a documentary in 1986 (Schwartzman 1988, 354; Viveiros de Castro 1979, 56). According to the Kayabi, the Upper Xinguans currently receive much more support in the form of goods from researchers, NGOs, and foreign embassies than do the Lower Xinguans.[16]

Ironically, many of the nonindigenous goods that the Kayabi use come from trade with these traditional and more isolated Upper Xinguans. One Kayabi man explained that he was traveling to the Upper Xingu to trade his handmade necklaces for Western clothing because the Upper Xinguans always receive more goods from outside sources as a result of celebrating "so many rituals." I also noticed that when the Txicão, who live in the Upper Xingu, came to play soccer with the Kayabi they brought only consumer goods (such as soap, ready-made dresses, and fish hooks) to trade for Kayabi handmade necklaces, chickens, and produce.

Many Kayabi echo the commonly held view that the Upper Xinguans are representative of an older tradition. Some bring up the possibility that the Upper Xinguans were not as intensively or as quickly contacted as they themselves were and are therefore more like their own Kayabi ancestors used to be: they still wear little clothing and observe more ceremonies. Others describe the Upper Xinguans more pejoratively, as being more ignorant of aspects of Brazilian culture than the Kayabi. One young man described the Upper Xinguans as being generally more undeveloped than the Kayabi, as "cultural clean slates" of a sort.

All of these characterizations are somewhat consistent with SPI and FUNAI logic about the "prehistoric" nature of the park's indigenous residents. They are also consistent with and legitimized by references to the view of cultural differentiation expressed in traditional Kayabi stories. The Upper Xinguans are referred to as either being like or actually being the descendants of a group of people who, according to the ancestors' stories (*eyia porongyta*), came before the Kayabi. They were called the "People-without-Understanding" (Kawaip Kwaapa re'ema). These people did not know about the world; they were "like children" and had to be taught by a Kayabi culture hero that animals were edible and that enemy people could be killed and their heads used in Jawosi rituals. Several storytellers remarked that these ancient peoples were just like the Upper Xinguans of today. Upper Xinguans have an elaborate series of food taboos, which Kayabi tend to interpret as the result of not "knowing" that certain animals can be eaten. The Upper Xingu's reputation as a community where several language groups coexist peacefully also resonates with the ignorance that "People-without-Understanding" have about warfare.

In contrast to the Upper Xinguans, Kayabi have historically had the reputation of being more like nonindigenous Brazilians than like other peoples within the park. The Brazilian anthropologist Berta Ribeiro, for example, wrote in her book, *Diário do Xingu*, that two Polish filmmakers commented to her that "the Kayabi were peasants rather than Indians because they wore clothes, had no rituals, and lived in houses at a distance from one another and not in villages" (1979, 11). People in Kapinu'a are well aware of this description. (Stone-Arm owns a copy of this book, and some of the younger men have read it.)

In part the Kayabi share this identity of having "lost their culture" with others in the Lower Xingu who are more familiar with the national society and Portuguese language. The ethos at Diauarum Post, serving the Lower Xingu, contrasts markedly with the romanticized image of the Upper Xingu as Schwartzman captures in the following passage: "The Xingu of the picture postcard and artistic photo essay is the traditional Upper Xingu, and the Upper Xingu in full ceremonial dress. Most of the residents of Diauarum wear clothes most of the time, many wear old clothes, and Indians in old clothes or warm-up suits are the antithesis of the image of the Xinguan that has grown up since the time of the Villas Boas" (1988, 343).

Even within the Lower Xingu, however, the Kayabi historically have had the reputation of being somewhat more acculturated than their neighbors. In 1992, for example, I heard one visitor joke appreciatively that arriving in a Kayabi village "feels like arriving in civilization after being in other northern villages." In part this reputation may stem from the fact that several Kayabi have been groomed since childhood by the Villas Boas to have positions of authority within the park. These men are very familiar with Brazilian customs and, since 1984 when the Xinguans took over the park, have worked in positions of leadership, which require that they skillfully interface with Brazilians and foreigners of all sorts. These individuals not only are fluent in a type of Brazilian lifestyle but are to some extent international diplomats.

Kayapó individuals from the northern part of the park have been in leadership positions to an even greater extent than Kayabi individuals, but they do not share the same reputation of acculturation as the Kayabi. Although many Kayapó are skillful at maneuvering in Brazilian society, such Kayapó customs as body painting and photogenic rituals are often upheld by non-Indians (as well as by some Kayapó) as unflattering contrasts to Kayabi practices. In part this is due to a general tendency for Kayapó individuals and communities to eagerly and assertively stress their distinctiveness in all sorts of interactions.[17] Kayabi, on the other hand, give the impression of immensely enjoying the pleasure of "passing" at certain moments for non-Kayabi.

In addition to quickly adopting the sorts of traits that many other indigenous peoples have done in other colonial situations in order to obtain a modicum of respect, Kayabi are also attentive to many finer points of colonizers' behavior (see also Hemming 2003, 146). The Kayabi who are familiar with Brazilian etiquette are quick to use it in interethnic situations. The owner of a motel in the town of São José do Xingu at the periphery of the park remarked, for example, that the Kayabi are "so polite," in contrast to other Xinguan Indians who pass through. I also heard a Kapinu'a chief who was a fluent speaker of Portuguese correct the Portuguese of younger men. On another occasion, this chief commented to a group of women that Portuguese should not be spoken unless it was spoken well. (Women rarely speak Portuguese, though some understand it.) Some of the more cosmopolitan Kayabi men are also skillful in carrying on a Brazilian type of interaction with visitors—that is, one with a very quick and exuberant greeting and a prolonged good-bye— which contrasts with the usual Kayabi suppression of emotion displayed at these junctures.

While Kayabi individuals have been attentive to the styles of *civilizados*, or whites, they have also been assuming traits from the Upper Xinguans— the denizens of "culture" in the Xingu. Chief João told me that when the Kayabi first moved to the park everybody began to cut their hair in bangs like the Upper Xinguans (although now it seems that mainly young adult women cut their hair in this fashion). Women are also lengthening the time of their puberty seclusions in self-conscious imitation of Upper Xinguan rites of passage. Chief João explained that he had even designed the layout of Kapinu'a village in imitation of a round, Upper Xinguan–style village.

At first glance, one might be tempted to make the argument that the Kayabi seem more like civilizados than many other groups in the park simply because they have become more assimilated due to their frontier history. Likewise, one might be tempted to conclude that they look to the Upper Xinguans as models simply because they want to garner the same resources possessed by those who are understood to "have the most culture" in the park. While in some respects both are undoubtedly the case, the matter is not so simple. Kayabi show a long-term pattern of seeking out other groups (Oakdale 2001). Even before colonization and their move to the Xingu, Kayabi avidly sought out interactions with other ethnic groups in the eighteenth and nineteenth centuries, such as the Carib-speaking Bakairí, the Tupi-speaking Apiacá, and the Gê-speaking Rikbakstá (Grünberg n.d. [1970]; Hemming 2003, 143, 146; Oakdale 1996). Many Kayabi also actively sought out SPI posts and rubber plantations to pacify the whites. Much as Viveiros de Castro (1992) has pointed out for the Tupian Arawete and Tupi-speaking groups more generally, they exhibit a centrifugal dynamic; their center or point of orientation is outside the bounds of their society. This pattern appears to be continuing with the Kayabi's move to the Xingu and places them in a unique position with respect to the problem of how to negotiate "being Indian" and "having culture" in the park.

THE PERILS OF NEW-STYLE VILLAGES

I've changed my name to "Young-Man."
STONE-ARM, 1992
I've changed my name to "Money."
JACARÉ, 1992

One afternoon as I lay in my hammock, a young girl from Stone-Arm's neighboring household poked her head under my mosquito netting and said, "Come eat. Bring your plate." This sort of invitation usually happened once a day and sometimes more often during my stay in Kapinu'a. [1] On some days Jacaré's daughter, Thorn, had made a sweet pumpkin soup; on other days Chest's wife, Pretty-Eyes, had made a corn porridge. Many times a monkey had been killed, and one household or another had sent a young girl to invite people for monkey and manioc stew called *mutap*. Over the course of the wet season, when monkey is most frequently hunted, I even started to like this pungent, robust meat. As time wore on, I realized that I would almost never have to open the tinned foods I had brought from town. Indeed, the few times I did eat from them, the food tasted overly salted or sugared. On this afternoon I was being beckoned to eat small delicate fruits gathered from the surrounding forest along with roasted fish—both procured by some of Stone-Arm's many grandchildren.

As I entered his house, Stone-Arm was lying in his hammock, his pet *paca* carefully stepping on her delicate guinea-pig-like paws around the baby birds, housed in shallow gourds underneath his hammock. After his granddaughter handed me the food, Carol, his wife, brought me a low stool and handed me a plastic bag of store-bought salt with which to season my fish. While his adolescent granddaughters turned the fish on the fire, Stone-Arm told me that he had changed his name to Young-Man (Kunumi'uu) because when he asked the young girls in his household who they wanted to marry they all said, "I want a young man." Past generations of Kayabi women, as a rule, married men who were much their senior. Laughing with me at his joke, he surprised me by saying I could go tell his neighbor Jacaré about his new name. Stone-Arm and Jacaré, who were once quite close when they lived at a distance, had grown argumentative with each other and spoke only through intermediaries like myself, if at all, since becoming neighbors in the village circle.

Realizing that a momentary break in hostilities was rare indeed, I eagerly went to visit the elderly Jacaré as soon as I had finished eating. Upon arriving, he motioned from his hammock for me to sit down at his family's wooden table. Suffering partial paralysis from a recent stroke, Jacaré could not walk. Always very tidy, his white hair was cut short, and his hands, sporting several carved tucum nut rings, rested in his lap. While his wife and granddaughters looked over dress fabric on the other side of the house, I relayed Stone-Arm's joke, trying not to laugh as I did so. No sooner had I finished when he quipped, "You tell Stone-Arm I've changed my name too. I've changed my name to Money [Karan'uu]. That is what all the young girls in my household are asking for in marriage!"

As a result of their move to the Xingu Indigenous Park, Kayabi individuals have had to negotiate not only new facets of Indian identity and the concept of culture but also changes with respect to how they relate to each other. The park administration has encouraged smaller family homesteads to aggregate in large multifamily villages in order to provide people with more resources.[2] Living in large multifamily groups has brought new sorts of tensions and problems. For example, the senior male leaders of extended family homesteads tend to be extremely autonomous. Living in close proximity to each other has presented interpersonal challenges, as seen in the rift between Jacaré and Stone-Arm. Because senior family headmen all consider themselves to be equals, a challenge has also arisen with respect to choosing a leader for these new-style local groups. The solution that the Xinguan Kayabi reached, which echoes a more general pattern found throughout the lowlands (Brown 1993, 312), was to place young men in the positions of village leaders—men who are far away from holding positions of authority in their own families because of their young age. However, establishing men who are clearly under the authority of seniors at the household level as village leaders has led to a new set of tensions. These young chiefs are gaining increased access to resources procured from beyond the family, including consumer goods and education, while the elder headmen are losing direct access to these resources. Through their access to these goods the young chiefs are wielding more power than their seniors might like and are encouraging other young people to do the same. Both young and old leaders seem to be painfully aware of these new tensions. As they narrate their lives in ritual formats, they counsel others on

35

2. Extended-family houses in the village circle.

how to address the perils of these new interhousehold and intergenerational relationships.

Household Leadership

A household or "a place" (*wyri*) is led or looked after by a senior male family headman, called the *wyriat* (custodian or owner of the place). Prior to the organization of large villages, households were spread out along the banks of rivers. A household usually consists of the headman, his wife or wives (called in the singular *wyriara remireko* [the custodian's or owner's wife]), their own unmarried children, their married children and spouses living with them, and their children's respective children. Often a powerful headman will attract a few other more distant relatives as well. The power of a headman—his ability to keep his grown children living with him and to attract their spouses—rests on his ability to care for his followers, particularly with respect to providing food and shelter as well as fostering a sense of "conviviality" (Overing and Passes 2000).

While a good headman is viewed as one who provides ample food for his household, he does not produce food on the basis of his own efforts alone. Rather, his productivity is the result of his ability to attract followers and to involve them in food production. Bride service is the institution that

36

traditionally gives a family leader access to much of this labor power (see Kracke 1978, 71, for similar Kagwahiv concepts of authority). For the Kayabi, bride service involves a son-in-law living with his new wife's parents for a period of time directly after marriage. A young married man is in fact frequently called "someone who has a father-in-law" (aty'up ma'e) as well as "someone who has a wife" (kunumi'uu emireko ma'e). Sons-in-law are expected to dutifully carry out their fathers-in-law's requests with respect to farming and hunting as well as other activities such as house building. They are also expected to have a sense of shame with respect to their fathers-in-law and to feel pressure to perform tasks well in front of them. In addition, ideally they are expected to speak relatively infrequently in the presence of their fathers-in-law. Currently, sons-in-law do provide at least a few years of such submissive service, and a successful headman can extend this period for much longer.

A headman orchestrates his household's agricultural work. Though the headman often works along with others in the fields, setting a good example, the work of his household is conceptualized as being done for him, not along with him. Together members of one household farm one field or a series of fields in the same area. At the end of the dry season, after the tracajá turtle has finished laying its eggs, the headman organizes the men in his household to collectively burn the vegetation off the fields. Once the rain starts, he decides when the crops should be planted. He takes charge of organizing the harvest as well. Crops are later processed by the household as an organized unit under the direction of the headman and his wife, with manioc processing being one of the most time consuming.

Though the headman's wife directs some of the women's labor, particularly with respect to food processing, senior women are not understood to "command" junior women in the way senior men do their juniors. While the relationship between fathers-in-law and sons-in-law is markedly hierarchical, the relationship between different generations of women within a household is more egalitarian. Whereas women do not often speak about the uncomfortable nature of in-law status, men frequently do. These differences in gender relationships may be a result of the lesser sense married women have of owing a debt to their in-laws. Men are viewed as paying their parents-in-law for their labor, for carrying their bride as a baby (in the case of her mother), and for taking care of her as a child. Women, on the other hand, produce children who are in many ways more closely related to their father's family, as children are thought to be of the same flesh and ethnicity as the father. In addition, because of the period of bride service, women are usually subject to living with their in-laws only after they have been more fully integrated into the family, usually after they have given birth to one or two children.

The household headman and his wife also function as the center of redistribution. The majority of the game that a household consumes is caught by the headman's sons and sons-in-law. These men give their catch to the household headman or his wife. The women in the household then cook and prepare it as a group. Finally, at mealtimes, the headman's wife or another senior woman (one of her elder daughters or daughters-in-law) dishes out servings of the cooked meat (along with manioc flour) to each nuclear family living in the household. In other words, raw game is given to the senior head couple, and they redistribute it in cooked form.[3] Through this process, food is understood as having been provided by the headman.[4] Visitors judge a household on the basis of how much food and drink they are offered. Households with an abundance of food are seen as unified and strong.

Children are also signs of a household's strength—not only because children (and grandchildren) form the core of a headman's following but also because Kayabi children come to parents who can provide for them. According to Kayabi ideas about conception, unborn children choose their parents. They decide to whom they want to be born. By this logic a plentiful household will attract children more than an impoverished one. To suggest that they have an abundance of food and to attract a new baby into their womb, women often hang small, child-size gourd spoons on their hammocks.

When agricultural work and hunting have slowed down, the men of a household work together on large collective tasks such as house building. Like he does for agricultural labor, the headman directs this labor as well. For example, the younger men are directed to haul palm fronds for the roof or saplings for the walls from the surrounding forest. They also climb up onto the roof and tie the fronds together to make the thatch. Because a house is identified by the name of its headman, a large well-built house is clearly a sign of his power.

While it is recognized that newly married men owe their in-laws a few years of service and should be respectful during this time, there is a higher degree of autonomy within this relationship than one might expect. The most respected headmen do not simply order their sons-in-law about. Instead, a good headman also take pains to foster a sense of conviviality, which, as it has been recently defined in an Amazonian context, involves a "psychological, moral and practical state of collective being," "productive social play," and "freedom of personal thought and action," among other features (Overing and Passes 2000, xiii). A good headman, in short, makes his household an

38

emotionally satisfying place to live, not one in which his workers feel only a sense of hierarchy. Much as Joanna Overing and Alan Passes have described for other Amazonian peoples, Kayabi tend to stress the emotional or affective side of local group sociality (2000, 14). A Kayabi headman should be emotionally connected with everyone in his household and show an interest in the needs and problems of each member, no matter how mundane. Chief João explained that a good headman should understand his followers and, in fact, know what they need before they actually have to ask (see Lévi-Strauss [1955] 1975, 308, on the Namikwra chief of the Wakletoçu group).

A headman is held responsible for orchestrating a sense of well-being and happiness (-ekõẽãi) within his household as well. Those men who posses shamanic powers are particularly good at fostering well-being, as an important part of curing diseases involves bringing co-residents into a state of sociality with each other (as well as with nonhuman spirits). Headmen who are not shamans rely more on humor and their ability to "play around" with their followers to bring about a sense of happiness. While a headman's sense of humor is important in attracting sons-in-law to his household in the first place, it becomes especially important in keeping sons-in-law and their families around after the period of bride service has been fulfilled. Several men said that they continued to work at their father-in-law's household, rather than moving out on their own or back in with their own father, because their father-in-law "really knew how to joke around."

Portraits of Two Households

Each household seems infused with the personality of its headman. Each is, for example, named after its headmen as the "place of X" ("X" wyri). People say that when a person moves it is hard to become accustomed to a new household because each is so different. During my stay in Kapinu'a even I noticed that the ethos of each household seemed very different—especially those of Jacaré and Stone-Arm. Jacaré and his family emphasized their connections to Brazilian customs and their knowledge of a "civilized lifestyle," while Stone-Arm and his family presented an image of openness and fecundity associated with shamanic powers.

When I met Jacaré in 1992 he no longer considered himself to be the headman of his household, though others often referred to his house as "the place of Jacaré." After his stroke in 1991 he let his eldest son take over the position of household headman. Jacaré's wife, Julia, ran the household along with this eldest son. A slightly younger and very active elderly woman, she both organized the household and took care of her husband. Though she spoke no

Portuguese and my conversational Kayabi always remained limited, I came to realize that she had a biting sense of humor, particularly with respect to nicknames.

"The place of Jacaré" in Kapinu'a consisted of one large, oval, open-room long house with dirt floors, walls made out of very thin trees lined together, and a tall, thatch roof. [5] This house had several elaborations that suggested the family's connection to salaried positions in the FUNAI. The doorposts and lintel were, for example, splashed with store-bought, bright blue paint. The door was fashioned out of expensive, cut lumber and inside the family had a table and two benches made from the same. During my stay no other household in the village could boast such furnishings.

Behind this house was a cleared plaza space and behind that a much smaller house with a very low roof that the family occasionally occupied. During 1992 the family tried to dig a well in the back plaza area, a feat that no other family would have dreamed of attempting (nor seen the necessity of attempting). Jacaré's eldest son, after living in Brasília, however, was very familiar with Brazilian ideas about water cleanliness and thought a well would provide better drinking water than the river port.

In 1992–93 the household had more members than usual. For most of this time, Jacaré's two adult sons lived with their parents. The elder one, having retired from his position in the FUNAI administration of the park, lived in one portion of the large house with his wife and two small daughters. In 1992 this son's adult son also moved back from Brasília, where he had also spent a good portion of his life. While in Brasília he had married a nonindigenous woman. He had recently brought her and their baby to live in the Xingu "to be close to his grandfather." This couple brought a wooden bed, hung a few Bruce Lee posters, and made a place for themselves in his father's side of the house. Jacaré's younger son, who had a wife and young children, hung his hammock in the opposite side of the house. His adolescent daughter by a previous marriage also lived with them. Jacaré's daughter, Thorn, unusually did not live with her father and mother but rather lived with her second husband a few houses away. She and her husband did, however, participate in agricultural activities, cook, and frequently eat in her parents' household.

Jacaré's children's very existence is a mark of his friendship with influential non-Kayabi. His youngest son and daughter are twins. In the past, most Kayabi only allowed one child of a pair of twins to live. The other was usually killed and buried after birth. Jacaré explained that he had planned to do this when his twins were born. At the time, however, he was working at Post Leonardo, and Cláudio Villas Boas offered to give him a rifle if he would raise both of his children. Jacaré was very proud of all three (his twins and his rifle) when he spoke about them in 1992.

Jacaré had a fourth child who lived across the village—a son who was born to his first wife, a woman who died while giving birth to this child. Kayabi do not usually let a child live who, as they say, "has killed its own mother." Again, Jacaré was convinced by a Brazilian chief of post in the Teles Pires area to raise the child even though there was no female relative to nurse the baby. Jacaré himself fed the baby powdered milk supplied by the post. This son has lived most of his life away from other Kayabi and therefore speaks Kayabi only to a limited degree. He married a Nambikuara woman on his travels outside the park and brought her to live in Kapinu'a along with their several children.

Stone-Arm, in contrast to Jacaré, still claimed to be the headman of his household in the early 1990s. While no Kayabi know the exact date of their own or others' births, most people considered Stone-Arm to be older than Jacaré, possibly because he had so many more great-grandchildren. Despite Stone-Arm's age, he was quick to tell me that even though he followed the orders of the village chief to some extent, he too still "ordered" people as a leader. Stone-Arm was one of the most famous and powerful Kayabi shamans, and he knew that his presence was a key factor in attracting others to live in Kapinu'a.

In comparison to the household of his neighbor Jacaré, Stone-Arm's household was bursting with people and activity. In November 1992 his household had thirty-seven full-time residents, while Jacaré's at its peak had only seventeen. Very similar to Jacaré's in construction, the interior of Stone-Arm's house was partitioned by two walls of thin tree trunks. The largest room was occupied by the family of his eldest son and the other room by the family of his youngest son. The middle section was a communal cooking area and a place for long-term guests to hang their hammocks.

Behind the main house was a partially cleared patio much like Jacaré's plaza, but with the addition of a little shelter and roost for Stone-Arm's macaws and pet monkey. A smaller house was located behind this plaza, which Stone-Arm liked to call "his office" in Portuguese. Stone-Arm and Carol hung their hammocks here with several of their grandchildren. This small house also contained a clay oven topped by a large iron pan for toasting manioc. Most other households did not have their own toasting pan but rather used a communal pan located in the village center. Chief João once joked that Stone-Arm's household was a village all by itself.

Stone-Arm, as a shamanic healer and leader, took pride in raising and nurturing people and animals of all sorts. His household, for example, included a

Panará (Kren Akrore) man whom Stone-Arm adopted as a boy when he participated in the Panará attraction mission in the 1970s. This boy later married one of Stone-Arm's granddaughters. One afternoon when we were talking, Stone-Arm fondly pointed out which grandchildren were Panará rather than Kayabi. Stone-Arm's household was also often visited by non-Kayabi who came to receive long-term treatment for illnesses. Before my arrival in 1993, he said that two Kayapó from the far northern part of the park had been there. Jacaré's eldest son by his first wife, somewhat of an outsider in his father's house, was also a frequent visitor. Stone-Arm was tutoring him in the arts of shamanic healing along with his own son.

In addition to being filled with people, Stone-Arm's house, especially his small house or "office," was perpetually filled with animals of all kinds as well. Around the walls gourds and plastic containers were filled with several species of young birds. While most people in Kapinu'a raise birds, no one did so to the extent of Stone-Arm and Carol. These two cared for eagles, macaws, toucans, and hawks, as well as many others that I could not identify. Carol, an unusually large and somewhat rotund woman by Kayabi standards with long gray hair, was adept at holding baby birds to her chest and feeding them out of her mouth. One mature vulture they had raised by hand could often be seen sitting on the roof of their house waiting to hear Stone-Arm's handclap, his signal to come and be fed. Closer to the ground, Stone-Arm's tethered macaws repeated a shamanic chant for stopping rain or playfully called out his wife's name as she passed by.

Stone-Arm's passion for raising animals extended to dogs as well. All households have a few hunting dogs, but Stone-Arm's had at least twenty. This pack usually hung around the smaller house, waiting for the opportunity to sneak over the low stick partition that kept them outside and the younger children inside. Unlike so many others, these dogs were extremely well cared for. One wore a collar of corncobs to cure what sounded like a perpetual attempt to dislodge a fish bone stuck in its throat. Others had their paws deloused with precious kerosene, to the amazement (and scorn) of his neighbors, particularly Jacaré.

Both Jacaré's and Stone-Arm's households diverged from the more typical uxorilocal pattern in which young men live with their wife's family. Both men were able to attract their grown sons back to their own households, indicating that they were unusually powerful and respected headmen who were good at fostering a sense of conviviality, much as their jokes about their new names might suggest. The power that each of these leaders had to retain their followers, however, was slightly different. Jacaré promised familiarization and experimentation with more urban and Brazilian customs as well as access to purchased goods. The attraction of Stone-Arm rested largely in his renown as a shaman and his unusual openness and willingness to care for a variety of people and creatures.

Village Formation

Even household headmen less worldly than Jacaré and Stone-Arm have been aware for some time that providing adequately for followers involves providing more than shelter and food from the forest and agricultural fields. Many of their daily necessities are procured from outside their own household production. In Kapinu'a people continue to eat their own traditional foods, but most also use salt, which needs to be purchased. All families, to a greater or lesser degree, use kerosene for lamps made out of old tin cans to light their homes at night. Men need bullets and fishhooks for hunting. Women use some store-bought plates and cooking utensils. Both sexes wear clothing and rubber sandals. Many want the chance to learn or perfect their Portuguese, which many do not speak and most do not read or write. And, in addition to consulting shamans, many Kayabi also want access to Western medicines. The park offers access to some of these goods and services for people living in villages, but not for smaller family homesteads. The administration provides short-wave radios, motorboats, reserves of medicine, and regular doctor visits only to the most populous residential groups. As a result, many senior family headmen have adapted to the structure of the park and formed multifamily villages.

As a way of solving the difficult question of who should lead these new villages, the household headmen appointed young men, men who were still often doing bride service, to fill the position of village leader. The village leader is called both chefe (in Portuguese) and wyriat (the same word for household headman). To avoid confusion, I call a man in this position "chief." Much like other leaders in the Amazon (Brown 1993, 311) these younger chiefs are skilled in Portuguese, knowledgeable about Brazilian currency, and good at interfacing with various people and institutions outside of the park. As a result they have been able to supply village residents with a steady stream of consumer items and, at least in Kapinu'a, to procure materials to run a Brazilian-style school.

Aggregation in large villages and the delegation of authority to younger men did not happen all at once, however. Between the 1950s and the 1970s, when Kayabi families first began to move to the Xingu, the majority of Kayabi were spread out in isolated, extended family households. In the 1980s and 1990s families slowly came together to form multifamily groups. By the early

1990s there were three such villages. Kapinu'a, the largest, came together in the mid-1980s at a place called Big Rock, where Chief João's father, Chest, had already established a homestead. Chest, with urging from João and his other son, convinced Jacaré to move his family to the same location and form a village. Chest and Jacaré agreed that the village leader would be Jacaré's eldest son. Analogous to the FUNAI administration, they also chose an assistant to the chief, called, in Portuguese, an *assessor*. João was chosen for this position. At the time of their appointment, both the chief and his assistant were young men who had only unmarried children—unlikely men for leadership positions according to traditional structures of authority.

When Jacaré's eldest son received a salaried position working for the FUNAI in Brasília, João took over as the chief of the village. For his own assistant, he appointed Stone-Arm's youngest son, Marcos, who was at the time still living independently with his extended family at a location upriver. João admitted that he explicitly appointed Marcos as the assistant in order to attract Stone-Arm and his family to the newly forming village. Because Stone-Arm had a reputation as a very powerful shaman, João thought his presence would draw others to the village. João was correct: the village did grow after Stone-Arm's household moved there. By 1993 seventeen households resided in Kapinu'a (see Oakdale 1996 for a history of the other Xinguan Kayabi villages).

Though the Xinguan Kayabi previously lived in small extended family homesteads, living in large groups like Kapinu'a was not an entirely new pattern. In 1915, for example, the explorer Antonio Pyrineus de Sousa reported seeing Kayabi residential groups numbering in the hundreds (1916, 76, 84, 85). These earlier large villages were, however, different than the present Xinguan villages in that they were each composed of one large extended family. Like contemporary extended-family households, these more populous households were led by senior family headmen, not young men (85). Bird, one of the men who taught school in Kapinu'a, recounting what his father told him, said that when these senior leaders caught "whites sicknesses" and died, everyone spread out, the result being that in the early half of the twentieth century smaller extended families lived on their own.

New-Style Village Leadership

In many ways the new-style young village chiefs still function much like senior family headmen. As Brown points out, new-style leaders all over the lowlands are "drawn inexorably back" to the patterns of old-fashioned leadership (1993, 313). Like a senior headman, a Kayabi village chief is responsible for "taking care of" his followers, that is, those families who reside in his village. Also like a senior headman, his power is based on his productivity and ability to foster conviviality. To this end, chiefs too organize their followers in work and play. The young chiefs and the senior headmen, however, ultimately attract and keep their followers in different ways. For a senior leader, the core of his following is his family, people bound to him by kinship and bride service. A new-style village chief, on the other hand, because of his young age at the time of his appointment, has few children and no grandchildren or sons-in-law. People are not compelled to work for a young chief because of bride-service obligations, nor do they respect him on the basis of his seniority. Rather, young leaders attract and hold their followers by offering them access to the Brazilian economy and other services that come from the park administration (see Fisher 2000 for a parallel situation among the Kayapó).

In Kapinu'a village, young chiefs organize the labor of others much as senior headmen do at the household level. All of the people who reside in Kapinu'a, for example, consider themselves to be the followers or the workers (*oporowykyma'e*) of the same village chief, just as they would if they lived in the same household. In Kapinu'a, the chief directs all sorts of village projects but especially work on a communal field. In 1992–93 the collective field was planted with manioc and small banana trees. Most of the young married men in the village worked on this field (as well as on their own families' plots). Joining the village in fact entailed providing young workers for this field. Headmen "loaned" out the young men in their own work force (their sons and sons-in-law). Those headmen who could not spare any of the younger men in their own household or who simply had none donated manioc from their own fields to sell along with the produce from the community's field.

In many ways the village chief treats the young men of the village as he would treat his own sons-in-law, if he were old enough to have any. The young men frequently meet in his house in the morning, are fed a meal by his wife, and then go off together to work on the community field or to perform other community services, such as repairing the short-wave radio house or clearing the plaza of vegetation.

Again like a senior headman, a village chief presides over certain types of food distribution. If a hunter kills a large animal he frequently asks the chief to organize its butchering and distribution. Occasionally men from his work crew (as well as older men) will bring the chief game, just as younger men do for their household headman. Every so often the chief and his wife also sponsor a village-wide meal.

Yet chiefs, at least in Kapinu'a, differ from senior headmen in that they are primarily mediators between their local group and the national society (see

Brown 1993, 311). Most of the senior headmen speak less Portuguese and tend to interface much less routinely with non-Kayabi. João, for example, organized and oversaw transportation for the selling of manioc flour (*farinha*) from the community field to the nearby towns. To successfully carry out an operation such as this, a chief must know how to speak Portuguese, know how to bargain with people, and understand Brazilian currency. One of the most challenging parts of this process is obtaining the sacks to haul the flour. In 1992 João was able to arrange for sacks in advance from the buyer in town. Harvests could then be taken to a park post by motorboat or by the ferry operated by one of the NGOs in the Xingu. Arranging for transportation from the post to the towns at the periphery of the park where flour is purchased is another challenge. In 1992 João had to rent a truck to take the heavy sacks to town.

In exchange for their agricultural work, the chief provides his followers with consumer goods. He is in charge of using the proceeds from the communal field to buy bulk products such as salt and soap and then distributing them among the village households. On trips to larger urban centers, the chief is also expected to buy yardage of cloth, plastic sandals, knives, fishhooks, and flashlights. João and his wife, Pretty, kept a locked suitcase with a small reserve of these goods at all times. João also started a community bank account in Brasília to save for larger items and emergencies. Again, all of these transactions require knowledge of urban areas. While traveling with João I noticed that he was very savvy about the different techniques an indigenous person can use to get the best price in stores, including knowing the finer points about which ones work best in which cities.

While the chief is not the only source of goods—for example, a few households have access to the wages of younger men and a few sell their produce on their own—there is an understanding that anyone can ask him for goods they are lacking. As a result, the chief's household often has fewer goods than others (see Fisher 2000; Price 1981; Lévi-Strauss [1955] 1975, 311, for similar situations).

A new-style village chief should also be able to attract goods to his community from the park administration. Chiefs use their fluency in Portuguese (in ways that most older family headmen simply cannot) to direct park benefits toward their followers. They also encourage villagers to take advantage of what the park offers. In Kapinu'a this can be seen with respect to both health care and education.

The larger villages in the Xingu are all equipped with certain standard goods to facilitate health care. They all have short-wave radios so that in emergencies doctors can be relatively rapidly summoned from a post. Larger villages also have a pharmacy stocked with medicines. As of 1993 the village of Kapinu'a was having a "permanent structure" built by the FUNAI as a result of João's lobbying efforts to obtain such a building. This structure, with a cement floor, tiled walls, and metal roof, was to replace the wood-and-thatch hut that had been housing medicines. No other village in the northern part of the park had such a structure at the time. Kapinu'a also received a motorboat to better transport sick individuals to the post.

João (along with his older brother) encouraged Kayabi to participate in the indigenous health care program in operation in the Xingu Park. Run by medical teams from the São Paulo Medical School, this program trains indigenous health and dental monitors (Monitores de Saude and Monitores Dentista) in each Xinguan village. Volunteers from each village spend a few weeks at a park post getting trained in Western etiology and the administration of medicines. Kayabi individuals are some of the most avid participants in these programs, and in 1993 more than one-third of the participants in the entire Xingu were Kayabi. During the 1993 training session, four men from Kapinu'a attended as health monitors and three as dental monitors. The young men who assumed these positions first asked their household headman for permission; their services were in a sense "loaned" out by their family headman, much as they are when they work on the community field.

João also channeled the limited resources available for Brazilian-style education in the park toward his village. While he held office he attempted to keep a small Brazilian-style school running in Kapinu'a, a service no other Kayabi village offered at that time. Conscious of the role the school played in attracting people to his village, he often mentioned the school as one of the benefits of living in Kapinu'a in his public addresses. The FUNAI furnished a blackboard and a few schoolbooks, but the Brazilian-style school was run solely by Kayabi men, called education monitors (Monitores de Educação). These were, like the health and dental monitors, voluntary, unpaid positions. In Kapinu'a the education monitors were self-selected men who either had previous experience with Brazilian-style schooling (such as attending classes at the FUNAI while staying with a relative receiving medical treatment in an urban center) or had, since assuming their positions, sought out such training. In Kapinu'a the monitors built a small wood-and-thatch house as well as a long table and two benches out of cut lumber to be used exclusively for classes. The two monitors held classes in Portuguese and arithmetic in the mornings and afternoons every day except Sunday for most of the year. Classes stopped, however, during the most intense periods of agricultural work for several weeks or months. Attendance was completely voluntary. Children and adults decided for themselves if and when they wanted to attend. In 1992 thirty-four people attended regularly.

Much like a household headman, a village chief is also supposed to be emotionally connected with his followers and to foster a sense of well-being. The two men who held the position of chief in Kapinu'a while I was there, for example, mourned in sympathy with families who were grieving the death of a relative. Despite being only distantly related to these families, the chiefs and their wives went through some of the grief stages that close family members go through for an attenuated period. Likewise, the chief's emotional state was a concern for others in Kapinu'a. Women spoke about how they needed to give Chief João gifts of food for his own family's consumption in order to give him a sense of happiness. My neighbor and her daughter-in-law spoke about the undesirability of making him upset with improper behavior. Similarly, some commented that the hard work of clearing the plaza center was done to please the chief. This is not to say that there were not some who expressed complaints about particular village chiefs but rather that among supporters there was a general concern with each chief's emotional state and an assumption that the chief would be concerned with theirs.

The village chief, again like the household headman, also has the obligation to hold parties and to "play around" with his followers. The best sort of village chief is supposed to have nightly get-togethers in his house, to encourage people to undertake Kayabi festivals often, and, according to many, to sponsor frequent Brazilian-style parties with taped *forró* and *lambada* music, dancing, and card playing. João, for example, bought an enormous record player and speaker set with the hopes of hooking it up to a battery in order to sponsor unparalleled parties. He used his increased access to purchased goods to provide an even more intense type of partying and "playing around" than what could be found at the household level. A village like Kapinu'a perhaps needs intense and frequent parties, as the risk for interpersonal tensions is high.

New Tensions

Though beneficial in many ways, new-style Xinguan villages have also caused several new tensions and strains. In Kapinu'a, families are not used to living with each other in such close proximity, and some do not like the stress of interacting on a daily basis. In many ways the village seems like a collection of independent houses struggling to avoid each other. Some households in the village are divided with respect to the location of their previous homeland outside of the park—the upper or lower Teles Pires. In short, there is a constant threat that one (or several) of these households will break off from the rest, go back to living on its own, or join another group. Another tension exists between the younger and older generations—both within each household and between the new-style chiefs and the senior family headmen who placed these young men in power. As a result, people discuss whether moving to villages, and all that it entails, was the correct thing to do.

With respect to daily activities, the village of Kapinu'a appears to be a collection of households that are largely independent of each other. Each household has its own separate path leading from its door, through the plaza center, down to the river's edge. Household members tend to walk exclusively on their own path. The river's edge is similarly divided into separate bathing places, many of which are secluded from each other by vegetation. Individual households also farm and process food with relatively little interhousehold interaction. Many of the fields are located far from the village, and families have a second house located near them. As a consequence, some families live by themselves for several months while they do the most intensive agricultural work.

People from the oldest generations in each of the households are the ones who interact least in their daily routines (see Wagley [1977] 1983 for a similar situation among the Tupian Tapirapé). For example, while younger men and women from different families frequently come to the chief's house for recreation, to converse, to joke, and to make plans for working together, elder headmen and senior women rarely get together as a group. Among senior men who are of equal power there seems to be almost an active avoidance.

Jacaré and Stone-Arm have carried their avoidance to an extreme. Throughout my stay I never saw them visit or speak directly to each other even though they lived next-door in the village circle. Jacaré often peppered his conversations with insults about his neighbor. According to him, Stone-Arm did not know how to cure and used various items "from *civilizados*" in his shamanic treatments incorrectly. Furthermore, Jacaré thought Stone-Arm did not know how to take care of the (very substantial amount of) consumer goods that people, such as researchers, park personnel, and his non-Kayabi patients in the park, had given him: "He lets his birds roost on them."

Stone-Arm similarly voiced criticisms about Jacaré. According to Stone-Arm, Jacaré knew no ancestors' stories and instead made up stories about "tapirs brushing their teeth" for the SIL missionary-linguists to print in their books. [6] Jacaré knew about these sorts of comments and admitted that he did not know the traditional stories as well as others did. (When he narrated them, he often asked Julia to remind him of certain segments.) He attributed this to the fact that he had been brought up at a pacification post. Despite their

49

general animosity, at some point in their younger years Stone-Arm and Jacaré had been companions in the Teles Pires River area. Stone-Arm described for me late one night as we sat near the fire how they had once gone down to the river together when there was a full moon and tattooed images representing each other's names into their forearms. Stone-Arm recalled with fondness the scene of inserting black *genipap* dye under their skin with thorns to make a permanent tattoo. Stone-Arm also later convinced Jacaré to move to the Xingu in the late 1950s. After becoming next-door neighbors, however, such a relationship no longer appeared possible. Maintaining a sense of conviviality in spite of this sort of bickering is one of the challenges young village chiefs face.

In addition to the tension that exists among households, another major fault line in a village such as Kapinu'a lies between the younger and senior members within each household. The clearest commentary by seniors regarding their lack of control over their juniors surrounds discussions of contemporary marriage practices. Because households are in such close proximity in large villages, young people can interact with each other with much less supervision by their elders. They do not need to travel to visit each other as they did when households were spread out; rather, they can arrange to meet secretively if they wish. As a result, some parents complain that their children are choosing their own marriage partners rather than letting them arrange their marriages with appropriate cross-cousins.

While some arranged marriages still take place successfully, others have met with unhappy consequences. One such marriage was arranged by a headman named Amapá. Amapá, a fluent speaker of Portuguese, had worked in frontier areas outside the park. As a result, he was one of the first people to engage with me when I arrived in Kapinu'a. In addition to his familiarity with Brazilian society, however, Amapá also proved to be one of the most knowledgeable seniors in Kayabi ways. He had an excellent knowledge of myth and verbal genres, such as a complicated ceremonial greeting similar to others found throughout the lowlands (Urban 1991). In keeping with older patterns, Amapá had chosen a wife for his son without regard for his son's preference, a practice that most said was disappearing—parents now wait to see "who their child likes" before making marriage arrangements. No matter how much his son protested, Amapá would not allow him to marry the girl of his choice. As a result, the young man ignored his new wife for months and took every opportunity to travel and leave her for weeks at a time.

Other seniors complain about the shortened time of bride service. Fire-of-the-Gods said that his elderly father told him that bride service used to begin while the bride was still in her mother's womb. A young man would make handicrafts for his mother-in-law, such as large woven baskets or spindles out of turtle shell, in payment for the labor of physically forming and carrying his wife. If the child was a boy or did not survive, he would wait for the next baby. Then when a girl was born, the man continued to work for her father, hunting, doing agricultural labor, and building houses. During this time he lived with his wife's parents and was supposed to "raise" his wife along with them. (They very likely raised their son-in-law during this time as well.) More recently in the majority of households in Kapinu'a, men marry women who are closer to their own age and frequently only move in with their wives' families after they have conceived a child.[7] The contemporary period of bride service is therefore much shorter, as the grooms are not working for their in-laws while waiting for their wives to grow up. As Fire-of-the-Gods commented, rather than arranging marriages and having the right to years of respectful service, now parents have to try to "tie down" the young men who sleep with their daughters.

Finally, there is a tension in the larger villages between elder headmen and the younger chiefs. While in some ways senior headmen view the chiefs as one more member of their work force—the services they provide being their interactions with the park administration and national society rather than agricultural labor—in other ways they realize the chiefs are not at all like their own workers. Village chiefs are not fully under their authority as are their own sons and sons-in-law living in their own households. Also, a village chief has some limited rights over the labor of the senior headmen's young workers. These are the aspects that seniors find disturbing. Some senior headmen, for example, resent losing their young household workers to the communal projects that the village chief runs. Because their workers must assist the chief, their own projects often run short staffed.

That the chief functions as the distributor of consumer goods purchased with money gained from the sale of produce from the community field is potentially another problem. Many senior headmen are no longer the major centers of redistribution. At the same time, their more direct access to pur-chased goods is shrinking. Members of their households instead go directly to the village chief to ask for high-prestige, purchased goods.[8] For example, newly married men have long been able to give their parents-in-law a large hammock or pot as payment for part of their bride-service obligations. Out-side of the park, young men sought out work at ranches, at farms, at rubber plantations, with animal skin hunters, and at government-run posts to buy these kinds of items for their in-laws. Inside the park, however, newly married men have fewer options for wage work. While there are still some young men who do find work at Xinguan posts or travel outside of the park to earn money, most rely more heavily on village chiefs to procure and distribute consumer goods.

Yet another potential problem for senior generations is the village school. Several chiefs in Kapinu'a have encouraged Brazilian-style education. While many agree that a village school is beneficial in a number of ways, some seniors see it as contributing to their loss of control as well. As Fire-of-the-Gods commented, again paraphrasing his elderly father, "Now, when a man wants to get married the guy gives nothing. He comes with a 'naked' hand [that is, nothing in his hand]. No one knows how to make things now, only how to write. You see how things change." Comments about young men's lack of ability to make handicrafts is related to the disappearance of male initiation as much as it is to increased literacy. During initiation, boys were secluded within their home, where they learned handicrafts from their fathers and other senior male relatives. In Kapinu'a, most men who are under the age of fifty have not undergone seclusion. Men do still continue to weave baskets and make other traditional Kayabi items, but they begin making them at a later age and therefore do not know how to make them when they marry. They are, as many seniors say, "still young" when they marry.[9] Instead, boys in Kapinu'a spend significant amounts of time in the village school under the tutelage of village schoolteachers. In contrast to the older male relatives who teach boys traditional skills during seclusion, the Kayabi men who are in charge of the village school are relatively young men and are for the most part from different families than their pupils. These factors—that a significant part of the training adolescents receive is in the hands of these younger men and that these men are teaching them skills their elders do not control—make the school a potential problem in the eyes of seniors.[10]

The village school in the 1990s also introduced a new way of helping to choose a village chief. For example, when João stepped down from the position of village chief and his assistant, Marcos, took over, a village-wide vote was held to install a new assistant. It was determined through village-wide discussions that all the villagers, adults and children alike, should cast a vote. The man who eventually assumed this position, Fire-of-the-Gods, had been the education monitor. Rather than focus only on garnering the support of the senior headmen before the election, he also focused on the village children. He had actively been cultivating a group of young followers for several months by devoting time to joking and playing with his pupils after class. At one point he even secured boxes of toothbrushes and toothpaste from a dental monitor.

Rather than simply giving them out to his pupils, he held them in his care and three times a day walked through the village yelling "brush!" in Portuguese. This was the signal for the children to get their brushes and paste from him. After a week or so this routine gave way to a new one. Boys would gather with him in the evening, when most of the visiting takes place, and do exercises such as running from one end of the village to the other or practicing karate-like moves. (The village had a surge of martial arts interest with the arrival of Jacaré's grandson, who had studied one of the martial arts in Brasília.) While none of these activities lasted long they all contributed to this monitor's popularity among the younger boys from various households. This sort of camaraderie and play not only helped him win the election but will no doubt help him when these boys later begin to work for him as part of his work crew when he eventually becomes chief. The education monitor's advantage with respect to his position as the children's teacher was not lost on his opponent's family, who was quick to point out that he won because, when any of the children were asked who they wanted as the chief's assistant, they naturally said, "my teacher."

2

Autobiographical Narrative Performances

THE SELF-CONSCIOUS "INDIAN"

The important thing about leadership is
understanding the situation of the other.

CHIEF JOÃO, 1992

As São José do Xingu, the Brazilian town located just outside of the northern perimeter of the park, was preparing for mayoral elections, an event that involved many candidate-sponsored festivities, Chief João called a village meeting in Kapinu'a. In his meeting João addressed the dangers of drinking alcohol when visiting São José. In the course of describing the problems that could ensue from drinking, he admitted that he himself had drunk beer in town and that afterward others had counseled him not to do so. Sitting in the audience, my first thought was that his admission was rhetorically just about the least effective thing he could have said. How, I wondered, could his admitting that he had done what he was advising others not to do convince people to behave appropriately? After listening to other comments by João and other leaders, however, I began to see that his admission fit within a more general pattern of leading followers in a nonauthoritarian manner. His account of his own past behavior, combined with the fact that villagers knew him as someone who currently did not drink, provided a model for others of how to move from wayward to correct behavior.

In this chapter I focus on two examples of public addresses given by leaders that also include autobiographical accounts. These addresses concern how the speakers have navigated facets of Brazilian Indian identity at play for inhabitants of the Xingu Park. Much as elsewhere in lowland South America, notions about Indian identity coming from sources external to indigenous communities are increasingly influencing contemporary self-representations (Conklin 1997, 2002; Conklin and Graham 1995; Jackson 1989, 1991, 1995a, 1995b; Ramos 1998; Turner 1991, 2000; Whitten 1981). In one address Chief João describes his own confrontation with aspects of Brazilian Indian identity during his 1992 trip to Rio de Janeiro to participate in the Earth Summit, a global conference on the environment. In the other, the elder headman Amapá recounts how he reacted to facets of Brazilian Indian identity during his 1966 relocation to the Xingu. I compare these accounts with the advice these leaders give their followers concerning how to most powerfully engage with aspects of this imposed identity in the present.

While many Kayabi people living in the Xingu Indigenous Park appear to be conscious of their Indian identity in the eyes of Brazilians, not all have the same understanding of what this identity entails nor do they know all of the associated terms, such as *culture*. Many Kayabi are, for example, just beginning to think about themselves in terms of the category "Indian" (see Jackson 1991). The two men who appear here, however, are leaders with shrewd appreciation of the many facets of Brazilian Indian identity at work in the Xingu as well as ideas about what this entity called "culture" might entail. Their comments display what Terence Turner has called a historically "appropriate" social consciousness involving "an awareness of the ambivalent import of their 'ethnicity' as a pretext for subordination by the dominant society, but also a potential basis for the assertion of collective autonomy" (1991, 293). In the addresses presented here each man draws on opposite sides of this "ambivalent import." The young chief's comments point to the subordination of an unreflexive Kayabi by the dominant society, while the elder headman's focus is on shared ethnicity or "culture" as a basis for group autonomy.

Although the speakers gave their addresses several weeks apart, they were in effect in dialogue with each other. In addition to making statements about how to most effectively engage with facets of contemporary Indian identity, they also made claims as to which sort of leader, young or elderly, is most effective for the present. Both made the argument that leaders should possess the most current and up-to-date knowledge about Indian identity and know how it works within the contemporary world. Indianness and culture, as others have pointed out (Jackson 1995a, 4, 14), are not fixed with respect to what they entail but rather are dynamic and changing. According to João, youths, who are more in sync with the present, clearly understand what Indian identity currently involves better than their seniors do. According to Amapá, elders, with their years of accumulated experiences, understand it better.

Political Oratory

The style of discourse I call "public address" or "political oratory" is classified by the Kayabi under the more general verb *porongyta*. *Porongyta* is usually translated (into Portuguese) by Kayabi as the equivalent of "to converse." *Porongyta* refers to the activity that takes place at the meetings called by the village chief in his house as well as to the talks that older heads of extended families give to younger people. This term also refers to the telling of myths or ancestors' stories, which are thought of as the ancestors' conversations (e'yjia porongyta). While translated generally as "to converse," the term porongyta implies moral admonitions or instructions on how to live. For this reason the type of teaching done in the Brazilian-style school in Kapinu'a is not considered porongyta but rather a process of learning how to speak. Apparently, learning Portuguese does not involve the same sort of instruction on how to live correctly as leaders' conversations do.

Though they do not necessarily have to be so, leaders' addresses are often autobiographical. In the course of addressing problems and giving advice, headmen and chiefs often mention their own experiences. Much like João's commentary on drinking, some provide negative models, a means of identifying with the wayward and showing the correct way to reform. Some, in contrast, provide positive models. They are displays of ideal, adult male comportment, such as the ability to travel and to experience firsthand other peoples and ways of life. For example, upon returning from a trip, a leader is expected to give his followers an account of where he has been, what he has seen, and whom he has encountered. Addresses also frequently include references to the activities and travels of Kayabi ancestors, including mythic characters. One former village chief explained that bringing up past stories from one's life or those of the ancestors is part of offering counsel: "In my point of view, leadership is not of the style that whites talk about. For me leadership is a type of counsel. He makes things clear: 'don't do that, you have to live like this,' and [he] brings up stories of the past."

Before discussing the formal characteristics of leaders' addresses, let us first discuss what they are not. While many have noted that leaders in Tupian groups usually possess a facility with language of one kind or another (see, for example, Kracke 1978, 69; Clastres [1972] 1998, 105; [1974] 1987; Fausto 2001, 223, 255; Lèry 1990, 113), lengthy discussions of the formal dimensions of political oratory are noticeably few in Tupian literature. This, perhaps, is not unrelated to the nature of Tupian political oratory. It has the appearance, when compared to the oratory of other Amazonian peoples, especially the Gê-speaking ones, of being nonexistent as such. Gê-speaking peoples such as the Shavante, Suyá, and Kayapó employ dramatic techniques such as standing in the village plaza using imploded lateral clicks, regularized phrases and cadences, or falsetto chanting.[1] Tupian leaders, on the other hand, often facilitate conversation rather than drawing attention to their own verbal prowess. Carlos Fausto, for example, describes how, during meetings, chiefs among the Tupi-speaking Parakanãs function like "jazz band leaders, people who set a tempo, but permit improvisations" (2001, 224).

Kayabi chiefs and headmen similarly exhort their followers to behave in ways that do not call attention to their verbal abilities. For example, they *porongyta* within homes, usually their own, rather than in the plaza. Only the most respected men seem to *porongyta* in a household other than their own. Speakers also observe no unusual or unique voice quality. The volume and structure of participation in chiefs' talks are likewise only slightly different from day-to-day conversation. Leaders speak only a bit louder than they would in everyday conversation. The speaker does, however, hold the floor while others listen. The chief or elder speaks uninterrupted for a certain amount of time and then, once finished, concludes with the words "it's finished" (*tepap* or *acabou* in Portuguese) or "it's finished, my part" (*tepap jema'e*). Village chiefs' talks then turn into a less formal conversation. The chief often asks people by name about their opinions, or individuals offer their own comments.

Village chiefs' talks can be large or small events. Often the whole village is invited. When a chief will converse with the community as a whole, a child is sent out to call each household, announcing "*wyriara porongyta*," and people come to assemble in the chief's long house. Often women sit at the periphery and carry on alternate, unrelated conversations with each other while the chief talks. Sometimes a leader's talk will be exclusively for the men or exclusively for the women. An individual of the opposite sex may join in these cases, but they sit at the periphery. A talk may also be held for the residents of two households who are involved in a dispute. Again in these cases no one is prohibited from joining, but not everyone is called to participate. In the case of disputes, the chief functions as a moderator or intermediary in terms of the dialogue as well as of any physical attacks that may take place between the two parties. [2]

When a chief or an elder family headman gives a *porongyta* to just one individual, the recipient usually sits expressionless, with eyes downcast, while the chief or elder looks and speaks directly at him or her. In the case of elders, I noticed the tendency for the speaker to get closer to the recipient than is usually done in ordinary conversation.

Two Examples of Leaders' Addresses

Let us now turn to the addresses, in which the leaders make reference to their own encounters with facets of Brazilian Indian identity. In the first example, the young chief João portrays himself as the model of a skillful, modern actor. In the second example, the elder headman Amapá uses his own past inappropriate behavior to convey a message about how to act in the present. In both cases the speakers are counseling others on the correct and most powerful way to behave with respect to aspects of Indianness.

Amapá and João have spent the majority of their lives in very different social contexts with respect to the national society. Amapá spent the first thirty years of his life in frontier areas to the west of the park. The much younger João, in contrast, moved to the park as a child. The differences between the two men's lives are particularly apparent in their ways of speaking Portuguese. Amapá, for example, uses the Portuguese that he learned as a youth in the Teles Pires River area. His reminiscence about moving to the Xingu is filled with vocabulary that recalls the logic that informed the national policy of assimilation. He uses terms like *serviço*, which I have translated as "job," to talk about teaching typically Kayabi rituals and practices—a term that indexes the SPI and later FUNAI notion that indigenous people should enter the nation as laborers (see Souza Lima 1992). He also uses the terms *caboclo* and *civilizado* to refer to acculturated indigenous people and nonindigenous people, respectively. In addition, some of the terms he uses to refer to indigenous practices sound derogatory from the perspective of a more cosmopolitan speaker. For example, he uses the term *gíria* (slang), an expression commonly used in the interior, to refer to indigenous languages. The younger chief, on the other hand, never in my memory used the same sort of interior-specific vocabulary when speaking Portuguese.

Amapá's narrative seems to betray more insecurity with respect to his Indian identity relative to the young chief. Again, this is likely a result of having lived in frontier areas for a lengthy period. For example, as an adult he experienced the 1981 "criteria for Indianness" created by Colonel Zanoni Hausen, a FUNAI advisor. This list consisted of sixty desirable Indian traits. The FUNAI revoked protection for those who showed less than 50 percent of these traits. The list was highly criticized, and it eventually dropped out of usage (Ramos 1984, 96).

Let us first turn to João's address. In June 1992 João came back from a trip to Rio de Janeiro, where he had participated in a conference held in conjunction with the Earth Summit. While ecologists, government officials from various nations, and representatives from NGOs attended the summit, indigenous representatives from Brazil and beyond attended a parallel conference. Eight Kayabi from the Xingu Park were invited to this event, including Chief João. Upon his return, he called the rest of the village for a chief's talk, as is typical after a long absence. Lying in his hammock, which was strung up in the center of his house, with villagers and myself sitting around the periphery, he told us about his trip—first in Portuguese, then in Kayabi. João explained to me later that he usually addressed his followers in two languages because a few men in the village could not speak Kayabi. One was a Kayabi man who had grown up with Brazilians, and the other was Stone-Arm's grandson-in-law, a Panará. João's command of Portuguese also was useful in that it signaled to the others that he was an effective mediator with the non-Kayabi world (see Graham 2002, 214; Jackson 1995a, 14).

Chief João explained that on his way to Rio he met the other Kayabi who were attending the conference. He described how, as they all rode down the highway on the bus provided for the occasion, the others nervously asked him what they were expected to do once they arrived in Rio. He told them: "When we get there, you're going to have to show your culture." (*Cultura*, a Portuguese term, was used in both the Kayabi and Portuguese versions of the story). Implying that some of the older men (who tend to be monolingual) in his traveling party might not know what *cultura* was, he continued: "That means you'll have to get up in front of thousands of people and sing Kayabi songs, completely naked." As a consequence of his joke, the chief explained, one old man from a Kayabi village downriver was so scared by the possibility of being asked to undress that he never left his hammock in the mock Indian village, called the Kari-Oka, that was set up on the fairgrounds to house the visiting Brazilian Indians. (All Kayabi men currently wear, at the very minimum, shorts, and many have full sets of traveling clothes indistinguishable from any other Brazilian.) Literally stuck in the space for Indian identity established by the national society, the old man missed the rest of the city completely. Chief João went on to joke that he, on the other hand, visited various places in Rio, including different beaches and neighborhoods, and even discovered a way to make a little money by selling the condoms being passed out freely to the conference visitors.[3]

João's address, though untraditional at first glance, is nevertheless typical of the kind of addresses given by good Kayabi leaders in several respects. First, it gives an account of the leader's mastery of foreign territories upon return from a period of travel. Second, it is an example of how a leader should joke or play around with his followers. While not everyone in the audience understood his story to the same degree, in general the crowd laughed as they listened. Not sure what to think at first, even I could not help but smile at the scenario he described.

In his talk, held a few weeks after Chief João's address, Amapá told about his relocation to the Xingu Indigenous Park in 1966. Amapá had previously lived in the state of Pará along the lower Teles Pires River. In 1963 the upper waters of one of the Teles Pires River's tributaries, the Paranatinga River, suffered a diamond rush, called the "Paranatinga." Six thousand miners were reported to have moved into this area (Grünberg n.d. [1970], 31). Soon Kayabi areas on the lower Teles Pires, where Amapá lived, were also experiencing an influx of miners. In 1966 the Villas Boas brothers arranged air transportation for Kayabi living in this area to resettle them in the Xingu, as they had done in previous decades for Kayabi living in other locations on the Teles Pires. Amapá came to the park by plane with this group of refugees.

Amapá told me about his arrival in the park while he and I were sitting inside João and Pretty's house, visiting and avoiding the midday sun. People usually gathered informally inside the chief's house at almost any time of day and into the night. On this particular afternoon, João and his family were away at their fields, but we were joined by a younger man from another household, Paulo, who operated the short-wave radio in Kapinu'a, as well as by a group of younger boys. Amapá and Paulo were letting me tape their opinions on a variety of subjects. It was Paulo's comments that directly prompted the headman to describe his 1966 move to the Xingu.

Lounging in the chief's hammock, Paulo explained to me that older men simply do not understand much and that younger generations have had to take over because they can read, use money, and operate various sorts of machinery, for example, short-wave radios. He was repeating sentiments that I had heard Chief João express from the very same hammock on other occasions. In response, the headman, sitting on a wooden bench, reached down to the dirt floor and picked up a crumpled magazine page that the group of adolescent boys had dropped. He then said in a much louder voice, "Boys of today only know paper." The others quickly stopped their horseplay and became quiet and attentive as Amapá held the floor.

The text of Amapá's address below is segmented into prose paragraphs to facilitate reader comprehension.[4] At the outset, paragraph breaks correspond to turns in the characters' quoted speech. Later they correspond roughly to changes in topic. Frequently the end of a topic is signaled by a request for a back-channel response from an interlocutor. Those lines that were delivered at a significantly higher volume than others are set in boldface type (see Tedlock 1983, 46). Paragraphs are grouped according to scenes to aid the reader in following my later discussion of Amapá's narrative. Scenes correspond to shifts in time.

Scene 1

When I first arrived here it was really lousy. I complained to Cláudio Villas Boas.

"Ah, you really are accustomed to whites aren't you. Hell, here in the Xingu that doesn't exist. You have to get used to your own people. De-educate a little," [Cláudio Villas Boas said.]

Scene 2

Later, people here [said], "You came here and you ruined people. You know whites more. You know more how to speak with whites. You don't have to be teaching other people how."

"Let him be. He'll learn things slowly." That's how Cláudio spoke to me.

He didn't **like** that I asked for so many things from him either. I used to say, "Oh, I want this and I want ammunition, I want soap to wash clothes, I want thread to sew, I want . . ." It was lots of things that I said. He did not like it.

"**Ah, you** spend a lot. It's true. You turned into a really civilized person. I'm going to call a plane for you to go [back to the Teles Pires]," he said.

Then, the one who did not allow it was Orlando [Villas Boas].

[Orlando said,] "Why did you order him to leave. You're really foolish. You can't do this. **Let him talk, later he'll get accustomed.**" He continued, "Not around you. You don't have to even spend much time with him. Soon when everyone is gathered together, the other groups, [when] there are no more wild Indians. After that he'll go to the city and [you'll] never [see him] again," he said to him.

"Okay," [Cláudio said.]

But he didn't like me. He almost ordered me to go once again.

I said, "I am really going. **There is nothing here. There is no soap.**"

Scene 3

In the first time, you see, Suzanne, people didn't have anything. Nothing. Nothing. They didn't know how to eat mangos. They didn't eat potatoes, those other kind from whites. They didn't know how to wash clothes. **Nobody had sandals, just the foot right on the ground.**

Scene 4

Today no, today they have everything here. They all have sandals. The boys all have sandals, everything. You don't have the Indian always just using our own things. That's why I talk to people, "Let's not finish it early. When we are alive talk to sons, grandsons, nephews, to people in groups. Get them to understand not to finish that, ours, everything." Understand?

In this here you can't finish. In this, the most important. The most truly important is the business about **parties** [rituals], **real Indian parties**, all of it. Only once in a while if you want to learn with boys like those there [he gestures toward the village plaza], learn what you're **going to learn** there in the middle of the city. How it is he [the white] dances. So what, he dances.

Now the older ones like me, the older ones **carry the Indian music** so it doesn't stop. Go **turning it over** to sons, to grandsons because he dies and there is another guy, because the oldest one dies. Then he goes carrying the job forward to **teach** another, right? For it not to be finished, right?

Therefore you don't need to finish it **all at once** like I said to that one over there, other people there, **"It's over.** You don't know anything, not even how to **speak**, to speak in slang." Those who speak more Portuguese do not know how to speak in slang. They only speak to their son in Portuguese. Right?

"Ah, son do that. Oh, my son **do that."** No, that's not it. You have to speak in slang **for it not to be finished.** Order more learning, work. It is our job. It's our culture. In order not to do away with this. Then you're stronger, more strength for us. You **do away** with this, speak more white. The white says today, **"That one is not an Indian anymore,** he's already a caboclo. He's already civilized." And then, **"He speaks more Portuguese. He learns more, speaks more Portuguese."** Right?

[End of quotation of whites' speech is unclear.] **"If you don't have anymore Indian** you don't have anymore value." Understand? That's the way it is.

What this older headman has done here is to skillfully place the sorts of skills and knowledge the young man is boasting about into his own past. Much like Chief João's story about drinking beer, Amapá describes himself as having behaved improperly. Like the young man to whom he is speaking, he was also entranced with white goods and skills. He describes how he surpassed his own youth by listening to the counsel of others and by devoting himself to Kayabi skills. His life provides a model to Paulo for how to move beyond white skills and knowledge. Throughout the talk he never directly confronts or comments on Paulo's own behavior but rather comments on his own past, describing how he changed.

Amapá's story is a good example of the way autobiographical narrative can be used to guide the behavior of others in a nonauthoritarian manner. Leadership in Amazonian societies has frequently been described as "indirect" or "oblique" (Brown 1993, 309; Clastres [1974] 1987; Lévi-Strauss 1967; Kracke 1978; Rosengren 1987). Waud Kracke, for example, writes about the Tupian Kagwahiv, "The manner in which work is directed seems deceptively unimperative to our Western sensibilities, accustomed as we are to commands being given and carried out even in positions of modest power" (1978, 42). This style of leadership, as many have noted, corresponds with the emphasis placed on personal autonomy. Leading by exemplary behavior is usually cited as the central way that leaders direct others in this oblique manner in Amazonian communities (Brown 1993, 309; Clastres [1972] 1998, 105; Kracke 1978, 42; Price 1981, 694). Leaders' use of autobiographical narrative for the same ends, however, has been mentioned less frequently in the Amazonian literature. But narratives, like actions, can provide a pattern for others to follow.

Leading by example, through action or autobiographical narrative, however, is not completely uncoercive (Kracke 1978, 43). Followers can clearly feel the rhetorical power of these acts. For example, though Amapá's message to Paulo was indirect, embedded in a story about his own experiences, it was clearly received by the young man. Paulo abruptly swung himself out of the chief's hammock and left after Amapá was finished speaking.

How to Be a Powerful Brazilian Indian

Amapá and João use their stories about their confrontations with Indianness to direct others in an indirect manner on how to behave with respect to this kind of contemporary identity. Although their techniques are different, both men provide an image of what they believe to be the most powerful way to "be Indians" in the present (Jackson 1991, 131). João's story about his trip provides a positive image of himself as someone who is fully in control of all facets of this identity as it is experienced in the Xingu. Amapá's account is more complicated, as he provides both negative and positive models for how to behave as an Indian. Despite these differences both men present their current selves as models for effective, powerful engagement with this identity in the contemporary world. The other characters, including past selves, are their foils.

In his account Chief João is clearly the most fully able character. He has the skill to maneuver around the city of Rio at will. His traveling companion, the old man from a village downriver, provides the contrast. By the end of the story, this character literally becomes stuck in his hammock inside the mock Indian village set up on the conference grounds. This image of the old man resonates with the previously practiced initiation rites of adolescent boys in which they were secluded within their house (and ideally within their hammock) for a period of time. In the story, then, the old man becomes like an adolescent. The seclusion is particularly degrading for the old man because his house is the mock Indian shelter, the Kari-Oka.

Kari-Oka was very likely chosen by conference organizers as the name for the Indians' shelter because the term *carioca* refers to an inhabitant of Rio de Janeiro.[5] It is also a word that has a Tupian sound. Tupian Indians have historically been considered the linguistic group that represents the "Indian" side of the mosaic of Brazilian national culture (Urban 1992). *Oka* is "house" in many Tupian languages, and *kari*, at least in Língua Geral, a trade language based on the Tupinamba language, referred to the colonizers (Waud Kracke, personal communication).[6] Currently *kari*, in Kayabi, is a vocative (a noun that indicates the person addressed) used by men when speaking to their female relatives. For a Kayabi audience, the name Kari-Oka might sound familiar but slightly strange. It might even have the connotation of being a house for women. The sense that the old man's ignorance and fear put him in an undeveloped adolescent and even female position is heightened when the listener learns that the items the chief was selling on the street were condoms.

For Amapá, it is his own past that provides the unflattering contrast to his current maturity. He represents himself currently as the one who speaks to grandsons, nephews, sons, and "people in groups" and who "carries Indian music" for the next generation. His younger self, upon coming to the park, in contrast, was someone others spoke about as "ruining people" because "he knew more how to speak with whites." His past self also annoyed the directors of the park, the Villas Boas brothers. Similar to the old man stuck in the mock Indian village, the younger Amapá, because of his behavior, comes very close to being physically unable to move. He is almost "sent back" to the Teles Pires by Cláudio Villas Boas.

As well as portraying their present selves as the most powerful characters in their narratives, Amapá and João also present strength and power in the present as following from a similar combination of different kinds of knowledge—that which is traditional, or passed down through the generations, seemingly unchanged, and that which is historically specific. In each case, it is a combination that another person, either a more elderly or a more youthful character, does not fully possess. These men are implying that they are powerful because they understand what is uniquely Kayabi and have an extensive knowledge about the national society, including their role within it as "Xinguan Indians." The young chief, for example, presents himself as going to Rio both as a self-conscious representative of Kayabi distinctiveness and as someone who knows how to manage in the city. He describes himself as even knowing how to trick the city folk in their own territory by selling them items that they themselves are passing out free of charge. Furthermore, he displays the fact that he understands very well the role that Indians living within the Xingu play within the nation as some of the most "primitive," "innocent," and naked of all. In his story, however, even the character of the old man is aware of the stereotypic identity of Xinguans as primitives. After all, this is what scares him into his hammock for a week. What really sets the narrator apart is his full understanding of the use of such terms as *culture* in the current national and international context (see Jackson 1995a, 1995b, for the importance of these terms in Colombia). He knows that at present representing one's "culture" in an urban context does not necessarily involve being unclothed. The old man's knowledge about "Xinguan Indian" identity is a bit outdated or provincial at best.

The headman Amapá also displays the fact that at present he has the knowledge and skills characteristic of both whites and Kayabi. For him, different periods in the life cycle correspond to expertise in these different sorts of knowledge. As a youth he was an expert in living as a white. Amapá depicts his current self, however, as having surpassed this earlier "white stage" by taking the advice of Cláudio Villas Boas and heeding the comments of other Kayabi. He gradually changed or "de-educated" himself of white habits. Now he is the one who knows Indian music and who speaks his indigenous language. He does not, however, completely deride learning about whites. According to Amapá, it is acceptable "once in a while" to learn things in the city such as white-style dancing "with boys," provided people don't forget about what is "ours." He treats being absorbed with only Brazilian culture as merely a phase of youth. For him, adult knowledge is built on an understanding of white as well as Kayabi practices.

Much like the young chief, Amapá portrays himself as understanding how Kayabi practices fit into the national context. Also like the young chief, he explicitly links this understanding with having strength in the present. He points out that when people maintain Kayabi practices there is "more strength for us." And he continues to comment that if "you don't have anymore Indian you don't have anymore value." As it is for the younger chief, whose joke turned on both his own understanding and the old man's ignorance of the term *culture*, for Amapá, understanding what is "our culture" in the national context becomes crucial for having power in the present. He equates culture, however, with the process of elders like himself teaching the younger generations how to sing Kayabi songs, hold Kayabi rituals, and speak the Kayabi language.

Enacting Power vis-à-vis the Audience

The relationships between the characters in the two narratives call into play certain relationships between the generations at issue in their respective speech events. The chief and the headman are not just those characters in their stories who possess the most agency and knowledge. Rather, through aspects of their oratory they also enact how their knowledge is superior to that of certain members in their audiences—specifically those who are of a different generation. For the young chief, the use of the Portuguese term *cultura* is one of the principle means of doing this. The headman, on the other hand, uses quoted speech and the presence of the tape recorder to this end.

As noted previously, Chief João gave his address in both Portuguese and Kayabi, as he typically did when speaking in formal meetings. In both languages, however, he used the term *cultura* rather than any sort of Kayabi translation for the concept. His use of this term seems to be especially effective in enacting his superiority over the two groups in the audience. On the one hand, elderly, monolingual speakers who do not often leave the village do not know the term *cultura*. Those who are not familiar with the term *cultura* would sense themselves to be in the position of the old man, who, it is implied, does not understand the term either. This type of audience member would miss much of the humor of the joke. On the other hand, the joke would be more effective for those who had some recognition of *cultura* but who were not entirely sure of its reference. Though I heard the term used by the chief and other well-traveled men, I also heard many other, less cosmopolitan men ask for clarification on the meaning of this term. The chief relies on these less cosmopolitan men— who spend the majority of their time in Kapinu'a (rather than working at posts or traveling in the city)—because they make up the work force for the common field. They are also the group of individuals who seem to be simultaneously most convinced of the benefits of interacting with the national society and most painfully aware of their own shortcomings, especially with respect to their ability to speak Portuguese and to transact money effectively. Listeners who were slightly unsure of the meaning of *cultura* would sense themselves uncomfortably close to the old man of the joke and would sense the urgency of relying on the chief for successful interactions (financial and otherwise) outside of Kayabi communities.

The senior headman's narrative similarly calls into play intergenerational relations between himself and the young man Paulo. When Amapá describes his youth as a period during which he too was well versed in nonindigenous skills and lifestyles, he does so from the point of view of past interlocutors. He quotes Cláudio Villas Boas as having said, "Ah, *you* really are accustomed to whites. . . . *You* have to get used to your own people." The Kayabi in the Xingu also say to him, "*You* came here and ruined people." His use of the second-person singular in direct quotation has the effect of making his comments seem as though they may have been the responses of powerful whites and fellow Kayabi to his present interlocutor—Paulo. In this particular situation,

69

sitting with my tape recorder in hand, I was the sort of white that the Villas Boas brothers were: a relatively wealthy individual interested in Kayabi distinctiveness. The quotations from the Villas Boas and the Kayabi of the past could be read as typical responses that Amapá and I might have made to Paulo's boasts.

Amapá furthermore presents his current self as the means to overcome these negative evaluations. He is the one who can teach the Kayabi skills necessary for the young Paulo to have "value" in the eyes of whites and fellow Kayabi. As I tape-record Amapá's words, I am a means for Amapá to actually enact how non-Indians "value" his knowledge as an elder (see Graham 1995 for a similar case). He literally commandeers the tape recorder for his own ends and draws attention to the fact that representing Kayabiness to whites, not fluency in Brazilian culture, is crucial for survival in the present context.

Placement of the Narrator in Human Development

Kayabi myths or ancestors' stories provide two alternate views of humanity's (that is, the Kayabi's) trajectory over time. According to one view, people learn more and more about the world as time passes. Humanity as a whole matures much like an individual, whose knowledge also develops with age. According to Kayabi theories of development, children "do not understand." Only as a person matures does he or she "understand" and "know." According to this model, current generations understand the world much better than previous ones (see Basso 1995 for similar notions among the Kalapalo). In many ancestors' stories, previous generations are depicted as being like children in comparison to those that follow. For example, the culture hero Tujarare, who gave rise to the Kayabi, married into a people called the People-without-Understanding. Like children, the People-without-Understanding did not know how to use language appropriately, what foods were edible, or how to perform certain rituals until they were taught by their young in-law. This progressive trajectory found in Kayabi ancestors' stories fits nicely with Brazilian-style discourse about progress and development.

Ancestors' stories provide the opposite trajectory as well: that at the beginning of the cosmos knowledge and power were the most complete. In these early times, humans lived alongside extremely powerful, nonhuman beings and had access to their knowledge and abilities. Since these first times, these nonhuman beings have gradually moved away from the Kayabi. As the generations have passed, the Kayabi have become less knowledgeable and weaker as a result. That Kayabi myths should offer two paradoxical visions, one of human progress and development over time and one of increasing weakness and distance from original power, is not entirely unusual in mythology and can be found elsewhere in the Amazon (see Whitten 1976, 49).

In political contexts, such as chiefs' talks, leaders and others who aspire to positions of leadership tend to draw predominantly upon the progressive trajectory. Men often employ the rhetoric that no one taught them, or in Kayabi caused (mo) them, to do things but rather that they understood and were able to do things by themselves. As João once said, with his father sitting at his side, "My father has taught me nothing. Everything I have learned I have learned on my own." They also bring up stories about how previous generations did not and do not understand all the trappings of contemporary life. At one gathering, for example, João told a story about an old man who did not fully appreciate the use of paper money and rolled cigarettes with his money, ultimately smoking all his earnings. Another man at the same gathering told a joke about an elder who took a younger, much more cosmopolitan man's billfold in order to steal his identification card. He supposedly had hopes of using it to place a vote in the mayoral elections in São José do Xingu. The joke revolved around the fact that he took the identification card, which theoretically could be used only by the man whose picture it featured, but gave back all of the money, which could easily have been used by anyone.

While it is tempting to assume that political leaders evoke only Brazilian notions of development and progress, these younger men also make reference to Kayabi ancestors' stories as they present the view that knowledge increases over the course of the generations. The first chief of one of the larger Xinguan villages, for example, suggestively bestowed the name of Tujarare on his village when it started to come together in the 1980s. The name of Tujarare, the young culture hero who taught his parents-in-law a more advanced way to live, evokes the image of a new, more advanced social order developing through the innovations of a younger generation.

In João's and Amapá's addresses, this progressive trajectory is similarly evoked, though each utilizes it in a slightly different manner. João, in his humorous story, presents the character of the old man as vulnerable to fear and ridicule because he has an outdated knowledge of what Xinguans are expected to do and an inability to understand Portuguese. For João, it is the most recent generations that are more in sync with the present. Amapá, on the other hand, indicates that older people, because of their accumulated experience, understand the present better than younger ones. He not only tells about the experiences of his own lifetime but also simultaneously indexes the times of the ancestors. In this way Amapá's "life" gives the impression of expanding over several epochs of time—his current self is the culmination of all the generations' accumulated knowledge.

According to several ancestors' stories, the people who inhabited the earth before the present epoch were pitiable creatures who had absolutely nothing. They had no fire but rather cooked their food in the sun. They also had no tools and ate only what they could gather from the hearts of palm trees. Several ancestors' stories begin by recounting this time of scarcity: "Along time ago, we had nothing. There was no fire. There was nothing. We fried animals in the sun. We left them on top of the grill to fry in the hot sun because we didn't have any fire. We really had nothing" (Ferreira 1992, appendix 26, my translation).

Amapá's comments in his address about the Xingu when he first arrived are remarkably close to the recounting of the first people's scarcity. He says, for example, in scene 3 that "people didn't have anything" and that they did not know how to eat foods like mangoes and the varieties of potatoes that were introduced by Brazilians. The "first times" of mythic scarcity and the early years of the park are identical. The present time, however, is a moment of plenty, when "boys have everything." When Amapá describes the prior state of life in the Xingu in ways that are very similar to the descriptions of prior epochs in ancestors' stories, his own lifetime in the park becomes parallel to the whole process of human development.

In ancestors' talks or myths, the lives of culture heroes are tied to important developments. Tujarare, for example, brings several important advances to the People-without-Understanding. Prior to Tujarare, the People-without-Understanding did not know how to refer properly to animals. They called them by the wrong names—for example, deer were called "owls." Tujarare taught them the correct names. He also taught them that animal meat could be eaten as well as how to perform the rituals for male initiation. Amapá, in his own story, is a similar type of culture hero. He tells the next generations about Indian parties, teaches them music, and orders them to speak Kayabi.

In addition to drawing on ancestors' stories, Amapá also uses non-Kayabi terms and concepts to explain the progressive trajectory. For example, he employs the Brazilian categories of índio, caboclo, and civilizado in his reminiscence. According to the nonindigenous logic of social evolution, índios should progress to caboclos and finally to civilizados. When talking about his own life, Amapá reiterates the notion of progress associated with these terms but inverts these stages. He represents himself as progressing from acting like a "civilized person" to acting like an "Indian." In scene 1, upon Amapá's arrival in the park, Cláudio Villas Boas comments that he "turned into a really civilized person." The Amapá of today in the Xingu Park in scene 4, on the other hand, speaks

Kayabi and sings Kayabi music. With this inversion, Amapá never represents himself as an Indian in quite the same terms as members of the national society might (see Albert 2000 for other examples in which these Brazilian terms are revalued by indigenous people). He is never the "primitive Indian" in need of development nor the untouched "hyperreal" Indian of the industrialized world's fantasies (Ramos 1998, 277).

Different Stances with Respect to the National Society

Despite their similarities, the older headman and the young chief have different stances with respect to the power of the national society to define them as Indians. The young chief's joke celebrates his own movements around the city and his agility concerning the identities that have been dealt to him as a Xinguan Indian: unlike the old man from upriver, João can literally "step out" of the constraints of the Kari-Oka. The elder headman, on the other hand, presents himself and his interlocutors as trapped within a system of values imposed from without. It is the park directors and the whites who are portrayed as dictating what is of "value," leaving he and other Kayabi individuals only to react.

In part, the difference between these two men's stances toward the power of the national society to define them as Indians may be the result of their different life experiences (see Ramos 1988, 1998, for a similar point with respect to other indigenous leaders' speeches). It may also be the result of the different interests at play for the two men in their respective speech events. The headman uses the image of the dominance of the national society over indigenous peoples to establish his dominance over his young interlocutor, while the young chief employs the opposite image—his freedom from the constraints of Indian identity—to assert his claim as a new-style leader.

The older headman's narrative is very much at the service of his attempts to establish himself as an elder within Kayabi society. I argue that he subordinates his presentation of himself as an "Indian" to his own agenda of establishing authority over a younger generation of Kayabi men like Paulo. For example, he uses the voice of the park founders and the whites to legitimize his position as the imparter of Kayabi knowledge to younger people. The various commands made by Cláudio Villas Boas to Amapá the younger are the very same commands that Amapá the older is attempting to carry out vis-à-vis the younger generations. It is as if the words of Cláudio Villas Boas—who says to Amapá when he first arrives in the park in scene 1, "get used to your own people"— have imbued the current "culturally conscious" Amapá with the authority to teach younger men.

73

Over the course of his story, Amapá gradually merges or fuses his "voice" (Bakhtin 1993, 199) with that of representatives of the national society. Through this technique, he appears to channel the obvious power of the national society to support his own claims. At first his "voice" and those of the two Villas Boas brothers are distinct; they all (Cláudio, Orlando, and Amapá) have different perspectives on the park and on Amapá's behavior in the park (scenes 1 and 2). Later, in the beginning of scene 4, the voices of the whites and Amapá seem to merge but in a way that still shows a dissonance. He invokes the voice of whites and of Kayabi without quite merging the two in an example of what Bakhtin would call "vari-directionally double voiced" discourse (1993, 199). This odd juxtaposition comes out particularly well when Amapá refers to the present as a time of plenty: "You don't have the Indian always just using our things." The two voices stand in contrast here, as "the Indian" is juxtaposed with "our things." It is as if he were speaking from the position of a non-Kayabi and a Kayabi at the same time.

At the end of scene 4 the boundaries between the whites' perspective and Amapá's perspective are even more blurred. In a quotation of his own words to other Kayabi, Amapá signals that a segment of quoted speech from whites is being embedded in his own counsel. The end of the quoted speech is, however, ambiguous. The listener does not know when the whites' words end and when Amapá's words begin again: "The white says today, '**That one is not an Indian anymore**, he's already a caboclo. He's already civilized.' And then, '**He speaks more Portuguese. He learns more, speaks more Portuguese.**' Right? [End of quotation of whites' speech is unclear.] '**If you don't have anymore Indian** you don't have anymore value.' Understand? That's the way it is."

The line "If you don't have anymore Indian you don't have anymore value" either could be a continuation of the whites' speech or it could be Amapá's own words. The beginning of this statement was delivered at a much higher volume, as was the obviously quoted speech of white characters that precedes it (and much of Cláudio's and Orlando's earlier speech as well). This suggests that it is a continuation of a non-Indian's quoted speech. On the other hand, it is also framed by Amapá's responses to his present interlocutors: "Right?" and "Understand?" This ambiguity produces the effect that he and the whites are speaking from the same position. They are the ones jointly setting the terms for the sort of behavior that is valuable to others. Furthermore, he finishes with the words "That's the way it is," implying that his perspective and the perspective of whites are not partial ones but rather the only perspective.

Amapá's stance contrasts sharply with the young chief's stance in his joke about the Earth Summit. Rather than merging his perspective with that of the whites, he uses the image of his challenge to the domination of the national society to support his own challenge to the authority of the elderly household headmen. He hints at the limitations of having one's culture defined by the dominant society, of being "stuck" in an Indian space. His joke implies that this limitation might be one of the dangers of being led by senior family headmen in the current environment. Leadership by the elder family headmen is in many respects considered "traditional" or the status quo. The chief, in a sense, goes against this traditional hierarchy of authority by being a young leader of a multifamily local group. The image of João unconstrained by the Kari-Oka of the national society is therefore particularly fitting. He invokes the image of the dominance of the national society in order to present himself as an iconoclast—the appropriate sort of leader for the present.

As the leader of Kapinu'a in 1992 João was extremely popular among most households. He seemed to be able to organize impressive amounts of work and to settle disputes quite satisfactorily. Some of the young chief's success must have come from the way he challenged the national or international society rather than using its dominance to assert his own. For example, he almost never used my presence as a member of a more economically empowered society to secure his own position over other Kayabi, as Amapá did in his address. On the contrary, in public settings João made a show of my subservience to him and to Kayabi needs, ordering me to buy goods for the village, to prepare some of my food for other villagers who wanted to try it, or to figure out math problems that had come up in discussions over community finances.[7]

THE HEALING POWER OF
SHAMANIC CAREER NARRATION

*Listening to the shaman's song is just like walking around
[in the spirit world] personally.*
A PARTICIPANT IN A MARAKA CURE, 1992

One afternoon in March, in the middle of the rainy season, João informed me
that his household would be going on a trip to Diauarum Post. A shaman from
another village, Monkey-Leg, was going to perform a Maraka cure there for
Jacaré, who was suffering from soul loss. Jacaré had been living at Diauarum
for the past few months while his son was working as the chief of the post.
João told me that the residents of Kapinu'a, including myself, were all invited
to come and participate in the event. As I was quickly preparing for the trip,
rolling up my hammock and wedging cans of sardines in my bag (just in case
food was in short supply at the post), I could hear him urging the shaman
Stone-Arm to come. Stone-Arm, however, steadfastly refused. I knew there
were tensions between Stone-Arm and Jacaré, but I wondered too if senior,
virtuosic shamans like Stone-Arm and Monkey-Leg tended to avoid each other
as well.

As I was walking down to shore to board one of the village's motorboats, I
couldn't help but notice that, even though I had tried to pack light, my bag was
conspicuously large compared to others' small hammock bundles. Somehow
I squeezed myself and my luggage into the boat, wildly swatting the tiny biting
bugs that plague the Xingu in the rainy season, much to others' amusement.
Once the boat began its slow journey to the post, the small breeze it created
kept the bugs away, and everyone, including myself, started to take on a festive
attitude. Much like Stone-Arm's previous Maraka, the whole affair had the
feeling of a party rather than a trip to the hospital, as one might expect for "a
curing ritual."

During Maraka cures Kayabi people get a glimpse of normally invisible
cosmological domains through the performances of their shamans. Very ancient, powerful spirit beings live in these domains. Applying terminology used

elsewhere in the Americas, I translate the Kayabi names of some of these beings, the Wyra Futat and Karuat, as Masters of the Game. The Masters of the Game control and watch over all of the fish and game in the rivers and forests. During Maraka cures shamans travel to these beings' homes underwater, up in the sky, deep in the forest, or at the horizon to retrieve the human souls that they have taken. Jealous of human life, these beings take human souls whenever the opportunity presents itself. Most frequently they attack in retaliation for Kayabi improprieties in hunting or the preparation of meat.

While they dream, shamans search the cosmos for the human souls that one or another of the Masters of the Game has taken. A Maraka cure is held for the shaman to wrest a soul away from one of these beings and replace it within a human body, often with the aid of benevolent spirit beings called Mait. Before this climactic ending, however, a shaman will sing about where in the cosmos he has traveled in dream and what he has found there. Often shamans will preface these accounts of recent travels by telling about their earliest dream experiences as healers. Maraka cures therefore feature the officiating shaman's autobiographical dream narratives. They present a kind of résumé of his cosmic travels and successes as a healer.

These shamanic autobiographical accounts also present a perspective on how to act in an empowering manner for other participants. Like family and village leaders' addresses, they offer a perspective on the perils of contemporary existence and present advice on how to overcome them. The counsel offered through these accounts is, however, presented in the idiom of health. Through their autobiographical accounts, shamans stress that health and well-being follow from maintaining continuity across generations and between different epochs of time. This continuity will connect the present generations with much more ancient power beings who control health, life, and death. According to shamans, as time passes, each generation becomes more tenuously connected to these beings than the one before it. Discontinuities between the generations make this connection weaker still. As a result of each generation's differences from the generation that preceded it, people become less able to influence these beings. Shamanic cures therefore offer what I call a "degenerative perspective" or, in other words, the view that humans' access to power is waning. Healers thereby critique and counter the more "progressive" perspective presented by secular leaders, namely, that access to power is increasing as humanity matures and distances itself from past ways of behaving.

In Maraka, shamans give an account of how their own dreams and emotional states have become identical with those of past personages over the course of their career. Presenting their own experiences in this way, they engage in what could be termed a process of "traditionalization" with respect to their own subjectivity; in other words, they work to link themselves to a meaningful past through their narratives (Bauman 1992). As shamans align their own states with those of their predecessors, they also give their audience members the sense that their own subjective experiences are aligned as well. According to Maraka participants, each audience member should sense an identification with the experiences and emotions of the shaman. Ultimately, this aligning of the shaman, ancestors, and audience members is portrayed as bringing health and strength to the patient and community. In this chapter I focus on how this identification takes place in the Maraka that Monkey-Leg performed for Jacaré at Diauarum Post in March 1992.

Shamans

Monkey-Leg is considered to be the most powerful type of Kayabi shaman, a pājērete (great or true shaman). A pājērete is viewed as ikwaapat (being in the state of complete knowledge). This title comes from a great shaman's acquaintance with the whole cosmos, with the domains of the Masters of the Game and other spirit beings that are imperceptible to average people. Always elderly men, great shamans are recognized as some of the most knowledgeable persons in a Kayabi community. Because they understand the whole cosmos, they have power over human health and fertility. The nonempowered, by and large, seek them out, especially when they are sick or infertile. Even when there is no crisis, great shamans are still sought out for guidance on how to live most healthfully. Much as Fernando Santos Granero has pointed out for many other Amazonian leaders, their "life-giving mystical knowledge and powers" are crucial components of their authority over others (1993, 215; see also Santos Granero 1986). In the early 1990s among the Xinguan Kayabi, Monkey-Leg shared this title only with Stone-Arm. Several other men and women, however, had lesser, more specialized, shamanic powers.[1]

Great shamans spend a large portion of their time interacting with spirit beings rather than humans. Most of these interactions take place as the shaman dreams and travels to their homes, though spirits occasionally come to visit him in the human community as well. In addition to trading and fighting with the Masters of the Game to win back the human souls they have taken, shamans also socialize with them. These beings are themselves shamans or, in Kayabi phrasing, are in a state of empowerment (ipājē) and know how to perform all sorts of curative procedures and transformations. Shamans thus spend time learning from these beings. They also study and socialize with the Mait, the more benevolent celestial beings who are considered to be the distant grandparents of the Kayabi. Both Stone-Arm and Monkey-Leg, for example, are married to Mait spirit women as well as to Kayabi women, and they spend long periods eating and visiting at the homes of their spirit in-laws.

Shamans, both great and novice, say that they become thin as a result of eating with the spirits rather than eating human food. Some shamans I spoke with were embarrassed of their excess weight and made a point of saying that they were usually much thinner. Stone-Arm even refused to tutor one woman in the arts of curing, even though she said she was having vivid dreams of spirits, because he thought she was "too fat" to be a shaman. Monkey-Leg, however, had little to worry about with respect to his weight. When I met him he was an extremely diminutive elderly man, so small and frail that I was told his robust young wife often carried him like a baby. Another man, appreciative of Monkey-Leg's mischievous sense of humor, remarked that he heard the old shaman tell park doctors once that he was "two years old" when they asked him for his age.

When shamans like Monkey-Leg interact with spirit beings such as the Masters of the Game, they cross a huge space-time divide. These spirits live far away from Kayabi villages and are the remnants of beings who lived in earlier epochs, or "earths" in Kayabi phrasing. As among other Tupian groups (Cormier 2003, 90), the past is as much a place as a time. Through their dream travels, shamans revive relations with these former beings and repositories of the past. They therefore negotiate relations with "others" much like contemporary village leaders do except the stakes are much higher, as the "others" that shamans confront are ancient nonhumans who can take away or give back human lives.

In contrast to new-style political leaders, shamans achieve their position only after a long apprenticeship under their elders, one that continues in dream even after specific elders have passed away. Unlike village chiefs or headmen, I never heard these men say that they learned any of their shamanic techniques "on their own." Rather, they first work as apprentices to older ones, accompanying them on their dream travels and codreaming along with them for a period of time. After learning how to interact with spirits, a shaman can then travel on his own, learning directly from these beings or bringing the souls of their patients back from the spirits' clutches. Even when a more experienced shaman dreams on his own, however, he is still not alone. The spirits of dead shamans come to help him. I was told more than once that a shaman's claim never to have seen other elder or deceased shamans in his dreams is a sure sign of feigned, rather than genuine, shamanic powers.

Because a shaman serves as a conduit of ancient and other worldly power, a shaman's ability is fundamentally different in kind from that of a skilled chief. Though a shaman knows how to talk with spirit beings and to persuade (or force) them to help the living, just as an able chief knows how to talk with those in the park administration and with NGOs, a shaman is not conceptualized as a fully autonomous locus of ability in the same way as a chief. The impersonal or superpersonal nature of the power of a shaman is particularly evident in Kayabi discussions of witchcraft or the use of shamanic power to cause harm. Kayabi shamans are rarely accused by other Kayabi of using their powers for their own selfish ends to harm Kayabi persons. Kayabi criticisms about their shaman tend to focus instead on their lack of knowledge about the spirit world. If, in the odd case, a shaman is suspected of causing harm, the blame is placed on his spirit familiar (his *rupiwat*), the spirit being who acts as a guide and shows him the way to the homes of the Masters of the Game, rather than on the shaman himself (see Ribeiro 1979, 144).

The manner in which shamans speak about first beginning their career also indicates that they are conduits of power and not powerful in and of themselves. Shamans describe themselves not as actively wanting to become empowered but rather as having been chosen by a spirit being, such as the Master of Monkeys or the Master of the Tapirs. Spirit beings interact with people of their own choosing. When I asked shamans and non-shamans if they had ever wanted or currently wanted to become empowered, I was given the automatic response that they absolutely did not because shamans suffer too much during their dream travels. As I increased my interviewing about shamanism, people often asked me if I wanted to become a shaman. Conditioned by previous negative responses, I could not help but answer in the negative. This seemed to always bring signals of approval, as if I had answered in the most socially acceptable manner.

Likewise, the fees that shamans charge for cures are considered to be requested directly from their spirit familiars, not a result of their own desires or greed. To not pay a shaman is viewed as dangerous for the shaman because the spirit familiar may inflict harm upon him if it does not get the items it requested. This sort of impunity from malevolent or selfish intent given to Kayabi shamans is not given to chiefs. On the contrary, their activities are frequently scrutinized for evidence of self-interest. As a result, shamans' households tend to be quite wealthy with respect to goods in contrast to chiefs'.

Maraka

A Maraka is held only by senior shamans (the *pãjẽrete*). The event unfolds in the following way: in the case of a prolonged or serious illness, people begin to suspect that the patient's soul ('*ang*) is no longer present within his or her body. If left untreated, soul loss is believed to cause death. A great shaman is called by the patient or the patient's family to come and speak with the afflicted person and to determine whether his or her soul has been stolen. The shaman talks with the patient about where he or she has walked, what he or she has encountered, and what he or she has eaten.

The most obvious causes of soul loss involve the treatment and preparation of game. The Masters of the Game are vengeful when one of their charges is not treated properly. A shaman therefore inquires whether the patient has met any animals that have an unusual appearance or behave unnaturally. Remarkable animals are either one of the Masters of the Game in disguise or one of their special pets. A hunter who has killed one of these animals is a sure target for soul loss. Similarly, someone who has laughed at a dying animal or has spoken rudely to an animal will incur their wrath.

If a shaman determines that his patient is suffering from soul loss, he sets out to find his patient's 'ang, traveling in dream to the guilty spirit's home either underwater, deep in the forest, or at the horizon. For a period lasting from a few hours to several months after consultation with his patient, the shaman searches for his patient's soul while napping during the afternoon or sleeping at night. After the shaman has determined the location of his patient's soul, he prepares to hold a Maraka cure. At this point he needs the cooperation of the patient's family. The patient's female relatives make special, labor-intensive delicacies for the event. The patient's male relatives form a chorus and sing and dance with the shaman during the cure.

Maraka are understood to be battles between the shaman and the spirits over the patient's '*ang*. For Kayabi they recall a mythic battle between two brothers and a monster called 'Angjãng (see also Travassos 1984, 147). [2] According to the ancestors' stories, the 'Angjãng killed innumerable people by tricking them into dancing with him around a hole with a spike embedded in the bottom. He would tell people to grab his thin arm, which was really his more powerful arm, and then as they were dancing he would push his partners to their deaths at the bottom of the hole. After discovering that the 'Angjãng had killed their father, the two brothers set out to kill him. Refusing to hold on to his thin arm when they danced with him, they succeeded in pushing the 'Angjãng into the deadly hole. After killing the 'Angjãng and his wife, the two

81

brothers liberated a small human boy whom the couple was keeping as a pet in a penlike cage.

People often say the spirits keep human souls as pets in the same way as the 'Angjãng couple kept this small boy as a pet in a previous epoch. The shaman, like these two brothers, is responsible for liberating human souls from the spirits' bondage. As the two men who worked on Maraka tape recordings with me said, the shaman is like "a type of policeman"—he tracks down lost souls and the spirits who have taken them and restores order.

Each Maraka consists of one great shaman singing about his spirit encounters for several consecutive nights.[3] The singing takes place for several hours in the late afternoon and evening on the first few nights and then continues on the last night from dusk until dawn. During the late afternoon of each day of a Maraka, the shaman smokes his pipe, swallowing, or as Kayabi say "eating," smoke as he does so. Continuing to smoke, he begins to sing while a small chorus of the patient's male relatives and others gathers to accompany him. In both of the Maraka that I witnessed, the shaman began singing in his own house and then later moved to the patient's house. Once a shaman enters the patient's house, more men come to join the chorus. Soon people begin to bring their hammocks so they can alternately doze and listen to the music over the course of an evening's performance. Others prop themselves up against the walls or sit on the floor or on low stools. People come and go throughout the event. The patient is present, but lying off to one side in his or her hammock. Over the course of the event, men and women take drinks of a sweet tapioca beverage made by the patient's female relatives that is usually present in a large pot in the house where the shaman is singing.

The shaman and his male chorus are clearly the focus of the event. The chorus is made up of men of all ages from the various households in a local group as well as any visitors. Over the course of a night of singing, the composition continually changes as men drop out and others step in. Women do not, at present, usually sing in the chorus.[4] Men in the chorus repeat each of the lines the shaman sings verbatim along with him as well as singing a repeating refrain of vocables (discussed later). Men singing in the chorus also attend to the shaman's needs, filling his pipe and catching him if he faints or, in Kayabi phrasing, "is knocked down by the spirits." In this respect Kayabi Maraka are different from other Tupian Maraka traditions in which the lead shaman interacts mainly with other shamans or with his wife.[5]

The first few songs of an evening's performance are sung seated, but once spectators and chorus members from other households begin to arrive, the men dance together as they sing. They dance in a closed circle, in rhythm with the music, each holding the hand of the man next to them on both sides. They lead with their right foot and bring the left in line with it. Their dancing is said to recall the way the 'Angjãng danced with the two Kayabi brothers when he fell to his death.

At the close of a Maraka, during the dawn of the final morning of singing, the shaman replaces the patient's soul within his or her body. The soul first reenters the earthly community through a ball of cotton thread that is placed within a basket on the ground near the shaman. The soul is attracted to a partially unwound thread and then through this thread enters the cotton ball. (In Jacaré's Maraka, however, thin strips of store-bought cloth were tied to poles to attract the soul back into the ball of cotton.) The shaman then picks up the basket and passes it over the body of the patient. The 'ang reenters the patient's body, and the cure is complete.

Maraka cures are always considered successful in terms of attracting the soul back to the patient's body and away from the spirits. In the case of a patient who continues to suffer or dies, however, they may not attract the soul back to the body for very long. In these cases the shaman is not paid by the family. When the patient is cured in a more lasting way, the shaman can ask for a large item such as a well-made basket, a hammock, or even a substantial store-bought item.

Self-Representation in Maraka

In addition to providing descriptions of distant cosmological domains and the location of lost souls, Maraka songs provide accounts of shamans' interactions with spirit beings. The majority of songs describe a great shaman's journey into various spirit villages as he searches for his patient's lost soul. He sings about how he talks during his travel with the spirits with whom he has established an alliance (his *rupiwat*) and asks them for further information about the location of the lost soul. He describes his encounters with these different beings in detail, telling how they look, sound, and move and how he, in turn, effectively speaks and acts toward them.

Maraka then conclude with songs describing how the shaman steals from, fights, negotiates, or trades with the offending spirit to regain his patient's soul. These portions of the dream songs could be said to recount the experiences of both the shaman as well as his patient, as the patient's soul is involved in the encounter. Patients are, however, completely unconscious of where their souls have been until they hear a shaman sing about it in a Maraka. Their souls are, furthermore, frequently metaphorically referred to by the shaman as an object rather than an active, experiencing subject. Monkey-Leg, for example, referred to Jacaré's soul as "the eagle claw" in this March Maraka.

While the major portion of a Maraka concerns the shaman's dream travels to find his present patient's 'ang, the officiating shaman will also talk and sing about the dreams he experienced during previously successful cures. At the outset of a night of Maraka singing, for example, a shaman begins with a spoken account of how he first became empowered, how he was originally made sick by the spirits, how he was cured, and how he was tutored by a senior shaman of the past. Next he will sing about dreams that he had previously had in some of his own successful past cures. In this way the initial part of each Maraka contains a kind of professional history or résumé of the officiating shaman.

Though he seems to be fully conscious and interactive with others, a shaman is said to be literally "sleeping on his feet" as he sings his dreams. Some say that shamans dream once while sleeping in their hammocks and then re-dream as they sing publicly in a Maraka. Others say that they dream only once, at the same time as they sing for their audience. Even past dream travels are considered to reoccur (that is, they are re-dreamed) as the shaman sings about them again. As one man explained in Portuguese, they too are happening "live."

Maraka songs are, in fact, compared to live radio transmissions. As one man said, shamans are like their radios. Despite the fact that Maraka songs are sung in the first person, from the perspective of the traveling shaman they are understood to be repetitions of music originally produced by the spirits. Shamans are said to "imitate maraka" (maraka -'ang). These songs are not, however, moments when the spirits speak.[6] Rather, Maraka songs are understood to be sung in the voice of the shaman. A shaman's Maraka music is somehow "authored" by the spirits (who are also the "principles") as well as by the shaman (who is also the "animator") (Goffman 1981). As William Hanks (1996) points out with respect to Mayan shamanic performance, an attempt to assign clear participant roles from a "purely synchronic perspective" misses the sociohistorical nature of the problem from an indigenous perspective. The shaman's performance of Maraka songs is understood by Kayabi individuals as necessarily having been preceded by other dialogues and perceptual processes. Maraka songs are by their very nature secondary reflections or "mirror" images of distant realms that are being passed on yet one more time to others, who because they do not dream of these places cannot hear this music directly.

How Maraka Cure

When descriptions of different cases of Kayabi soul loss are compared, this disease can be linked to emotional isolation, particularly with respect to fellow household members. As cures for illnesses ultimately caused by emotional estrangement from coresidents, Maraka appear to work by restoring a sense of identity or empathy among members of a household. Maraka cure individual persons, therefore, by attending to their network of social relations. As such, Maraka are events that play a part in healing not only persons but also the basic agricultural and social unit of production in Kayabi society, the household. Much as Donald Pollock (1992, 31; 1996) has suggested for the Kulina, sickness is a sign of social relational disorder much as it is among the Ndembu (Turner 1969, 1982). In this way, shamans are leaders who organize social harmony, as headmen and chiefs do with their work projects and parties. Before turning to how the shamans do this, I describe a few cases of soul loss.

Persons who are the target of gossip, are left without care, sense a strong feeling of loneliness or mourning, fight with others, cry uncontrollably, or have been badly frightened are all likely candidates for soul loss. The Wyra Futat and Karuat spirits take advantage of these sorts of estrangements, particularly if these individuals have also mistreated game or met one of the Masters of the Game's special pets. People speak about an assumption on the part of the spirits that the person has not been demonstrably valued or cared for by the living and therefore can or should be taken away to live in the spirit world. Immediately after the death of one very old man, for example, his family members commented with anxiety that they should not have left him alone that day. They had all gone to their fields to farm. They continued to explain that he may have wanted something such as a drink of water and no one was there to attend to him. The logic seemed to be not that a drink of water could have saved his life but that he had been clearly left in need and his 'ang was therefore taken by the spirits.

Travassos also reports cases in which soul loss is seen as having been caused by a lack of proper care. She writes that one man was diagnosed by Monkey-Leg as suffering from soul loss because his wife gossiped about him continually. According to Monkey-Leg, this man's 'ang was taken by Kūjãmutat, or the True Woman. This spirit often takes men's souls in order to keep them as her own husbands. The implication in this case seems to be that the woman's lack of proper care for her husband resulted in her losing him to Kūjãmutat. Travassos also describes a case in which a shaman diagnosed a young boy as suffering from soul loss because a spirit saw his mother beat him (Travassos 1984, 134).

During my stay in Kapinu'a, João and Pretty's mentally disabled son was diagnosed by Stone-Arm as having had his soul stolen because he fought with his siblings incessantly. In his case it would seem that the victim made himself vulnerable because he could not agree or identify with the perspective of his playmates but rather was consistently at odds with them. Quarrelsome persons are in general thought to be more susceptible to soul loss.

Maraka restore a sense of empathy among coresidents by fostering a sort of distributive identity on the part of each audience member with the experiences of the officiating shaman. Participants all have a shared experience through their participation in his adventures. In other words, the shaman's songs produce a type of "para-experience" for his audience members. Kayabi describe Maraka as an experience in which they go to the places the shaman sings about and see what he has experienced in distant spirit villages. One audience member said that the visions of the spirits are so vivid for some people that they are often overcome with emotion and begin to cry during Maraka singing. Men who are embarking on shamanic careers themselves find the music particularly evocative.

With respect to nonempowered participants, people seem to understand Maraka as producing the same effect for everyone present. When I asked Jacaré about his own experiences during his Maraka cure, he commented that I had been there as well and that I should know what he felt since I had also listened to the music. He explained that his experiences were the same as those of all the other people who had participated. If soul loss is the result of an individual's sense of emotional isolation, the sense of this uniformity of perception may be one of the essential components of a successful cure.

The identification with the experience of the shaman that audience members (and patients) report recalls the empathy or understanding that secular leaders say is necessary between themselves and their followers. The audience's identification with the experience of a shaman in Maraka, however, requires an acceptance of a type of perception that is radically distinct from the everyday perception of the layperson.

Shamans, especially great shamans, have unusual perceptive abilities. They are able to see as well as hear spirit beings. The nonempowered can only hear the spirits. [7] Any swimmer, for example, may hear the music of the Masters of the Fish, the Karuat, but only shamans (who know the Karuat) actually see these beings and know what their underwater villages look like. Similarly, nonempowered people can speak with spirits when they meet them in the forest or when they visit their village, but only shamans can actually see them. They see spirits hovering in the air in places where the average person sees nothing. As one man explained about spirits, "When they are with us, we don't see them, only the shaman can."

Shamans can also see the spiritual dimensions of common objects. Stone-Arm explained that when a shaman enters a house, where most people see normal objects such as mortars and pestles, baskets, and benches, a shaman often sees the souls of these things. The objects appear "like people." Shamans also see the souls of individual animals hovering around their carcasses in the garbage midden behind the houses, whereas non-shamans see only their discarded bones.

Shamans are also able to see intrusive objects that angry spirits place under people's skin to cause pain and discomfort. The Masters of the Game as well as the spirits of individual dead animals throw projectiles into people's bodies in retaliation for the pain caused during the hunt. Though the nonempowered feel the discomfort of their presence in sharp pangs or dull aches, these objects are invisible to them. Unlike other lowland traditions of exorcism, these objects do not usually become visible once they are removed from the body. Kayabi shamans tell their patients that they have just extracted a tooth, a bone, a lump of beeswax, or a piece of hair and then carry the invisible object out of the patient's house. Often they will scream from "the heat" of the object as they carry it, but rarely do they produce a visible object to show their patients. In part this special shamanic perception is aided by tobacco. Smoke allows shamans (but not laymen) to perceive more than they would be able to see without it.

The power of shamans is, in fact, described in terms of sight. A young, novice shaman, for example, was described in the following way: "He is not very empowered, he dreams normally but he sees some things." Great shaman, on the other hand, can "really see." These men often describe their own power in Maraka songs in sight-specific terms. Stone-Arm, for example, described his own experience of entering the world of spirits in dream as a process of gradual illumination. According to him, the first sensation is darkness. Then one sees one's spirit associates (the rupiwats). He said these beings have large eyes like flashlights and smoke cigars. One sees their eyes and cigars as spots of light in the darkness. These beings show their human shaman associates the path to various spirits' villages. According to Stone-Arm, when one enters the villages the darkness disappears, as if it were daytime. Several shamans emphasized the lightness or brightness of the spirits' homes.

When shamans talk and sing about their visions of spirits, they use an unusual tense and evidential construction indicating that the manner in which they "see" these beings is not equivalent to the manner in which they see the ordinary world. Empowered speakers usually use the particle *ra'e* when recounting their interactions with spirit beings. *Ra'e* is one of a series of particles otherwise used to speak about past events not experienced firsthand. It is used to speak about events learned about through hearsay. *Ra'e* also usually indicates that an event took place in the most proximate past. Most empowered speakers curiously use *ra'e* to speak about interactions with spirits whether the event took place a moment ago, occurred several years ago, or is currently taking place. This particular use of the particle *ra'e* gives the sense that spirit interactions happen in a timeless realm that is just slightly removed from normally experienced reality.

Shamans give the nonempowered access to this normally invisible spirit world through song. Their Maraka music is understood as having the power to create visual images for those who hear it. The microhistory of each performance could be thought of as a synesthetic chain in which sound repeatedly produces visual images. The spirits' Maraka songs are first heard by the shaman in dream. These songs produce visual images for the shaman. Then through his rendition of this music for a second time and the choral repetition of his music for a third time, his human audience also comes to "see" the spirit world.

Maraka is not the only sort of verbal performance thought to lead to a visualization of the narrated events. Images are produced for listeners in other situations as well. When traditional stories are told, for example, listeners are described as being able "to see" before them (-*esak*) the recounted mythic events. Kracke (1987 and personal communications) has noted a similar phenomenon among the Tupian Kagwahiv, as has Basso (1995) among the Kalapalo. During Kagwahiv and Kayabi myth telling, audience members often gaze out in the distance beyond or in front of the narrator, a gesture that may be related to the process of visualizing the narrated events.

Listening to Maraka, however, involves a very intense sort of visualization—or possibly the visualization of intensely powerful beings. That people are reported to cry because of the beauty of the spirits supports the notion that the visualization involved in Maraka is of a different order than the sort of visualization involved in myth telling. I never heard anyone comment after hearing traditional-style stories that, for example, they felt as though they had been to the places the narrator had described. Ancestors' stories describe a state of being that has come to an end, and though the "mythic" characters still exist (somewhere in the cosmos), their way of life has changed. Maraka, on the other hand, describe repositories of the past in their present form. This may explain why participants are able to feel as though they "have been where the shaman has been."

The repetition involved in Maraka singing very likely plays a significant role in encouraging people's identification with the shaman's travels. As Janet Hendricks has pointed out with respect to a Shuar man's life history, his own repetition of portions of his text was used to draw the audience "into an emotional frame of mind," one that generated sympathy for his point of view (1993, 219). Given that it is the male chorus who repeats the lines of a shaman's Maraka songs, sympathy for the point of view presented would likely be even more intense. Uttering Maraka songs is understood to be a particularly powerful act, and one is not supposed to sing them outside of the context of a cure. During Maraka performances the men who sing along in the chorus report much more vivid participation in the shaman's experiences than the women, who do not sing. Men spontaneously report feeling as though they were seeing exactly what the shaman was seeing and having the sense that they too were traveling along with him. Women, on the other hand, comment more on the beauty of the songs.[8] Even those people who do not sing but come with their hammocks to doze while the shaman and his chorus sing, however, may have their own dreams shaped by these songs.

Monkey-Leg's Maraka

Let us now turn to the way in which Monkey-Leg brings the perceptions of ordinary persons to approximate his own shamanic perception of spirit beings and spirit villages through his spoken and sung narratives in his cure for Jacaré.

Diagnosing Jacaré

While living at Diauarum Post, Jacaré was diagnosed by park doctors with a case of colic, perhaps a complication from his paralysis. According to Jacaré, the medicine they were giving him was not working and he felt that there must have been another reason for his malaise. He and his family members decided to consult a shaman. They chose Monkey-Leg from a village close to Diauarum, a man who was distantly related to Jacaré. Jacaré's sons told me that they spoke with Monkey-Leg from the post by short-wave radio for several weeks, advising him on Jacaré's condition as well as discussing the circumstances surrounding the onset of his illness.

Monkey-Leg, at some point during his consultations, determined that one of the Masters of the Game, the guardian of tapirs, Tapira Futat, had stolen Jacaré's soul. This had happened, according to him, because his daughter, Thorn, had oversalted a piece of tapir meat she had served to her father.

According to Monkey-Leg, salt annoys all of the Masters of the Game, and oversalting Jacaré's tapir meat had provoked Tapira Futat to take Jacaré's soul. In light of other cases of soul loss, Monkey-Leg's diagnosis of Jacaré's illness pointed to a problem in Jacaré's household: an interpersonal rift between Jacaré and other members. His diagnosis also suggested that this family overindulges in non-Kayabi foods—problems that are not unrelated.

Thorn's lack of care in preparing her father's tapir meat indicated a more general estrangement between her nuclear family and her natal family. When Jacaré's family lived in Kapinu'a, Thorn, her second husband, and their children lived in a separate nuclear family residence. They were the only nuclear family in Kapinu'a to live separately, that is, not with the husband's or the wife's living parents. As her husband was the senior health monitor in the village at the time, they lived in a small house near a wood-and-thatch building used as the pharmacy, located a few houses away from Jacaré's house in the village circle. Because of her husband's connections to the park's medical personnel, their household was quite well stocked with nonindigenous goods (including a solar energy panel). Though they participated in agricultural activities with Jacaré's household and spent time cooking and eating there, they also functioned as an independent unit. When Thorn and her family moved for a period to Diauarum to be with her parents while her brother was serving as chief of the post, she and her husband traveled frequently back to their own house in Kapinu'a for lengthy stays. The rest of her extended family, on the other hand, lived more regularly at Diauarum.

By diagnosing the overuse of salt as part of the cause of Jacaré's illness, Monkey-Leg also was implicitly warning Jacaré's extended family against the excesses of administrative life. Jacaré's son, who had been the first chief of Kapinu'a, obtained the position of chief of post after concluding his tenure as village chief of Kapinu'a. Because this job was a salaried position, it was a route to obtaining an abundance of "white" goods such as salt, sugar, coffee, and gasoline. Working at the post also gave Jacaré's son a pivotal position with respect to the redistribution of goods coming into the park from outside. Likewise, Thorn's husband, as senior health monitor, also had unusual access to and contact with nonindigenous goods. Though the position of health monitor is voluntary, the person filling this position controls a large number of items from NGOs, including Western medicines. Living at a post and being nodes of distribution of store-bought items seemed to have augmented this family's reputation of embracing a nonindigenous lifestyle. As a family well connected to Kayabi external sources of goods and positions, Jacaré's family members could be tempted to forget their identity with, or to attenuate their

90

connection to, their elderly father (or father-in-law). This situation was particularly dangerous in light of the fact that nonindigenous goods have a smell that the Masters of the Game find attractive.

Pinpointing salt as the cause of Tapir Spirit's anger is, however, a sign of extreme conservatism. While most Kayabi would agree that Brazilian foods like coffee or sugar do weaken a person and attract spirit beings, many do not categorize salt in the same way. These other Brazilian foods are called in Kayabi "odorous foods" (komikasing). Many say that store-bought salt, on the other hand, actually lessens spirits' anger and enables a person to eat more kinds of game than they could before it was available. Prior to Kayabi's access to salt, meats from different kinds of animals would fight in the eater's stomach, causing a fatal type of cramping. Salt, according to many, deadens the spirits of individual animals after their deaths. The conservatism of Monkey-Leg's diagnosis is in keeping with his general reputation as someone extremely wary of non-Kayabi objects and lifestyles. In the early 1980s Elizabeth Travassos (1984) described him as counseling against listening to Brazilian music because it was unhealthy for young children. Stone-Arm, on the other hand, was not nearly as vigilant with respect to non-Kayabi goods, foods, and music.

Curing Jacaré

After Monkey-Leg spoke to Jacaré's relatives about his condition and after they repeatedly asked him to hold a Maraka at the post, he finally agreed. The upcoming event was then announced over short-wave radio. In Kapinu'a, Chief João urged fellow villagers to attend. Several families obliged by paddling their canoes or, like I did, by loading into one of the villages' motorboats and traveling to the post. After arriving at Diauarum, Chief João then used the motorboat (and, more important, the village's precious gasoline) to pick up Monkey-Leg. Jacaré's two sons and his son-in-law (as well as myself) accompanied the chief to pick up the elderly shaman and bring him back to the post—a trip I will never forget. As rain clouds threatened a downpour, Monkey-Leg knelt at the front of the boat, blowing, singing, and chanting for the rain clouds to move away. Despite his small statue, his performance had an incredible intensity, and no rain fell while we were traveling on the river.

Monkey-Leg began his Maraka in his own village prior to traveling to the post. That Jacaré was at this point lying prone at Diauarum Post is yet more evidence that Maraka are about transforming the perceptions and experiences of family members as much as those of the patient. [9] When we arrived at Monkey-Leg's village, a group of people were gathered in his small wood-and-thatch house to greet Jacaré's relatives. Eventually Jacaré's male relatives formed a chorus and Monkey-Leg began to sing his dreams. Directly before singing, however, Monkey-Leg told us about how he had become empowered. In part his narrative was for my benefit. I had asked en route to Monkey-Leg's village if I could record Monkey-Leg's songs and had inquired as to whether he might talk about his empowering experiences, as Stone-Arm had spontaneously done at the beginning of a Maraka he had just held in Kapinu'a. João said he would ask Monkey-Leg to tell his story and assured me that this was a regular part of Maraka performances.

After he visited and drank fermented manioc kawĩ, João, as promised, asked Monkey-Leg how he had become a shaman. In the rising humidity, as he lay in his hammock, Monkey-Leg told his audience about how he had gone to an abandoned homestead to look for annatto plants to make red body paint when he was still living outside the park on the Peixes River. While he was cutting the annatto, a spirit knocked him down and made him sick. My taped transcript of his narrative begins as he is telling his family members who are accompanying him on the trip to Diauarum Post about his sickness. The abbreviated nature of many of the episodes in Monkey-Leg's account is likely a result of the fact that many of the listeners have heard this story several times and are generally familiar with the main episodes. [10]

At different points Monkey-Leg directs parts of his narrative to various audience members, including Chief João and myself. When he does this, he uses vocatives. I have translated these as "guy," "girl," "guys," or "you people." The use of vocatives is extremely common in spoken Kayabi and does not have the somewhat stilted feeling my translations do in English. While my choice of English translations is not perfect with respect to vocatives, I have tried to use terms that are neither overly archaic nor overly contemporary (see Tedlock 1983, 44).

Format of Presentation

The transcript of Monkey-Leg's Maraka narrative is presented in a format based on Robert Moore's format (1993), with some elaboration. According to this mode of presentation, each vertical column represents speech in a "distinguishable . . . event frame" (219). Column A, which is justified with the left margin, contains speech related to the event of narration. This includes Monkey-Leg's asides to his audience and his audience's responses. Column B contains representations of the narrated characters' behavior told in a way that ties the behavior directly to the event of narration. As such column B represents not a "distinguishable event frame" but a mediation between two event frames. In Monkey-Leg's spoken narrative, techniques for mediation include demonstratives such as "here" and "like this." In the sung portion, the personal pronoun I frequently ties the events being narrated to the event of narration (discussed later). Column C contains representations of the narrated characters' behavior (other than their reported speech and onomatopoetic sounds). Because this narrative is about Monkey-Leg's own experiences, the main character is Monkey-Leg himself, but as a much younger man. Finally column D, which is furthest to the right, contains the directly quoted speech of narrated characters and Monkey-Leg's onomatopoetic representations of the sounds of various narrated actions. I have left these onomatopoetic words untranslated (see Tedlock 1983, 44). Quoted speech that connects the narrated event to the event of narration is, however, represented in column B.

Representing this text in columnar fashion is useful for pointing out how the unusual dream events Monkey-Leg describes are made vivid for his audience or tied to the ordinary experiential realm of the layperson. My discussion therefore focuses on the lines represented in column B. The Arabic numerals corresponding to these lines are set in boldface type. Where possible, I indicate the gestures that accompany the narrative presentation, as they play an important role in aligning the narrated and narrating events.

In the spoken portion of the narrative, lines have been broken and numbered according to pauses (Tedlock 1983). Lines often end with vocatives directed toward audience members, such as those I have translated as "guy," "girl," "guys" and "you people." Vocatives indicate a momentary completion of an utterance. In fact, rather than the term *vocative*, the SIL linguists use the term *final word*. One of the Kayabi men who worked with me on translations (and who had previously worked with SIL) felt that these words did, indeed, signal a type of momentary closure. Because I have broken the text into columns representing discourse modalities, a few of what I have termed "numbered lines" unfortunately span more than one line on the printed page.

Ritual speech in indigenous South America is famous for its formalized response patterns. Many ritual genres, for example, require the speaker or chanter to be accompanied by an addressee, who responds in formalized ways (see Sherzer 1983, 198–200; Urban 1991). Even though many of Monkey-Leg's lines are directed at audience members by virtue of the fact that they contain vocatives, only rarely does an addressee actually respond to them. Kayabi myth telling follows the same pattern. Although these kinds of stories must be told to an addressee, the addressee responds only intermittently.

To facilitate comprehension in English, I have grouped numbered lines together at higher levels into scenes. In the spoken part of the narrative, shifts in scenes generally correspond to shifts between dream and waking reality. Scenes that are italicized occurred for the main character in dream; scenes that are not italicized occurred for the main character in normal, waking reality. In most cases I base these divisions on the presence of Kayabi tense and evidential markers. These give a clear indication as to whether the events are occurring in ordinary reality or in dream. In some places where these particles are lacking, I base the divisions only on the inferences of the two men who helped translate this narrative. Scene 7 is, however, an exception. The action recounted in this section has been categorized as a scene unto itself because it relates to a time in Monkey-Leg's life that is very different from the action that precedes it.

The Text

Columns:

A   **B**   C   D

Scene 1

1 "I am not going. You are not going to take me," I said to them [the spirits].

2 "I may die today. I am going to be taken," I said to them [his relatives].

3 Then I fainted

4 Over this way I caught, I caught my arms. [He demonstrates his fall in his hammock. "This way" ties the narrated and narrating events.]

5 I really did not perceive anything when he [the spirit] ran, guys.

6 Way over there he [a spirit] knocked me down, guys.

7 Pop. [The sound of something coming together in his hand.]

8 "What has come together in my hand?" [He is referring to something that the spirits have given him. He looked at his hand, thus tying this past happening to the present event.]

9 Way over there I fainted maybe.

10 "I don't hear any music, people." [Monkey-Leg is quoting himself speaking to his family. He is asking why they are not performing a Maraka cure for him yet.]

11 "Be quiet, husband. You are really bothering me, husband. How are we going to sing Maraka?" [He is quoting his wife answering him.]

12 Pop. [The sound of him falling into a canoe.]

13 Into the canoe, I was really bad, guy.

94

14 I was not well.

15 Then I went,

guy.

   16 Tooo. [The sound of him traveling over water.]

17 Then I got better [I] am saying,

guys.

18 Then maybe they carried me in their arms.

   19 Poaa. [The sound of his family putting him into
     the canoe.]

20 Into the canoe.

21 They arrived at our village.

22 I had a fever.

23 He took me in the canoe.

24 He brought a canoe for me, it seems.

25 They rowed really well.

26 Then I was worried we would miss him [his older brother
  who was a shaman],

guys.

27 My deceased older brother, Eroit, was with his Maraka
  music.

   28 "He is treating someone." [Monkey-Leg is quot-
    ing one of his companions.]

   29 "Who is?" [Monkey-Leg is quoting himself as
    responding.]

   30 "Your older brother."

31 Then maybe they surely brought me,

guy.

   32 "He has been sick for a while," [his companions
    said to his older brother].

33 Then they took me,

guy.

34 I did not hear [perceive anything] as I was taken,

guys.

35 I was taken, taken and then embanked.

36 She [his wife] spoke to my younger brother, Myaiwa,
  "Come. Look at Shorty [one of Monkey-Leg's names], my
  husband's brother."

Scene 2

37 *He [his brother Eroit] took him [the spirit] into the Maraka music
  all night until dawn.*

38 *It was strange,*

95

guy.

39 *This same time [of day], he [the spirit] brought a canoe for me.*
   40 *"Get in."*
   41 *A canoe was brought for me,*

guy.

   42 *"Get in."*
   43 *Turbulent water was underneath it,*

guy.

   44 *Inside there was a jeju fish.*
   45 *A black jeju was in there with me.*

Scene 3
46 Ah, truly.
47 A moon passed.
48 A moon passed.
49 I was feeling poorly.
50 But still I went to sit in my hammock, lowering myself
   into it.
      51 Hup. [The sound of falling into the hammock.]

Scene 4
52 *Then I really heard only Maraka music all night until dawn,*
   dawn, dawn.
      53 *Hyy ariiim.* [The sound of the music.]

Scene 5
   54 "Someone who knows how to sing Maraka,"
they maybe said then.
55 I did not eat anything.
56 Some women really worry about people when they are sick.
   57 I went to sit in a hole.
      58 "I am going to escape them [the spirits], their
        people,"
I said back then.

Scene 6
59 Haa, here, smoked game laid out. [He gestures with his arm to the
   side of his hammock, linking the narrated and narrating events.]
60 "There, there is smoked game laid out," [the spirits] said to me. [He
   looks at the ground near his hammock.]
61 "There, there is smoked mutum bird laid out." [The spirits are still
   speaking. He looks at the ground in another place near his
   hammock.]

62 "There, there is smoked jaku bird laid out, guy." [The spirits are still speaking. He looks at the ground in yet another place near his hammock.]

63 Here, smoked monkey laid out,
guy. [Monkey-Leg is now speaking to someone in the audience. He gestures near his hammock.]

64 To the side, a lot. [He gestures to the side.]

65 Here, kawĩ drink,
guy. [He gestures to the other side.]

66 Woo

67 Haaaa

Scene 7

68 Thus I stayed,
guy.

69 Thus I stayed.

70 [Chief João asks:] Was it hard to get better, guy?

71 It was really hard going,
guy.

72 It was hard.

73 Then my deceased younger brother perhaps arrived into our village. My deceased older brother, Eroit, came into our village, perhaps came they say.

74 "Make smoked foods for him, bring him a pig, leave the carcass for him so he can get well," he said.

75 Then maybe right away back then they slaughtered wild pigs, slaughtered pigs, and brought them.

76 But the grill was brought first, the grill,
guy.

Scene 8

77 "Hyy, here is your food laid out." [His brother is speaking to the spirits.]

78 Then they [the spirits] came and joined together,
girl, guy.

79 "You are well." [The spirits are speaking.]

80 Here, my gourd dish underneath me. [He gestures under his hammock.]

81 They brought me handicrafts, a gourd bowl,
guy.

82 An arrow, an arrow decorated with string woven in designs, and toucan tail feathers,

97

guy.

83 Haa, over here a diadem above me. [He motions over his head.]

84 Here, sweet potatoes were brought for me in my dish, roast sweet potatoes. [He gestures under his hammock.]

Scene 9

85 I spent a lot of time in the hammock, curled up [that is, sick].

86 Look at all those fat people going outside to urinate. [He is commenting on a few men leaving the gathering at this point.]

Others break out in laughter.

Scene 10

87 Then I heard only Maraka music.

88 Jaguar bone,

guy. [He is referring to bones used to make a flute used in healing.]

Scene 11

89 From them I got better,

guy.

90 Hm uua

91 I got up on my feet a little.

92 Then my older brother's wife came to me,

guy.

93 " 'Come,' your older brother says to you, husband's brother."

94 "What is it?"

I said.

95 " ' "Come blow, take out spirit things," say to him,' he said." [Monkey-Leg is quoting his brother's wife as answering.] [Blowing and the removal of spirit projectiles from people's bodies are the first curative techniques learned by novice shamans.]

96 "Oh no, I am not even strong yet." [Monkey-Leg is quoting himself.]

97 People steadied my hands and took me just the same.

98 They took me and arrived with me,

guy.

99 "How are you?" [Monkey-Leg quotes his brother as asking.]

100 "I am going to die."

101 "No, you are turning into a shaman." [His
brother answers Monkey-Leg.]
102 Then, here between his shoulders the jaguar bone [flute]
turned into my lizard. Here sitting inside his shoulders.
[Reaching behind his neck he shows where this happened on
his own body.]
103 "You grab it so you can be the same as me, I say.
In my place, I say." [Monkey-Leg is quoting his
brother, Eroit.]
104 "How are they going to come to me?"
I said,
guy.
105 Then he put my hand thus, the way people put their hand on
people [to cure]. [He demonstrates.]
106 Tok [The sound of the objects spirit put in
people's bodies uniting in his hand.]
107 Then a large one came.
108 Ja ooo
109 Then I really grabbed it,
guy.
110 He gave it to me,
guy.
111 Ooo
112 Then, here I am going around [as a shaman],
guy.
113 Here [is where] I went around in the past,
guy.
114 Hmmm
115 Then, here I am going around [as a shaman],
guy.
116 [Man in the audience comments:] Hmm
117 I am going around,
guy.
118 It seems as if it was from the beginning but it wasn't
from the beginning that I went around as a shaman,
people.
119 Here, I am going around lying,
guy. [This is a standard statement made by the most powerful shaman. It
should be read as indicating the opposite.]
120 Ha paa. Thus, I was in the past,
guy, girl. [He directs this comment to Chief João and me.]
121 [Man in the audience comments:] Uhuh.

Scene 12

122 But when I was well, strange how people are.

123 My frog was singing in my port inside a pool of still water.

124 "Haa, I am not going to go get it to eat. You all go get it for me." [Monkey-Leg is quoting himself as having asked the younger people in his household to go get this frog for him.]

125 But how people do not obey others.

126 I went.

127 I got up on a log, like this on a hill of refuse [washed in from the river] I got on top of a log. [He got up on his knees and demonstrated in his hammock.]

128 I'll put my hand out for him, I thought to myself.

129 Like this, seated on a hill of refuse, seated, guy.

130 I put out my hand for him. [He puts his hand out.]

131 I went way over to the other side. [He motions with his arm.]

132 Po [The sound of falling into the water.]

133 "Haa, where am I going."

134 I really went where the river flows into another, maybe floated on my back. Soon I was with Maraka music as I floated.

Scene 13

135 Hoo, just like this, those incredible houses are the same as houses for people. [He is visiting the Masters of Fish, the Karuat, who live in villages underwater. At this point he made a sweeping gesture with his hand and arm toward the walls of his own house.]

Scene 14

136 "The houses underwater are just like these houses, you all," [I] said in the past, guy. [He is quoting himself telling people about his dream voyage in the past.]

137 Strange

138 Ho

139 Thus I went around in the past, guy.

140 [Man in the audience responds:] Hmm

141 Ho, I am finished, guy.

142 Let's sing [I] say, until evening, [I] say.

After Monkey-Leg finished his narrative, people continued to drink from the pot of *kawĩ* and talked about how strong it was. (As a responsible host, João thought I should not be given anything fermented during my stay in the Xingu. Much as on other occasions, he declined in my stead all gourds of fermented *kawĩ* offered to me. Although curious about its taste, I was ultimately quite thankful for his concern, as well as glad to forego drinking anything that might, in fact, give me one more round of stomach problems.) After a bit more conversation a few people left the gathering. Finally, Monkey-Leg began to sing about his dreams. Jacaré's male relatives got up and sat behind his hammock in order to accompany him as a chorus.

According to the belief that all Maraka songs merely repeat what the shaman hears from the spirits, the following columns would technically be considered reported speech. According to my format, they should therefore be represented in column D. I have chosen, however, to indicate from the outset that all of this song is possibly a type of quoted speech and to treat it in a manner similar to his spoken narrative.

I have also divided this section into scenes. Unlike the spoken portion of his narrative, the scenes here do not correspond to waking and dreaming experiences since all of this sung portion is technically considered by Kayabi to be a dream. Instead, scene changes here correspond to relations between different participants (Hymes 1981, 171) or, as in the last scene, when spirits move inside his body, to radically new ways of relating to previously introduced participants. Dividing the sung narrative up in this manner, again, is done to facilitate reader comprehension. In this section Monkey-Leg describes a very complicated series of interactions that hopefully become clearer by segmenting the narrative. Initially, in scene 15 (lines 143–70) Monkey-Leg is singing about his interaction with his human chorus. These lines are represented in column A, with the exception of line 168, which is quoted speech and is therefore represented in column D. In scene 16 (lines 171-87) he begins to talk about, quote, and interact with spirits. In this scene there are two dramatic pauses in Monkey-Leg's singing. These occur when Monkey-Leg is listening to what the spirits are saying. Finally, in scene 17 (lines 188–97) the spirits are within him and he is speaking as someone who has spirits seated within one of his hands. The lines in scenes 16 and 17 are represented appropriately in columns C and D, depending upon whether they are descriptions of action or quoted speech, with the exception, of course, of those lines that tie the narrated events to the event of narration; they are represented in column B.

Each of the following lines was sung by Monkey-Leg alone. His chorus did, however, sing along with him at the conclusion of each numbered line, a repeated refrain of vocables: "hii hi hii hi ha ha." I have not reproduced the choral repetitions.

Columns:

A   **B**   C   D

Scene 15

143 Hii hi hii hi ha ha hii hi hii hi ha ha hii hi hii hi ha ha hii hi hii hi ha ha

144 *I don't know how I am going to go.*

145 *I don't know how I am going to go.*

146 *For those who are accompanying.*

147 *I don't know how I am going to go.*

148 *For those who are accompanying.*

149 *Singing Maraka as I go for those who are going to accompany.*

150 *Everything is going well for those who are going to accompany.*

151 *I don't know how I am going to go.*

152 *After I go around visiting.*

153 *After I go around visiting.*

154 *Singing Maraka while going, for those who are going to accompany.*

155 *In the state of singing Maraka while going, for those who are going to accompany.*

156 *Visiting, visiting.*

157 *Well-being, well-being.*

158 *Comes for you all.*

159 *Well-being.*

160 *I go about singing Maraka.*

161 *After I visit another place.*

162 *After I arrive.*

163 *After visiting.*

164 *After I arrive.*

165 *I don't know how I am going to go.*

166 *I go singing Maraka, I go singing Maraka.*

167 *For those who are accompanying me, for those who are accompanying me.*

          168 *"It will go well once again, it will go well once again,"*
    [I] *say.*

169 *In this plaza, in this plaza.*

170 *I go singing Maraka, I go singing Maraka.*

Scene 16

[Pause]

         171 *Those* [spirits] *are talking among themselves.*

     172 "What is happening to us now?" [that is, why is the shaman singing?], *those said.* ["Now" ties Monkey-Leg's interaction with the spirits to his presence in the human gathering.]

173 I don't understand right away. I don't understand right away.
[Monkey-Leg is speaking about himself. The "I" "not understanding" is in both the narrated event (with the spirits) and the narrating event (with humans).]

174 When they speak to me. [The "me" to whom the spirits are speaking is a participant in both the interior and exterior speech events.]

175 When they speak softly.

176 When singing Maraka, when singing Maraka.

177 When singing Maraka, when singing Maraka.

178 Everything is well when they speak softly.

179 For me when they are talking among themselves.

[Pause]

180 "On which side are we going to arrive?"

181 "On which side are we going to arrive?"

182 "For you?" [The spirits are speaking here. The "you" refers to Monkey-Leg but also could refer to the audience members.]

183 "I am calling," [I] *say.* [The shaman is speaking. The "I" "calling" and "saying" is again a participant in both the narrated and narrating events.]

184 Well-being.

185 "On which side are we going to arrive?" [The spirits are talking to each other.]

186 "In your hand." [One spirit answers.]

187 "I sing/imitate again," [I] *say.* [Monkey-Leg is speaking to the spirits. The "I" "singing" and imitating is again a participant in both the narrated and narrating events.]

Scene 17

188 "Well-being once again,"

[I] *say.*

189 I am with my music. [The "I" singing is again a participant in both the narrated and narrating events.]

190 *In this plaza.* [This is the human village's plaza.]

191 I am with my music.

192 In his plaza. [Monkey-Leg is referring to the spirit's plaza.]

193 I am with my music.

194 I don't believe it. [The "I" "not believing" is again a participant in both the narrated and narrating events.]

195 I am with my music.
196 Well-being. [Given previous lines, this could refer either to the
human or spirit plazas or to both simultaneously.]
197 hii hi hii hi ha ha hii hi hii hi ha ha [The chorus and Monkey-Leg end by
singing this refrain together.]

At this point the singing stopped, and Monkey-Leg packed up his hammock
and got ready to leave for Diauarum Post.

Bridging Perceptual Fields

Over the course of this initial portion of his Maraka Monkey-Leg moves from
recounting his experiences from the perspective of a nonempowered person
to narrating his experiences from the perspective of an empowered healer. His
gradual shift in perspective creates a bridge between the normal perceptual
field of his audience and his own enhanced perception. For example, at the
outset of his spoken narrative in scene 1 (lines 1–36), Monkey-Leg's spirit
encounters are narrated exclusively from the perspective of a layman. Like the
nonempowered, he describes himself as unable to fully see or understand the
spirits. He says in lines 5 and 6 that a spirit knocked him down but that he did
not understand what was happening to him. In these initial accounts he omits
all but the most basic details about the spirits and their activities. Instead, he
portrays himself as perceiving these events only through the physical pain of
sickness, just as any nonempowered person might.

In contrast, his later dreams and visions are more vividly reenacted or represented. He gives detailed descriptions about what the spirits presented to
him, such as a canoe with a black jeju fish sitting in it, smoked game, or an arrow fletched with toucan tails and fancy woven designs on the shaft. In scenes
2 and 6 he also includes the directly quoted speech of the spirits—a technique
that gives the audience an increased sense of "being there" (Hendricks 1993,
182; Tedlock 1983, 167). Later, when Monkey-Leg begins to sing and the spirit
interactions begin to take place in the present, within the space of his body, he
continues to directly quote the spirits' words and to evocatively describe their
speech. By scene 16 he even describes the subtleties of their search. In line 175
they are "speaking softly."

As he narrates his experiences, Monkey-Leg uses demonstratives such as
"like this," "this time of day," or "here" accompanied by gestures to tie his
dreams and visions to the ordinary world inhabited by his audience. To some
extent the use of such demonstratives is a standard technique, likely used
by skillful storytellers everywhere to encourage their listeners' engagement.
Kayabi narrators, for example, repeatedly employ phrases translated as "just

this same time of day" to tie a mythic story to the event of its narration. The interesting aspect of Monkey-Leg's narrative, however, is that he uses relatively few of these aligning phrases when speaking from the perspective of a layman but uses them more when describing his past and present Maraka dreams and visions. Furthermore, at the outset of his account, he only uses one such phrase when referring to his limited perception of his dreams (line 4) and uses none at all when describing his experiences in "ordinary reality." In other words, he is not interested in facilitating visualizations of all of his past life for his audience, only the parts that concern his visualizations of spirits.

His "ordinary" experiences are, moreover, narrated in an unusual tense and evidential construction that may even hinder a listener's visualization of them. In Kayabi he uses the particle *nipo* or *nipo a'e* to tell about his past ordinary or nonempowered experiences. I have translated this as "perhaps." *Nipo* is used to indicate uncertainty or probability to refer, for example, to an event that has not yet occurred, and *nipo a'e* is used to indicate that an event was not experienced directly but rather learned about through hearsay (SIL 1991). In several passages Monkey-Leg gives the impression of having been only semiconscious and almost blind to events in the ordinary world. He portrays himself as relying on others to tell him about his own experiences. For example, the reported dialogue between Monkey-Leg and the person who first brings him to be cured (lines 28–30) gives the impression that Monkey-Leg could perceive almost nothing in the ordinary world: he needs to ask his companion, as they approach the village, to tell him exactly who is singing Maraka. In later passages the ordinary world continues to be described as only indirectly perceived by Monkey-Leg, while the spirit world becomes increasingly more vivid.

As he tells about his dream experiences, Monkey-Leg creates a "centered space" (Hanks 1996) around himself. Beginning at line 59 he describes the placement of the foods the spirits bring to him in relation to his own position in his hammock. Then, when describing the handicrafts they bring to him, he continues to point to the area around his immediate physical presence in his hammock. He demonstrates how items were placed below him and hung above his head (lines 80–84).

Finally, in the last few episodes of his spoken narrative and during his sung account, he contracts or "pulls in" this centered space even further. He makes his own body the focal point. In lines 102–9 he shows his audience how he cured his elder brother by demonstrating the procedure on himself: he reaches behind his head and touches the area on his back where a lizard appeared for him between his brother's shoulders. He declares that it was "here" where he saw this lizard and began to pull the intrusive items out of his brother's back. In line 102 he says, "Then, here between his shoulders the jaguar bone turned into my lizard. Here sitting inside his shoulders." Later during his singing he focuses the audience's attention on just one of his hands. Near the end of this first song (at line 186) he quotes the spirits as announcing that they are now "in your hand." At this point, the hand that moments earlier had been used to indicate where the spirits had put their gifts on the floor of his house and then had demonstrated how he had performed an exorcism on his brother's body now becomes the actual seat of the spirits at the present moment of narration.

Over the course of his performance, as he "centers" the space of the house to a greater degree, Monkey-Leg's situates his body as the mediator between the spirit world and the ordinary world occupied by his audience. His body becomes a portal to this other, normally invisible world. When he sings, particularly after the spirits are explicitly brought in as participants (line 171), his use of the pronoun "I" is a powerful means of linking these two worlds. The "I" "not understanding" (line 173) or "being spoken to" (line 174) or "calling" (line 183) is simultaneously a participant in an empowered interaction within his body and his tangible or ordinary interaction with his human chorus. The normally inaccessible world of the spirits existing in the very distant domains of the cosmos implodes within the space of Monkey-Leg's body and subjectivity. This process "carries" with it the "space" inhabited by the audience members and pulls them into a meditation on the interior space of Monkey-Leg's body.

The gradual shift from the perspective of a layman to that of an empowered healer and the centering of space around the shaman's body are standard techniques used in Maraka performances. Like Monkey-Leg, Stone-Arm also began the second day of one of his Maraka in 1992 with a spoken account of how he became empowered. He too first anchored his account in the ordinary perceptual field of the average person. He began by pointing to scars on his body. Next he told about how his older brother cured him and then about his encounters with the spirit being who watches over sloths, the Master of Sloths. Next he presented these encounters more vividly by quoting from a past dialogue between the sloth spirit and himself, reenacting how they had exchanged names with each other. His account thus also moved from the perceptible—that is, his scars—to the normally imperceptible visions and conversations with the sloth spirit. This kind of centering of space and use of the body as a portal to normally invisible cosmological domains is found throughout the Amazon. The narrative construction of a cosmos within the body of shamans has, for example, been documented among other lowland peoples such as the Yanomami (Chagnon 1997; Lizot 1991).

Constructing a Continuity between the Generations

While Monkey-Leg gradually draws the audience into alignment with his perceptions of the spirits, he also simultaneously aligns his own subjective state with that of a member of the past generation—his deceased elder brother. The spoken and sung portions of the narrative align Monkey-Leg with his brother in different ways, but the underlying message is that the power of the distant times and spaces inhabited by spirits is reached by establishing continuity across generations or by replicating one's elders.

In his spoken account Monkey-Leg describes how he and his elder brother literally exchange places with each other. Initially Monkey-Leg recounts how he was a patient in his brother's Maraka cures (scenes 1–8). He tells how his wife called his elder brother to come and treat him. Later, however, in scene 11, the roles invert. His elder brother's wife comes to Monkey-Leg and asks him to cure her husband. In line 93 he quotes her as saying, " 'Come,' your older brother says to you, husband's brother." Later still, Monkey-Leg quotes his older brother as explicitly stating that Monkey-Leg is to be his replacement. As Monkey-Leg attempts to cure him he says, "You grab it so you can be the same as me, I say. In my place, I say" (line 103).

An even more vivid proof that Monkey-Leg has become like his elder brother or "has taken his place" follows in Monkey-Leg's performance at the post. The first dream he sang at the post was one that he originally dreamed along with his brother years ago, when his brother was still alive. According to audience members, Monkey-Leg often begins his Maraka performances with this shared dream. While most Maraka songs are sung in first-person singular, this one switches into first-person plural (exclusive) at several points. Also unlike most dream songs, in which a shaman meets only one spirit at a time on his "path" to different spirit villages, here he and his brother meet a double manifestation of the eagle spirit. The same series of events is described as taking place for both men, each with their respective eagle interlocutors. Through this song Monkey-Leg and his brother become mirror images of each other. A few lines of Monkey-Leg's song that show this shift to first-person-plural pronouns are as follows:

> The eagle with a rash was on his feet.
> He shook himself.
> We caught the itch.

Over the course of subsequent lines, it becomes apparent that there are two eagle spirits each simultaneously affecting Monkey-Leg and his brother in exactly the same way. After describing how they got an itchy rash from the eagle who was ruffling its feathers, Monkey-Leg sings that there are two eagles. Bird and Fire-of-the-Gods, who helped me translate this song, explained that the action Monkey-Leg describes is happening in tandem for the two men.

Because the dream was shared, Monkey-Leg presented a portion of a song that the deceased may well have sung when he was alive. Whether members of the audience had previously heard the song or not, the effect was that the experience of a subject of the past was being relived by the singer, brought back to life in a sense. Previously dreamed dreams like this one are supposed to be heard and seen again for the singer as well as the audience, just like the first time they were dreamed. They are "just a little further away." Members of two generations—one that is now gone and one that is currently a member of the senior age group—are represented as tangibly overlapping in their dream states.

While Monkey-Leg sang about mirroring his brother's experiences at Diauarum Post, the male chorus (which still included Jacaré's relatives) sang along with him. In these later songs they followed the standard style of Maraka singing by repeating verbatim each line of the shaman's first-person dream narrative and then singing a repeating refrain of vocables. As is typical, the men who formed the chorus were for the most part younger than the elderly Monkey-Leg, due to the fact that only the most senior shamans can sing Maraka. This repetition by the chorus was, therefore, an interaction in which younger men repeated the words of an elder verbatim. Because Monkey-Leg was at the same time repeating the words of his elder brother, the younger chorus was mirroring an elder who was, in turn, a reflection of a member of the previous generation. This mimesis connected all of them to the very powerful times and places of the ancient Masters of the Game, beings who were created much prior to humans and are, therefore, closer to the origins of the cosmos.

Toward the end of this introductory section of his Maraka, Monkey-Leg returned to using a first-person-singular pronoun. This initial portion was only the prelude to a whole night of singing in first person about his successful experiences with spirits. After this introduction, the character of his elder brother disappeared and Monkey-Leg described only himself standing in front of the two eagles. Near the end of this episode he sings the following lines:

> I am calling for you all.
> The eagle who makes a wind on his feet.
> In this plaza.
> Everything is fine.

In these lines the incorporation of Monkey-Leg's elder brother into his own identity (or of himself into that of his elder brother) is complete. To use Greg Urban's distinctions with respect to the different types of "discourse 'I's," here Monkey-Leg comes to assume a "projective 'I' " or a "non-ordinary self" that aligns him with the past "I's" of specific ancestral figures (1989, 43; see also Graham 1995 for a similar instance in Xavante ritual.)

Later at the post, after finishing the account of his past successful cures, Monkey-Leg sang about the current location of Jacaré's soul in the dream world. As the night wore on, Jacaré's male relatives continued to sing in the chorus, repeating Monkey-Leg's words verbatim, and ultimately came to have the sense that they too were "walking around in the land of the spirits." Through their repetition of Monkey-Leg's dream narrative they came to identify with the shaman's and Jacaré's soul's unusual experiences in the spirit world (while Jacaré was also coming to identify with his own soul's travels). All of these identifications took place through the medium of Monkey-Leg's sung dreams—dreams that were portrayed as having been ultimately based on previously shared adventures with his elder brother. The dream experiences of subjects from distinct generations (both past and present)—Monkey-Leg and his elder brother, Eroit, as well as Jacaré and his sons and sons-in-law—overlapped within the performance of Monkey-Leg's sung dream experiences.

This overlap, which produced the effect of the narrating subjects (both the shaman and each member of the chorus) being made up of "multiple subjects," is similar to Laura Graham's (1995) description of Xavante men's *da-ño're* singing—speech that is represented as an emergent intersubjective production. Because Maraka are cures for an illness caused by emotional isolation and the individuation of experience, this sort of intersubjectivity can be said to be associated with the state of human well-being (*jaruete*) that Maraka are supposed to engender in a community. Health and well-being come about by connecting members of different generations through their shared experience (or musically created "para-shamanic experience") of spirit domains.

Jacaré's daughter, Thorn, may not have had quite the same sense of "para-shamanic experience" as her male relatives did because she, like all of the other women, did not participate in the choral singing. Instead, in addition to her own dreams, which may well have been influenced by the shaman's singing, she may have come to identify with Jacaré by carrying out a standard female role in Maraka. She, like the other women involved, lavishly cared for the patient by preparing the special foods required for the occasion. Before a Maraka is held, women from the patient's household invite the women from other families to work along with them. Thorn, her mother, Julia, and other women at Diauarum collectively prepared large pots of a sweet manoic drink called mo'yfet as well as other delicacies such as a toasted manioc-peanut "cookie" called kanape. These foods are viewed as being made "for the spirits" or to "attract the spirits," yet all of the participants eat the delicacies.

Monkey-Leg's spoken account also suggested how shamans and non-shamans should behave toward elder generations outside of Maraka cures in order to encourage this cross-generational connection. He portrays his own incorporation of his elder brother's experiences as having come about through obedience. According to the spoken account of his dream life, he only begins to assume his brother's place after he follows his brother's directions. In scene II (line 97), despite being shaky from illness, he responds to his brother's request and goes to cure him. Then, despite his self-doubt, he tries to follow his brother's directions and cure (line 105).

The scenarios in which Monkey-Leg is obedient to his brother can be seen as parts of a larger pattern—a pattern that Urban calls a "parallelism of speech-action relations" (1991, 60). Commands, seven in all, issued by either Monkey-Leg, his wife, his elder brother, or spirits are all carried out by other characters. Even in the cases in which the orders are joked about or ridiculed, they are followed nonetheless. For example, Monkey-Leg asks for a Maraka to be performed for him (line 10), and his wife arranges for one to take place; Monkey-Leg's wife asks Monkey-Leg's brother to look at her husband (line 36), and he does; the spirits tell Monkey-Leg to get in their canoe (lines 40, 42), and he does; Monkey-Leg's brother tells the village to smoke a pig (line 74), and they do; Monkey-Leg's sister-in-law asks him to cure her husband (line 93), and he does. As a consequence of the translation of various characters' speech into action, the young Monkey-Leg recovers from sickness and becomes an empowered healer.

The obedience of people in the past is contrasted with the account that followed, a story about recent disobedience by the young people in his household. He concluded his spoken narrative with a tale of how he had asked his younger family members to go get a frog that he heard singing by the river, but that they had ignored his request (lines 122–25). He says in line 125, for example, "But how people do not obey others." The failure of his family members to carry out his request is a sharp break in the sequence of speech-action parallelism. By this point in his narrative, Monkey-Leg had already recounted how seven verbal commands were carried out and how beneficial results had followed.

Elderly healers frequently say, quite blatantly, that they are the last link for the living to the powers of health, implying that younger generations cannot equal them. Here Monkey-Leg communicated this message more subtly and implicitly (see Urban 1991, 267). The youth in Monkey-Leg's household are portrayed as missing the chance to become empowered by refusing to obey. His comment "but how people don't obey" ties this narrated event with the present: people behave now just as they did when this incident took place, that is, in a way that limits their access to the past.[11]

Shamans as Unique

Paradoxically, the obedience to and replication of previous generations lead to a sort of unparalleled uniqueness for great shamans in the present. They are fond of proclaiming that they are unlike any other living person. Likewise, each Maraka song is conceptualized as a completely unique entity. Even a past cure that has been sung about innumerable times by an elderly great shaman as a part of his "résumé" is thought to be sung slightly differently each time it is recounted. As one man explained, "Sometimes just few words or phrases are changed, but it is always different."

A great shaman's claim to singularity is a result of his relationship to spirit beings. Each great shaman has an individualized set of spirit associates (his *rupiwat*), a unique set of powers that are available only to him. These nonhuman spirit beings live in various far-away domains: underwater, at the horizon, deep in the forest, or in the sky. Shamans visit with these beings in their homes and learn about their distinctive ways of life and powers. As no two shamans are familiar with exactly the same set of spirits, they each know about a very different segment of the cosmos.

Given this emphasis on uniqueness, it is understandable that great shamans like Monkey-Leg and Stone-Arm would avoid each other. They have different understandings of the spirit word. Their singularity is, however, only possible by virtue of the fact that they first obeyed and came to replicate the experiences of elder shamans. Continuity across the generations provides the base from which their distinctiveness in the present can be established.

HEADMEN'S SONGS
AND THE END OF MOURNING

People breathe deeply again and become happy.
FIRE-OF-THE-GODS, DESCRIBING
THE EFFECTS OF JAWOSI SINGING, 1992

After I had been living in Kapinu'a for several months, João told me one afternoon as he and Pretty swung in his hammock that they had lost a baby son just a few months before my arrival. He had taken the baby outside the park to be treated at a hospital, where the baby was diagnosed with malaria. In João's opinion the malaria had weakened the boy and had allowed his soul to be taken from his body by one of the Masters of the Game. After watching the chickens peck at the dirt floor beneath the hammock for awhile, João admitted that he delayed my permission to enter the park for months as a result of simply being too upset to host a visitor. Never having met João and Pretty before moving in with them, and not yet knowing the contours of Kayabi mourning, I could only sense the depths of their sadness retrospectively, by thinking about how much more lighthearted they had become as the months passed.

Just as sickness and health are not prerogatives of individual persons, neither is the process of moving away from sadness and mourning after the death of a loved one. Others, particularly the affines and cross-cousins of mourners, bear this burden. After an appropriate period, they give the mourners gifts, make them food, and encourage them to socialize. One of the most spectacular means of encouraging an end to mourning is a performance of Jawosi-style singing. Jawosi features the songs of adult men. Most are about heroic encounters with non-Kayabi enemies and are often based on and generated by the singers' own experiences in war or travel. Kayabi understand this ritual and singing style to have originated in a mythic war and have traditionally held it in conjunction with warfare. [1] Consequently, in the literature several have labeled this event as a war ritual (Grünberg n.d. [1970], 127; Travassos 1993). [2] Jawosi singing, however, is significant for Kayabi people in many other ways as well. Here I explore the comments of those who remarked that Jawosi helps alleviate the sadness (-arasing) experienced with the death of a relative and treat it as pertaining to war insofar as warfare is also connected to the process of mourning. This chapter, therefore, focuses on the relationship between Jawosi singing and the end of mourning and examines how singers' autobiographical narratives figure into this relationship.

Like the other genres of autobiographical narrative I have discussed, these songs suggest a means of having strength and power in the present. They are sung, for example, explicitly to move mourners from a state of debilitating sadness to one of happiness and strength. In these performances strength is presented not as the result of the living having a clear continuity with past generations, as in Maraka cures, nor as the result of one generation surpassing and distinguishing itself from the previous one, as in political oratory. Rather, strength and happiness are the result of the living having a distance from their own dead and a strong identification with each other. Jawosi songs, therefore, present and enact a point of contact between what I have been calling the "progressive" and the "degenerative" perspectives—what could be termed a "presentist" position.

Unlike the issues of Indian identity, salaried positions in the park, or increased consumption of Brazilian foods, death is not an issue specific to the last several decades, though for Kayabi it is a problem specific to this latest cosmological epoch since in earlier times death, as we know it, did not exist. Jawosi songs confront the persistent problem of death through accounts of interethnic relations, many of which are characteristic of, or interpreted as characteristic of, contemporary times. These songs are therefore very much about how to have power in the present in light of historically specific as well as more timeless challenges.

My discussion concentrates on a series of Jawosi songs performed to help João and Pretty attenuate their sadness over the death of their son. This particular period of singing took place for three days in early April 1992. I focus on the performances that were considered the most virtuoso, those of the elder headmen. From among these I concentrate on the songs performed by those headmen who were most closely related to João and Pretty. The texts of these songs provide examples of interpersonal encounters for the mourners to emulate with respect to their own dead relative, while the formal aspects of the singing model a kind of empowering sociability and interpersonal involvement between households. Throughout the discussion I contrast the relationships that are described and encouraged through the singing with those that Kayabi understand the mourners to be experiencing.

Jawosi

Jawosi is a style of singing that can take place at various times in a Kayabi village like Kapinu'a. While Jawosi singing can explicitly be orchestrated to help a household end its mourning, it can also be organized to celebrate the arrival of visitors or the return of hunters or successful warriors; in the past it was also performed at the beginning of male initiation. On these various occasions, Jawosi singing is supposed to help people forget their dead relatives while simultaneously performing these other functions. As Fire-of-the-Gods explained, upon hearing the music "people breathe deeply again and become happy." The lungs in conjunction with the heart and liver are the seats of emotions such as happiness. [3] He continued that Jawosi should ideally help people to forget about their deceased relatives and "to complete their sadness." The music gives people a sense of healthful well-being. In keeping with their association with the end of mourning, Jawosi songs are not sung during the appropriate mourning period, that is, for several months directly following a death (see Grünberg n.d. [1970], 121). People say that during this time they are too sad to sing. When I first arrived in the Xingu in 1992, for example, I was told that no village would be singing Jawosi for several months because a senior man in another village had recently died. Similarly, a period of singing was cut short when an elder passed away in the dry season of 1993.

Jawosi singing consists of a group of women, mainly young unmarried women, asking each of the married men in the village to sing for them. The women serve as a chorus for each singer and collectively repeat the lines that the male soloist sings first. Singing begins in the late afternoon and can last from a few days to a few weeks. On the first few afternoons, the women go from house to house asking each of the married men to sing for them as they lie in their hammocks. In each house the chorus asks the most senior men to sing first and then the younger married men. After they have asked each one, they move on to the next household.

The initial few days of Jawosi singing serve somewhat as a rehearsal for later days or even later Jawosi. During the late afternoon, for example, some of the youngest married men practice singing without the chorus of adult women. A small chorus of young girls often gathers to accompany them. These young, newly married men sing extremely quietly. During these practice songs children stop to listen and generally hang around, but most adults continue on with their afternoon activities.

On the last few nights, however, Jawosi singing increases in intensity. Almost everyone gathers in one of the larger, traditional-style, rectangular houses. People bring their hammocks to hang. On these nights the focus is on the older men who are grandfathers and heads of extended family households. Again, the chorus makes its rounds, going from hammock to hammock to ask each senior man to sing for them. Men begin their singing while lying in their hammocks, but after a song or two they get up to sing while dancing up and down the central corridor of the house. The soloist takes several steps forward and a few steps back while the chorus follows in one or two rows behind him. The women dance side by side with their arms around each other's waists and shoulders alternately.

When the senior men dance in Jawosi they carry weapons or hunting implements such as bows and arrows, fishing poles, clubs, or shotguns (see also Grünberg n.d. [1970], 170). I was told that when heads were taken in battle some singers also carried skulls suspended by cotton string from poles as they danced. During these final days men are painted by their wives or by other men with unique designs in red annatto and black charcoal representing enemies or game animals. Others are painted solid red.

Self-Representation in Jawosi Songs

Jawosi songs are first-person accounts of heroic encounters with non-Kayabi individuals. In general, people characterized Jawosi as being based on the singers' own experiences. Chief João commented that they "are about the singer himself." He went on to describe some of his own songs about his travels among whites and around the Xingu Park. He said he sang the songs so that people would know where he had been and would say, "Wow, this guy traveled around here, around there." Similarly, when I asked a group of men why they sang Jawosi after coming back from a collective fishing trip, they told me that they wanted to sing about their experiences.

Jawosi songs can also be inherited from paternal relatives. Songs are described as being "left over" after people die. With respect to inherited songs, sets of brothers and paternal cousins, also called "brothers" in Kayabi, along with their fathers and grandfathers understand each other's songs most fully. These men often know exactly which experiences of which relative originally gave rise to a song. They also know more or less where the event took place and which enemy was involved. Members of other families are not usually aware of this sort of specificity. They tend to interpret all songs as relating to the life of the singer in terms of what they already know about him.[4]

Several aspects of Jawosi songs encourage audience members to interpret them as relating to experiences of the singer rather than to experiences of previous generations. First, most songs lack the tense and evidential markers ordinarily used when speaking Kayabi. These markers indicate whether an event was experienced personally and whether it occurred in the immediate, recent, or distant past. Their absence in turn gives the songs a timeless or free-floating quality. Second, Jawosi songs employ a standard set of metaphors to refer to generic kinds of interactions with enemies. While most adults who are not closely related to the singer can decipher the sorts of events to which the metaphors refer, they cannot determine anything very specific from them. For example, a reference to "chopping down a tree" is generally understood to mean killing an enemy. "Losing the blade" of one's ax or "losing" one's arrow are understood to mean losing one's own relative in battle. Songs about "making a kawĩ beverage" are about boiling down the head of an enemy to obtain the victim's teeth. [5] A hot kawĩ indicates that the enemy was violent, a cold kawĩ that the enemy was already dead when encountered or was a "pacified" Indian. Non-Kayabi are referred to as different sorts of animals; the different characteristics of the animal—for example, the color of its fur or feathers—give clues to his or her ethnicity.

While I believe that the lack of tense and evidential markers and the use of metaphors facilitate a presentist interpretation, my work on the translation of one particular song led me to a more profound reason for why audience members might interpret all songs, even inherited songs, as relating to the singers' lives: because singers themselves interpret them this way. Inherited songs are simultaneously about the singers' own lives and their relatives' lives. The song that led me to this conclusion was sung during a Jawosi held in August 1992 by an elderly man, Waist, who had been living in Kapinu'a for several years.

In the following version of Waist's song I have omitted the chorus's responses that follow each of his lines.

> I am standing looking at the oropendula bird's offspring.
>
> The oropendulas are standing grouped together, guy.
>
> I stay looking at the oropendula bird's offspring.
>
> Might we have a long branch to take the oropendula's child?
>
> This one moving is the offspring of a red oropendula.
>
> They [the birds] are arriving, guy.
>
> This one moving is the child of the white oropendula.
>
> The oropendulas are standing all mixed together, guy.
>
> Might we have a long branch to take the oropendula's child?

They have their children in any old tree.

They have their children in the mountains.

The oropendulas are standing grouped together, guy.

I always go to the oropendula's tree on foot.

I look at the oropendula's children with curiosity.

Bird and Fire-of-the-Gods, who translated this song for me (and who were between the ages of twenty-five and forty and unrelated to Waist), recognized it as one that Waist frequently sang. They both readily admitted that they did not know exactly to what event it referred, but supposed it was an account of something that had happened to him. They were reasonably familiar with his life experiences and thought the song was very likely about a trip Waist made to the FUNAI office in São Paulo. They knew this man had spent extended periods of time at FUNAI in urban centers undergoing medical treatment as a result of being inflicted with a skin disease common among Kayabi. They inferred with confidence that the white and red birds standing together in one place stood for the whites and the Indians who worked together at FUNAI. The line "Might we have a long branch to take the oropendula's child?" was interpreted, according to the standard metaphorical equivalents used to decipher Jawosi, to mean that he wanted to kidnap one of the children in São Paulo and take it back to raise. That a "long branch" is needed and that the birds are described as raising their children "in the mountains" were both interpreted as references to the tall buildings in São Paulo, where, they said, people live "like birds in trees."

When I asked the elderly Waist about this song he explained that he inherited it from his uncle. According to Waist, it referred to his uncle's travels. He said that this uncle lived in the Peixes River area and interacted with peoples who lived in the vicinity. [6] It was Waist's further commentary, however, that shed light on how an inherited song such as this one may also become the singer's own. In explaining this particular song to me he did not simply say that it referred to his uncle's experiences. He indicated that the song referred as much to his own experiences. Rather than being about the period of his medical treatment, he related this song to his experience of first coming to the Xingu Park as a much younger man after having lived away from his fellow Kayabi. He explained that his uncle had raised him until he was an adult and then had passed away. During this period his uncle taught him this song. Waist admitted that he did not publicly sing it until much later. As a young adult he went to live with the Bororo (another Brazilian indigenous people). He then moved to the city of São Paulo, where he reconnected with some of his Kayabi relatives, who convinced him to move to the Xingu Park. On the occasion of disembarking from the boat that brought him to a Kayabi village in the Xingu, Waist said he sang this song for the first time in his life. With this type of commentary, he suggested that his travel experiences outside of the Kayabi community among "red" and "white" enemies paralleled those of his uncle and that the song represented his life experiences as much as it did his uncle's. The two young men who translated his song for me were not so wrong in their interpretation, though they were unaware of the song's genesis. My sense is that other men who sing inherited songs come to understand their songs in a similar manner—as relating to their own experiences as well as to their relatives'. Inherited songs may be a sort of template that men use to understand their own experiences with other ethnicities (Oakdale 2002). They may mature into them, much as Waist did, through their own travel experiences, eventually making them their own.

Like Maraka songs, Jawosi songs are conceptualized as first having been overheard. In Kayabi, "to sing Jawosi" is "to repeat Jawosi" (Jawosia'ang). The singer is therefore never exactly the equivalent of the "author" of the songs even when the songs are generated by his own experiences. In the case of songs that recount an enemy being killed by a Kayabi warrior, these songs are said to "come from the bones of the victim," to "be emitted from them." The killer hears his victim's voice speaking to him after the encounter. The songs that recount the death of an enemy are furthermore sung from the point of view of the dead enemy rather than the Kayabi warrior.[7] When I asked about the origins of songs that do not recount a death (such as Waist's song), I was told that the "music can come from anything." The crucial aspect seems to be that it comes from the singer's interaction with something outside of himself.

The Kayabi warrior hears the songs and repeats them to himself before singing them publicly. In this respect, songs learned by Kayabi men that were first sung by relatives may not be so different from songs learned from firsthand encounters with enemies. Young men repeat their inherited songs quietly, almost to themselves, during the initial days of a Jawosi; presumably they do this for several years before singing them as loudly as the more senior men. Many of the songs actually make reference to this process of hearing the songs and repeating them to oneself. The women's choral refrain in one of Chest's Jawosi songs, for example, turns each of the soloist's lines into self-reflexive speech. One segment of Chest's song is as follows:

Soloist: While I cut down trees
Chorus: "While I cut down trees, while I cut down trees, I keep walking,"
I say to myself.

To add one more layer of complexity in the case of songs authored by a dead enemy, the dead enemy and the singer of the song are not clearly distinct persons during Jawosi rituals.[8] Jawosi singing is conceptualized as calling the dead enemy into the here and now through the singers themselves. In some songs this happens through the use of the victim's name. In the songs that mention the name of the dead enemy, the name does not carry the usual suffix ('i) to indicate that they are deceased. To call the name of any deceased person is understood to actually invoke their presence, and one would supposedly do this even more so without this suffix. I was told that people do not call out the name of someone who has died because one of their spirits, presumably their "body spirit" ('angjang), will think they are being summoned and will come to harass the living.[9] In the case of men who sing about an enemy they themselves killed, the use of the enemy's name blurs the distinction between warrior and enemy. Warriors often take, as one of their own names, the name of the enemy whose life they took. Even in songs that do not use a proper name, the singer comes to represent the enemy. The singer's body paint is, for example, a visual representation of the enemy.

Fire-of-the-Gods's Jawosi

By April 1992 at least six months had passed since the death of João and Pretty's son. Fire-of-the-Gods, who considered himself to be João's cousin, decided that he should organize a Jawosi to help João and his family recover their well-being. A Jawosi might have been held earlier, but an elder in another village had died recently, making Jawosi singing inappropriate for yet another period of time. Neighbor women mentioned that earlier they had held Brazilian-style Christmas and New Year's parties to help João and Pretty but that the Brazilian *farró* dancing at the New Year's party ended in a fight; rather than alleviating their sadness this unfortunate event had only made them more upset. It seemed only Kayabi-style singing and dancing could bring solace. A Jawosi seemed especially appropriate since a man from a village downriver had just come for a visit.

Fire-of-the-Gods also reasoned that a Jawosi would show me during my stay in the village that the Kayabi still had "their culture." While seemingly unrelated to João's mourning, this demonstration of culture was also part of recovering João's happiness. João often complained that others who had passed through the Xingu commented that the Kayabi had "lost their culture," and he was interested in showing me the untruth of this assertion. Fire-of-the-Gods reasoned that a Jawosi was a way to show João that the community was behind him in this endeavor. João considered Jawosi festivals to be one of the most powerful embodiments of Kayabi culture. One afternoon during Fire-of-the Gods's Jawosi he commented that, although Kayabi people use Western clothing and other nonindigenous goods and many can speak Portuguese, this did not mean they had become *civilizados*, for they still ate their own food and, most important, celebrated their own festivals such as Jawosi.

Fire-of-the-Gods, as the owner (*jat*) of this April Jawosi, began the event by going from house to house, asking the women in Kapinu'a if they would agree to sing Jawosi.[10] Several days later, in the late afternoon, a female chorus began making the rounds to each of the village's households to sing at least one song with each of the married men as they reclined in their hammock. A few of the women from the chorus convinced me to sing along with them. After some hesitation about both my linguistic and singing abilities, I finally agreed, and before long I was gleefully running with the other young women from house to house in the village circle.

On the last two nights, the singing culminated at Chest's (João's father) big traditional-style long house. On the penultimate night people sang and danced until well after midnight, and on the final night they did the same until a few hours before dawn. On the final night, other families came to Chest's house with pieces of meat to roast over small fires as they lounged, visited, and participated in the singing. Families tended to hang their hammocks together in clusters, and parents and their young children sat together. Next to the house a large fire was built, and older children ran excitedly in circles around the fire in the illumination of the unusual and festive evening. Again the women asked me to sing with them, and a young man offered to take over the task of tape-recording the music. On this night only the most senior men—those who were grandfathers—were asked to sing. They began in their hammocks but after a few lines got up and began to dance up and down the central corridor of the house. Despite their age, some of the oldest men danced very quickly, playfully varying their steps so as to trick the women's chorus following them. Little girls held onto the senior men's shorts or belts of polished tucum nut beads (which the older men continue to wear under their shorts) as they sang and tried to follow their steps along with the chorus. Boys hooted with approval after particularly well-sung songs and urged the women's chorus to sing louder at various points. A blast on a jaguar bone flute finally ended the singing at dawn.

All the songs that I present here were sung relatively soon after the sun went down and were sung by senior men close to João in one way or another. The first was sung by his father, Chest, and the second by Leg-Bone, Fire-of-the-Gods's father, a man whom João treated as an uncle (a mother's brother). To understand how these songs might have helped João and Pretty, some background on the couple's emotional or social state is needed. Thus I begin with a discussion of Kayabi mourning to show how the social relations that characterize the state of mourning are related to the social relationships described and enacted through Jawosi songs.

Understanding João and Pretty's Sadness during Mourning

Ethnopsychological approaches to the study of emotion have led to a fruitful disassociation between emotion or affect, the private domain, and the individual, on the one hand, and reason or cognition, the public, and the social, on the other (Lutz and White 1986, 429). Explorations of Amazonian notions of sociality and emotion have furthermore pointed out that the distinction between "the public" and "the private" does not fit well with Amazonian notions (Overing and Passes 2000, 5). Rather, for many Amazonians "emotion talk is also social talk" (4). In the following discussion of Kayabi mourning, attention to how a subject perceives (and is perceived) to be related to significant others in this social or sentimental way is a useful starting point.

According to Kayabi commentary, the sadness people feel after death (-arasing) is conceptualized as a state of intense connection and identification with their dead relative, an identification that entails an equally extreme estrangement from other living people. If this state is too prolonged it can cause the mourner to become weaker, to be less connected to the living, and ultimately to die. This state contrasts with at least one sort of happiness or joy (-ekõeãi), which seems to be fully possible only when living people are gathered together and feel a connection or identification with each other, such as when they are celebrating a Jawosi festival.

Directly after death the deceased's immediate family—spouse, parents, children, and siblings—shares a physical substance with the dead. A part of the "body soul" or "soul of the corpse" ('angjang ipirewat) is understood to cling to their bodies. In part this substance may come from their intense physical contact with the dead, an important aspect of a Kayabi funeral, much as elsewhere in Amazonia (see Conklin 2001, 69). When adults die they are placed in their hammock within their home and relatives are called from the surrounding area. During the days before burial, fellow household members spend time holding and crying over the body. Once all the relatives have arrived, the deceased is buried in the floor of their house, usually underneath the place where he or she slept when alive. Again, during the burial close relatives have intense physical contact with the deceased. Spouses or children might hold onto the body and let themselves be partially buried as a sign of their attachment to the deceased, eventually being pulled from the grave by one of their affines or cousins. After burial, children or spouses may also hang their hammock and sleep directly over the grave for a period of time.

In addition to their physical identification with the dead, mourners are also socially similar to the dead in that they become isolated from other living humans. This estrangement is most noticeable in the silence that occurs after death. When a villager dies the silence and estrangement overtake the whole local group, but as the days pass the silence is maintained only by the household of the deceased. Though I was not in the village when João's son died, I was present when the elderly Jacaré passed away in 1993. Jacaré had been taken to a Brasília hospital by plane after falling into a coma one afternoon. After several anxious days of waiting, the sad news of his death was received over the short-wave radio. Children boisterously playing in the plaza were called in by their mothers and told in a harsh whisper to be quiet; they were informed that the grandfather of a playmate had just died and that they should come inside. The nightly soccer game in the plaza was abruptly put to a stop and the young, grief-stricken men dispersed to their homes. A mournful hush overcame the entire village for several days.[11]

Jacaré's family maintained its isolation and silence much more intensely and for much longer. A grieving family does not visit other households for months, nor do they talk even among themselves very extensively for several weeks after the death. Jacaré's house was eerily devoid of human voices for weeks after he died. With the exception of an occasional child's voice, only dogs, chickens, and the occasional sound of a knife chopping could be heard from outside. When visitors such as myself arrived, Jacaré's family, particularly his children and wife, spoke in hushed whispers, if at all, from their separate hammocks.[12]

Rather than communicating with the living, a mourning household communicates in a one-way fashion with the dead. Adult women keen at sunrise and sunset for several weeks, "calling out," as Kayabi say, to the soul of the dead as it makes its way across the sky. Kayabi keening consists entirely of vowels, which begin high and then fall in pitch. It has a "high energy" or operatic quality that sets it apart from other styles of Amazonian keening (Briggs 1993). As Graham (1986, 87) points out with respect to Xavante keening, this type of nontexted vowel utterance explicitly displays intense personal emotion by not partaking in the sociability of language. The poignancy of Jacaré's wife's and daughter's keening brought tears to my eyes one evening as Stone-Arm, with his shaman's pipe in hand, described for me how he was watching his relative's 'ang depart across the western sky, with the aid of tobacco smoke.

Mourners' estrangement from others can at times also take the form of spatial distance. For example, Jacaré's grandson who moved to the Xingu from Brasília told me after his grandfather passed away that he and his wife would be moving away from the Xingu soon as a result of his grandfather's death. When Fire-of-the-Gods lost one of his brothers, a man who did not live in Kapinu'a but rather with the Panará, he also moved his wife and children temporarily to one of his father's distant fields. It was said that he moved away from everyone else because of his sadness over the death.

Hostility and arguments are also linked to the sadness that occurs after a death and further contribute to mourners' isolation. Death is supposed to cause survivors to become angry (-maratne) and argumentative (for a similar emotional response among the Yanomami see Alès 2000; among the Achuar see Taylor 1996). In part this anger is fueled by a stylized type of argument that is a standard part of Kayabi funerals. As a family holds and buries a body, they shout out the offenses others perpetrated against the deceased when he or she was alive. As they do this, they hold the body and place the deceased's belonging into his or her hammock—both signs of how they, in contrast to others, cared for the dead individual. Regardless of the routinization of airing complaints in this manner, it nevertheless appears to cause long-standing feuds to flare.

Kayabi understand that mourners' lack of sociability is caused by their meditation on the dead. João explained this point to me when I asked him why he would often leave social gatherings. One night, for example, I noticed that João, after becoming engrossed in conversation and smoking along with other young men who had come to visit, abruptly stood up, threw his cigarette down, and went to lay down in a dark recess of his house. Another night he was convinced to participate in a game of cards and joking banter. Suddenly he rose up out of his hammock and flamboyantly threw down his cards, causing them to flutter partially onto the ground and partially onto the box that provided the playing table, disrupting everyone's game. He explained these incidents in the following way: "Sometimes I am happy, talking, playing with others, smoking, and all of a sudden I ask myself, 'Where is my son, how can I enjoy these things when he is not here?' All of a sudden I ask myself, 'Why am I here? What is it that I am doing that a relative dies so suddenly?' "

Decreasing the connection with their deceased loved one and simultane-ously increasing their sociability with the living are not things mourners can do on their own. They require the actions of others, particularly in-laws or cross-cousins. In the weeks after a death these individuals wash mourners with sweet-smelling leaves and paint them with red annatto paint to remove the deceased person's lingering body soul. These people also give mourners gifts such as necklaces and baskets. Later they encourage mourners to social-ize and after a few months may organize a Jawosi to help the mourners forget their dead, much as Fire-of-the-Gods did for João and his family. According to Fire-of-the-Gods, in-laws should "bring the bereaved to a Jawosi festival, sing Jawosi and everything will return to normal. Paint him and end the sadness." Affines and others, according to him, need to plead with the bereaved, point out that "it's not good to stay in mourning" and that "you have to paint yourself with annatto."

The Texts of Jawosi Songs Sung for João and Pretty

In contrast to mourners' meditation on their lost love one and their iden-tification with the dead, the texts of the Jawosi songs focus on a different kind of dead—dead enemies—and present an image of extreme antisociabil-ity and nonidentification with these dead individuals. These songs feature an encounter between a Kayabi warrior and an enemy who is called back from the dead for the duration of the song. The lines of one song sung for João, for example, described the dead as singing from his grave: "I am covered with dirt as I lay in my hammock." Most songs describe the encounter between the Kayabi warrior and the non-Kayabi enemy before the enemy has died. In these songs the Kayabi warrior behaves in the most unsociable ways possible: killing, fighting, or kidnapping the non-Kayabi. The image of a Kayabi warrior behaving unsociably with a dead enemy provides a model for mourners to fol-low regarding the treatment of their own dead. Ideally, mourners' own dead, much as elsewhere in Amazonia, should become like enemies, "paradigms of sociological foreignness" (Taylor 1993, 654).

While many Jawosi songs refer to enemies in vague metaphorical terms (see also Grünberg n.d. [1970]; Travassos 1993), many of the songs sung for João and Pretty were about specific (named) enemies. They offered particularly powerful images of a warrior's understanding of and communication with his human victim, much as mourners have with their dead. Unlike mourners, however, the warriors featured in these songs remain unmoved and do not identify with their victims enough to act in a sociable manner; instead they treat them as enemies.

The first song I present here was sung by Fire-of-the-Gods's father, Leg-Bone. Everyone agreed that Leg-Bone's song concerned the deeds of the singer himself. It recounted, in the voice of a non-Indian victim, how he had died at the hands of a Kayabi warrior. Leg-Bone entered Chest's long house late in the afternoon, with his war club in hand and white bird down in his hair, perhaps in imitation of the enemy in his song or perhaps as an actual embodiment of this enemy. [13] Warriors who have killed come to have an intimate relationship with their victim: the blood of the victim fills the killer's stomach and necessitates a special diet and seclusion for a period of time. During Jawosi this same type of bodily communion may be revisited in a brief and more controlled manner. Just as cosmological spaces collapse within the body of the shaman in Maraka, in Jawosi subjects of different ethnicities (living and dead) may come together in the person of the warrior. Warriors like Leg-Bone are, therefore, men who have had an unusually close association with a deceased individual as a result of having shared blood. They also come to understand their battle encounter from this other individual's perspective. [14] Most important, they are able to disassociate themselves from this same individual. As a result, they present a powerful model for mourners on how to distance themselves from their own dead.

Throughout Leg-Bone's song, both men (Leg-Bone and the enemy) are described as understanding each other's perspective but ultimately as having irreconcilable positions, much as the living and the dead have. Because it is sung from the point of view of the victim, this song shows that Leg-Bone knows the thoughts of his enemy. The song in turn recounts how the victim also "understands," "foresees," or has premonitions about his killer. As a result, he tries unsuccessfully to feed, befriend, and "pacify" him. Ultimately the Kayabi warrior does not take the enemy's food and will not "be pacified." The sharing of food is one mark of a sociable encounter from a Kayabi perspective, and refusal of it is a clear signal of hostility. Though they understand each other well, the Kayabi warrior is described as not allowing for any kind of sociable encounter.

The choral repetition and refrain were repeated throughout the song. Here I include only the response from the chorus after the soloist's first two lines.

Leg-Bone: Just like this I always wander about. I make food for the one
who comes for me [my assassin].

Chorus: Just like this I always wander about. I make food for the one
who comes for me [my assassin], the one who comes for me,
the one who comes for me.

Leg-Bone: The one who comes for me foresees [plans] my death.
Chorus: The one who comes for me foresees my death. I make food
for the one who comes for me, the one who comes for me, the
one who comes for me.

I try to make him forget me. To no avail.

The one who comes for me understands me.

Just like this I always wander about. I make food for the one
who comes for me.

The one who comes for me foresees my death.

I try to make him forget me. To no avail.

I try to pacify him. To no avail.

The one who comes for me understands me.

Just like this I always wander about. I make food for the one
who comes for me.

I am definitely arriving, I think to myself.

You are foreseeing the one who comes for you.

The one who comes for you foresees.

I am definitely arriving, I think to myself.

Just like this I always wander about. I make food for the one
who comes for me.

The one who comes for me tries to forget about me.

Just like this I always wander about.

The one who comes for me tries to forget about me.

I try to make him forget me. To no avail.

The one who comes for me tries to forget about me.

For the one who comes for me.

The next song was sung by João's father, Chest. Like Leg-Bone's song, this
one also recounts an extreme kind of antisociability between a dead enemy and
a Kayabi warrior. In this song the enemy is a little girl who was kidnapped. [15]
As in Leg-Bone's song, the Kayabi warrior refuses to share food with his

3. Chest with his young daughter.

victim. The little girl is begging and crying to her captor for some honey. Kayabi children are rarely left to cry by adults, so the image of an unmollified child would be particularly antisocial from a Kayabi perspective. A song about behaving antisocially with a child is very fitting for João, who is trying to cut his ties with his own lost child. The child's name in the song, Kirikatu, also links this little girl to João's household, as some of the women in his house have "katu" as a part of their names. This song may indeed make reference to the event in which this name was first received by João's relatives from an encounter with a non-Kayabi. As well as taking enemy names for themselves, Kayabi warriors also brought names back for family members. These names are also passed down through the generations.

Each of the soloist's lines was repeated by the women's chorus along with a repeating refrain, but again I include this refrain only after the first two lines.

Chest: The singer is turning into a little girl.
Chorus: The singer is turning into a little girl. I cry to my captor, to my captor.

Chest: My captor is truly a great person, my captor.
Chorus: My captor is truly a great person, my captor. I cry to my captor, to my captor.

I feel hunger pangs.

The singer is turning into a little girl.

The first time that he runs with me I cry.

My captor is truly a great person, my captor.

I cry to my captor for some honey.

The first time that he runs with me I cry.

My captor is truly a great person, my captor.

He brings me from the forest of the *Awapey* people.

I have nothing to eat.

The first time that he runs with me I cry.

My captor is turning into a little girl.

My captor is truly a great person, my captor.

The captor brings Kirikatu [the girl's name].

My captor is truly a great person, my captor.

To my captor.

To my captor.

You were all quite a long time ago.

When your captor ran away.

Your captor was truly great when he brought you.

I always cry to my captor.

The first time that he runs with me I cry.

My captor is truly a great person, my captor.

I have nothing to eat. I cry for honey.

My captor is truly a great person, my captor.

I have nothing to eat.

I cry to my captor for some honey.

My captor is truly a great person, my captor.

The first time that he runs with me I cry.

To my captor.

Even though the Kayabi heroes of Jawosi songs are depicted as thinking about their enemies and understanding their position, much like mourners do with respect to their dead, they ultimately have no emotional attachment to them. In Leg-Bone's song the warrior is described as "understanding his victim" but killing him anyway. In Chest's song the warrior hears the kidnapped child crying but is unmoved and does not stop to give her honey. This kind of emotional detachment has been noted in the depiction of other Amazonian warriors, such as those found in Kalapalo stories about bow masters (Basso 1995) or those found in a Shuar warrior's account of his own life (Hendricks 1993). In the Kayabi Jawosi genre, a warrior's emotional detachment seems to be an image that helps mourners detach from their dead relatives, an image that plays an important part in helping them to forget and end their sadness.

In using powerful images of dead enemies to mute mourners' attachment to their own recently deceased relatives, Jawosi singing also shifts participants' evaluation of non-Kayabi. If the dead are equated with non-Kayabi, then non-Kayabi become equated with the dead. On the whole, Kayabi people impressed me as being very interested in other ways of life (see Oakdale 2001). It surprised me, therefore, that the overall theme of Jawosi performances was the sway that Kayabi ways of life have over other traditions and ethnic groups. In Jawosi songs individuals from other ethnic groups do not have any power or sway over Kayabi—all are overcome by Kayabi warriors.

It is interesting that Fire-of-the-Gods's Jawosi was one of the only times I was specifically asked to dress like a Kayabi woman. As mentioned in chapter 1, Fire-of-the-Gods first suggested with some humor that I go naked, but other women asked only that I dress like them, that is, that I wear a dress and have my face tattooed with black dye. They also invited me to participate in the chorus. Fire-of-the-Gods told me that foreign women—those, for example, who had married Kayabi men—were always asked to sing and that the men took great pleasure in the humor and irony of having them unknowingly sing about their own relatives in the opaque, metaphorical songs—a comment that definitely made me think about my own participation in a new way! The power of the Kayabi community over other communities is paramount in these events. Given this emphasis, João's focus on Jawosi (versus other rituals such as Maraka) as a sign of Kayabi "culture" becomes understandable.

Formal Dimensions of Jawosi Singing

While the text of Jawosi songs encourages mourners to view their dead as enemies, the form of the songs encourages sociability among the living. In contrast to the isolation of mourning, interpersonal involvement is crucial for the kind of happiness, strength, and well-being that Jawosi is thought to produce. [16] To understand how Jawosi singing brings mourners back into social life, it is helpful to understand Jawosi singing as a kind of ceremonial dialogue.

Jawosi are what Greg Urban calls "form defined" or "pragmatic ceremonial dialogues." The male soloists and women's chorus take turns singing in a regular fashion, producing a "palpable rhythm of alternation"; the chorus, however, does not contribute any new content during this alternation (Urban 1991, 127). The role of the female chorus is to repeat the male soloist's lines directly after him. For example, each Jawosi song begins in the following manner. Directly after the chorus asks a man to sing, he sings one short line about a heroic encounter. The women in turn respond with the vocable "*e'heeija*." This pattern continues for approximately two to four more turns. Next the soloist sings the words that the chorus will sing as a refrain. The women repeat these words after him. After this initial introduction of the women's refrain, the male soloist does not sing this part again. For the rest of the song, the women repeat the soloist's lines two times along with this refrain. This pattern is demonstrated by one of Chest's songs about "the sound of fish," a metaphor for the sound of battle.

> Chest: [Singing is too quiet to be intelligible.]
> Women: e'heeija.
>
> Chest: Enabling you [singular] to hear the sound that the fish make.
> Women: e'heeija.
>
> Chest: I am listening to the fish making noise, women, while lying down.
> Women: e'heeija, while lying down.
>
> Chest: I am really listening to the fish make noise.
> Women: I am really listening to the fish make noise. I am really listening to the fish make noise while lying down.

Chest: "You do not hear," you all say to me.
Women: "You do not hear," you all say to me. "You do not hear," you all say
to me while lying down.

As illustrated, the soloist supplies all of the content in a Jawosi song. The women's chorus has the key role of repeating his lines to produce a striking rhythm of alternation.

Like many other types of ceremonial dialogues throughout the lowlands, Jawosi singing encourages a sense of interpersonal connection among the living by iconically modeling the most secure domain of sociability—the household (Urban 1991, 144). The structure of the singing—a group repeating after one adult man—resembles the dissemination of knowledge among the paternally related members of a household. Each Kayabi patriline is conceptualized as a group that shares a slightly distinct set of traditions passed down from the elder to the junior members. Paternally related men share common versions of ancestors' stories, medicinal knowledge, and weaving designs. The versions of ancestors' stories told by other elders are not considered incorrect, but they are considered slightly strange and novel. And while men may try to learn other families' versions informally, during Jawosi nonfamily members sing the songs of each patriline in a more institutionalized way. The nonfamily members who sing other families' Jawosi songs are, however, women, not men, since men can only sing the Jawosi they inherited from their own relatives. The female chorus, made up of women from various households, repeats all of the different Jawosi songs, not merely those of their own fathers, paternal uncles, and grandfathers, as they make their rounds to all the households in a local group. This choral repetition of all the songs enables them to behave as if they have one shared body of songs, just like a group of paternally related men. The tendency to interpret songs as relating to the life of the singer also encourages a sense of shared tradition rather than each singer having differential knowledge about each of the songs.

The quality of sound the women produce when they sing Jawosi highlights their role as icons of interpersonal harmony based on a shared tradition or shared perspective. During Jawosi singing women sing in an unnaturally low pitch to match the pitch of their senior soloists. Women from the different households also try to blend their voices together into one unified sound rather than stand out as distinct entities. The lowest songs are considered the most beautiful. Much of women's commentary about the songs I tape-recorded regarded the inappropriateness or humor of hearing one singer over all the others. This blending of voices contrasts sharply with women's keening, where each woman cries out in a distinctive and independent way.

During the last few nights of Jawosi singing, when there is dancing, the chorus orchestrates their movements in accordance with those of the soloists. As with the choral repetitions, during Jawosi dancing the women follow the lead of senior family headmen. Even during some of the oldest men's playful tricks of speeding up or stopping abruptly, the chorus makes a show of trying to follow the soloists. At these moments they dramatize their attempt at imitation to an even greater extent. The women's chorus, therefore, plays a key role in providing a model for interpersonal harmony and identification among the living members of a local group. This may account for why Jawosi is considered to belong to women despite the fact that the soloists are men.

When a Jawosi is held between different communities, the invitation process is also iconic of a kind of solidarity based on a shared tradition or shared way of life. When others are invited, the host village sends out young messengers, called in the singular *piara*, to other households or villages. *Piara* is the same term used in Jawosi songs to refer to the Kayabi warrior, from the enemy's perspective, and is often translated as "assassin." These messengers, usually younger adult men, engage in an elaborate type of shadowing that involves imitating the daily routine of the headman of the household he is inviting. Each of these headmen is called a *pareat*, a term used to refer to the foreign enemies in Jawosi songs as well as to mourners who come to pay their respects after a death. The ideal of the messenger (*piara*) is to do exactly what his future guest (*pareat*) does: eat when he eats, bathe when he bathes, and even relieve himself when he does so. I was told that in some cases this shadowing lasts for several days or even weeks before the guests accompany their hosts back to the village that is celebrating the Jawosi. In the most elaborate invitation processes the *piara* also farms with the *pareat*, following his orders for harvesting or processing crops. This mimesis, like that of the singing and dancing, is similar in form (as well as in content, in the case of agricultural work) to the shared rhythm of life and work set by the family headman within a household group.

When the guests arrive with their messengers at the host village, the structure of mimicry becomes extremely complicated. During the last few nights, when the adult men are painted, the young messengers are painted solid red with annatto. This contrasts with the decorations of the guests and other senior men from the host village, who are painted with red and black designs representing the dead enemies. Many of the texts of the Jawosi songs contain a series of identifications between the black and red *pareat* and the red *piara*. Singing from the perspective of the dead enemy, guests and other senior men will sing about "their own" Kayabi assassins. Many times when they sing about "their own assassins" they are referring to themselves as younger men, as many songs are about their own exploits. In these songs the Kayabi assassin is called a *piara*, just like the young messengers. The senior men are, in these cases, singing simultaneously about themselves in the past and, in a sense, about the young Kayabi messengers from the host village. The young messengers' and the senior singers' heroic youth become superimposed. This complicated inversion is particularly apparent in Chest's song quoted previously. Painted as an enemy with black charcoal and red annatto, presumably as the little kidnapped girl, Chest sang, "The singer [the *pareat*] is turning into a little girl," and "My captor [my *piara*] is truly a great person, my captor." The title "great person" (*arete*) usually refers to seniors, not young men, so here the seniority of the *pareat* is being superimposed upon the future seniority of the young men who are playing the role of the *piara*. The past and future of the men's life cycles come together in one particularly powerful present moment.

The iconic model of solidarity based on mimesis and a shared tradition that is produced in Jawosi contrasts with the household individuation that is characteristic of the mourning period. Jawosi singing may help to alleviate the sadness after death at least in part because its formal dimensions are iconic of a sociability that stands in opposition to the isolation characteristic of sadness. The mimesis involved in the singing, dancing, and invitation process, for example, engages members of different households in a coordinated activity—a stark contrast to the mourners' individuation of routine after death.

Muting Connections with the Past

Jawosi singing not only helps mourners to manage their memories of their recently deceased and to reconnect with the living but also mutes the ties that the living have with past generations more generally. As one man explained, no matter when Jawosi are sung they help people forget about the dead. Although singers understand that many of their songs describe the exploits of past warriors and they remember learning the songs from a relative who is no longer living, Jawosi songs are not memorials or means of collectively remembering particular Kayabi heroes of the past. In this way they are different from Maraka songs, which explicitly state that a shaman is carrying on the teachings of a particular mentor of the past. To be sure, singers do think about the deceased relative who taught them a particular song. Chest, for example, said that he was saddened by the memory of his deceased elder brother when he sang about a particular enemy that he had killed. Others unrelated to him, however, did not recognize the name of his brother's victim and did not know the victim or the hero that first gave rise to his song. Most songs contain no clues to help listeners understand that the songs pertain to other lives lived in other epochs, leading listeners to understand them to be about the singer himself. And most listeners do in fact understand singers to be singing about themselves. They are a form of "historicity" (Whitehead 2003, xi) that incorporates the deeds of the dead into the lives of the living. In this sense they give the impression of being ahistorical.

Its lack of emphasis on the present's connection to the past makes Jawosi quite different from a thematically similar type of dialogue among another Tupian-speaking people: the sixteenth-century Tupinambá. Before they were killed in the village plaza, Tupinambá prisoners of war engaged in a dialogue with their captors during which they recounted acts of revenge, describing, for example, how they had killed and eaten particular relatives of their captors and would therefore be killed and eaten by them or how in the future their own deaths would be revenged by their own people (Carneiro da Cunha and Viveiros de Castro 1985). Manuela Carneiro da Cunha and Eduardo Viveiros de Castro have persuasively argued that, in light of the fact that revenge was the institution par excellence of Tupinambá society, these dialogues were a type of temporal consciousness. Through these dialogues describing a series of past and future revenge killings, "the memory" and "the future" of each group were given by their enemies (1985, 200). In Kayabi Jawosi, "the enemy" is also a focal point of orientation, but cycles of vengeance that represent temporality are by and large absent. Most songs, for example, recount in detail one particular valiant encounter, not a series of vengeful killings that give the sense of temporal depth.

The one Jawosi song I recorded that did recount a series of turns in a spiral of vengeance is an interesting exception. One of the songs sung by Stone-Arm during Fire-of-the-Gods's Jawosi describes a series of killings between Kayabi and Rikbatsá individuals from the Peixes River area.[17] This song is filled with quoted dialogue between particular, named people. With respect to describing a cycle of vengeance, its text is very similar to the Tupinambá dialogues that preceded plaza executions. My translators, however, both thought it was a "confusing" song and was "too long" and less beautiful than the other shorter songs describing one single, valiant feat. Songs that recount a series of killings may in fact be more archaic, as they are more similar to the dialogues of the Kayabi's distant relatives, the Tupinambá. A few men like Stone-Arm may continue to sing these sorts of songs because of their identities outside of Jawosi. Stone-Arm, as a well-known shaman, may have had an interest in showing his own connection to a historical chain of events (that is, a connected series of battles or killings), as this sort of linkage with the past is crucial to the construction of a healer's authority.

In the majority of Jawosi songs that describe one fleeting interaction with a non-Kayabi individual, this one interaction is a kind of abbreviation for relations with whole classes of enemies. In Leg-Bone's Jawosi song about the death of a nonindigenous Brazilian, for example, the encounter could easily be read as a condensed version of "pacification" or, better, the yet uncompleted pacification and incorporation of the Kayabi into Brazilian society (backing up João's claim that the Kayabi have not in fact "become civilizados"). The song describes how the white enemy tries to feed and "pacify" his Kayabi enemy. The Kayabi verb *tamotawa*—translated as "to pacify"—is the same verb used by Kayabi speakers when referring to the Brazilian pacification process. Like the encounter described in this song, many of the encounters between pacification teams and Kayabi also involved the exchange of food. In this song the more complicated nature of Kayabi relations with the national society is strikingly absent—relations that narrators were able to comment on with acumen in other genres. There is, for example, no account of how this death was part of the larger process of colonizing Kayabi territory.

Songs also usually lack any commentary about why a killing was justified in terms of the microhistory of the interaction. Leg-Bone's song, for example, describes the determination of the Kayabi killer but gives no account of his personal motivation. Some of the more elaborate spoken accounts of this event indicate that this song documents the execution of one of two Brazilians who had invaded Kayabi territory and committed violent acts against other Kayabi. Leg-Bone's song, however, includes none of this more immediate histori-cal background. In Jawosi a complex series of interethnic and interpersonal relations are reduced to one particularly dramatic and relatively timeless or "presentist" interpersonal encounter.

A focus on a timeless type of interpersonal encounter provides a way to sub-merge the event of death into a more all-encompassing cosmological process. These timeless sorts of encounters turn an individual death into what Raymond Fogelson has called a type of "latent event" (1989, 143). They urge participants to forget about individual deaths in much the same way as Fernand Braudel suggests the historian should exorcise the dangerously enchanting events of traditional history—those events that are on the scale of individuals—by viewing them as "momentary outbursts, surface manifestations . . . of larger movements" (1972, 210).

This larger process within which the deaths of both Kayabi and others become submerged is a type of transformation that continually occurs between different kinds of beings in the Kayabi cosmos. Philippe Descola has pointed out that Amazonian cosmologies often view "the universe as a gigantic closed circuit within which there is a constant circulation of the substances, souls, and identities held to be necessary for the conservation of the world and the preservation of the social order" (1992, 116). According to Descola, for some lowland peoples this circulation is understood to take place through predation between human groups, while for others it takes place as an exchange between humans and animals. The Jivaró are an example of the former. [18] For them only a set number of identities exist, and warfare involves capturing these identities from other humans (Descola 1992, 118; Taylor 1993). The Desana are an example of the latter. For them death is understood to transform people into animals, augmenting the number of game depleted by hunting (Descola 1992, 117). This latter category could also include the Wari' and the Kulina. For the Wari', ancestors' spirits present themselves in the form of white-lipped peccaries in order to be shot and eaten by their surviving human relatives and later to inhabit yet a second peccary body (Conklin 2001, 205–8). For the Kulina the spirits of the dead go to the underworld to be devoured by peccaries, reincarnated as peccaries, hunted, and eaten by their human kin (Lorrain 2000, 296; Pollock 1993).

While the Kayabi I knew never expressed a straightforward notion that humans upon death become game animals, commentary about childbirth, shamanic healing, and myths all clearly emphasize the process of recycling and transformation between the human and the animal worlds. Shamans, for example, sing about how human spirits are kept as pets or as foster children by the Masters of the Game before they are born. Shamans either offer to trade something for these souls or secretively take them so that Kayabi women can be impregnated. While I heard little commentary on what specifically happens to a person after death (in keeping with the value placed on distancing oneself from the dead), discussions about illness and shamanic cures also indicate that upon death the human soul becomes part of the animal community. All deaths, for example, are caused by one of the Masters of the Game animals stealing the soul ('ang) of a living person and taking it back to his home. If the soul stays with its captor and is not retrieved by a shaman, it is described either as being eaten or as living with its captor as a pet, hostage, child, spouse, son-in-law, or daughter-in-law. [19] For one type of being, animal or human, to gain new life, the other must simultaneously lose it. The birth of new human persons involves a loss on the part of the animals. Conversely, human death implies a gain on the part of the animal community.

For the Kayabi this cycling or exchange of life also takes place between different ethnicities. While ultimately blamed on animal spirits at the level of soul loss, the death of a relative is also often understood as having been facilitated by individuals from other ethnic groups. For example, directly after a death, Kayabi may blame themselves for not caring enough for their relative or for leaving him or her vulnerable to the attacks of spirits, but as time passes they tend to also blame particular shamans and witches from other ethnic groups. Often these are individuals who may have been visiting before the death occurred. These people are accused of intentionally working their magic to weaken the deceased and leave him or her vulnerable to spirits. Strikingly unlike many other Amazonian traditions of shamanism, the Kayabi never seem to accuse their own shamans of these sorts of deeds. Their own shamans only bring souls back into the Kayabi community, while shamans from other groups work to extract life from the Kayabi.

As Eduardo Viveiros de Castro has observed, ontologies concerned with transformation (and, by extension, the recycling or limited nature of life) are also marked by "perspectivism," or the idea that the world is inhabited by different kinds of persons who "apprehend reality from distinct points of view" (1998, 469, 471). "[N]on-humans see things as 'people' do. But the things that they see are different: what to us is blood, is maize beer to the jaguar; what to the souls of the dead is a rotting corpse, to us is soaking manioc; what we see as a muddy waterhole, the tapirs see as a great ceremonial house" (478). This means that the world and various sorts of events look differently depending on which side of this transformational process a subject is situated. Death for one kind of being, animal or other ethnicity, can appear simultaneously as new life for another kind.

I argue that a similar kind of logic can be used to understand Jawosi songs that recount the death of a non-Kayabi. In keeping with the idea that the cosmos has a limited supply of life, the death of a non-Kayabi person entails the possibility of new life for the Kayabi community. An event that appears as a loss from the perspective of an enemy is seen as a gain from the Kayabi perspective. It is interesting to note that many Jawosi songs are sung from the perspective of the defeated enemy, who describes his thoughts or even his relatives' thoughts about his own death. The application of the structure that most commonly occurs between animals and humans (that is, the balanced giving and taking of life) to different ethnicities may also explain why Jawosi songs frequently employ animal metaphors to refer to enemy victims.

This interpretation of Jawosi corresponds with the fact that Jawosi are associated with human fertility as well as with forgetting the dead. They were once, for example, part of making young boys into productive adults. In the past male initiation began with a period of Jawosi singing during which senior men brought out the bones of enemies that had been saved for such occasions. Boys were supposed to touch these bones for the first time, after which they "changed blood," a process that made them fertile. Much like male initiation among other lowland groups (Hugh-Jones 1979), Kayabi male initiation was a type of male menarche in which the boys' blood was encouraged to change by their seniors. After touching the bones the boys would go into seclusion in their homes and upon their emergence would be able to marry and legitimately father a child. As among the Tupinambá (Carneiro da Cunha and Viveiros de Castro 1985) death was understood as necessary for procreation and new life in a very concrete way (see also Fausto 1999 with respect to the Parakanã). In contemporary Jawosi festivals this message is more muted.

Jawosi are about changing peoples' perspective on death, about showing how past deaths of others (animals or enemies) have the potential to bring new life. Jawosi songs play with the notion of changing perspective: they are all about viewing warfare and death from a non-Kayabi and nonliving perspective. In this way they may help mourners to see how individual deaths are really part of a larger cycle of transformations. Also in this way they are antihistorical in the sense that they are concerned not with individual events of death but with much larger cosmological transformations. Their focus on the presently living is therefore a way to transcend either the progressive or degenerative trajectory and to view the passage of time and the passage of the generations in the cosmos from a much more distant vantage point. Mourners come to feel strong and happy, "to breathe deeply again," because they are connected with other living people at one moment in this process. This sociability among the living, in turn, allows for future transformations. Their own dead need to be forgotten, to become other, and others need to become transformed into new Kayabi lives.

Did It Work for João and Pretty?

According to the Kayabi, Jawosi singing is supposed to move mourners from weakening sadness to strength and well-being. It is supposed to simulta- neously help the mourners to forget about their own dead and reconnect them with the living. The content of Jawosi songs provides a model for the former, while the formal dimensions of the singing provide for the latter.

Songs also help mourners to see individual deaths as part of a larger, time-less, cosmological ebb and flow according to which beings are in a contin-ual oscillating process of transformation. Death comes to be seen as new life if one's perspective can be changed from one side of this process to the other.

A more prosaic question remains, however. How exactly did Fire-of-the-Gods's Jawosi help João and his family? In short, it did not immediately bring about an end to their mourning. Rather, "becoming happy" seemed to be a gradual process for them, with this Jawosi being only one step toward this goal. They needed a series of festivals and much urging to socialize and to finally put their sadness behind them. [20] During Fire-of-the-Gods's Jawosi, João came to watch but never sang himself. Instead, he retired to his hammock after a short stay. He was also never painted. Pretty stayed at home for the entire event. Unlike other evenings, during the nights of this Jawosi singing she lit nor fire nor any of her kerosene lamps. Their daughter, Little-Pretty, however, who was reaching puberty, could not resist the temptation to join the singing and had to be forcefully schooled in how to display her sadness. As I was arranging my tape recorder in their house before attending the Jawosi, I could hear Pretty telling her daughter in no uncertain terms to stay inside. Little-Pretty, however, eagerly ran off to join the others to sing in the Jawosi chorus. Periodically other children were sent to relay her mother's request that she return home. Finally Pretty came to get her daughter herself, dragging Little-Pretty away from the gathering to be sequestered again in their intentionally dark and dreary home.

One evening a few weeks later, when her parents and most of the other adults had gone down to the short-wave radio to speak with members of a distant Xinguan Kayabi village, Little-Pretty staged a small rebellion to her parents' mourning. She first called me out of my hammock, where I was writing, and then began to organize a "practice Jawosi" with her younger sister and three of her playmates. She ordered her mentally disabled brother to sing the men's part. He eagerly slipped into his father's hammock and assumed the pose of a self-confident senior man while humming a line or two in Jawosi style. So pleased to be included, he had a hard time enunciating the words because he was smiling so broadly. The girls grabbed me around my waist and sang out one of the choral repetitions I had heard the women's chorus sing. As soon as the adults could be heard leaving the radio hut, however, she excitedly ordered everyone to scatter.

Three months later, in August, João, Pretty, and their children finally par-took fully (and openly) in a period of Jawosi singing. By this time Pretty had given birth to another son. Stone-Arm determined that this son was animated by the soul (*'ang*) of the same son they had lost the previous year. The same soul had been received from one of the Wyra Futat and born again. Even if Fire-of-the-Gods's Jawosi did not have the power to end their sadness all at once, perhaps it had more subtly prepared them to accept this baby's birth as a moment in which life had recycled.

Understanding the Dialogic Nature
of Kayabi Narrative Performances

THE KAYABI LIFE CYCLE
AND THE DEVELOPMENT OF A DIALOGIC SELF

*Our lives are like logs on the fire; for some the log burns very quickly
and they die young, for others the log burns slowly.*

BIRD, 1993

A few weeks after Jacaré passed away, as Bird and I sat in the wood-and-thatch
school building transcribing some of Stone-Arm's Maraka songs, I asked
if Jacaré had been as old as Stone-Arm. "No," he said, "he was younger."
He continued to tell me that Kayabi people compare human lives to logs
on the fire. "Why some should burn so quickly and others last so long, no
one knows." That afternoon I watched my neighbor arrange her cooking fire
in Kayabi fashion—logs radiating out like spokes on a wheel with the fire
burning in the center. As each log gradually turned to ash and she pushed it
further in, I could not help but think about Bird's comments.

The autobiographical narratives recounted in the genres of political oratory, Maraka cures, and Jawosi songs do not give full accounts of the tellers'
lives, "the whole log," to use the Kayabi metaphor. They are not full-blown
autobiographies, works that capture a "formidable portion of an experience"
(Weintraub 1974, 822). Nor do they even, as most elicited life histories tend to
do, cover a wide selection of elements from a narrator's experiences. Instead,
they recount periods or moments in each of the narrators' lives—segments
that narrators and those listening find meaningful to share in large-scale social
gatherings and that are important for contemplating contemporary problems.[1]
How these narrated experiences fit into the contours of whole lives has been
left implicit.

Most Kayabi listeners would understand all of these accounts to be, at one
level, demonstrations of the knowledge and understanding that are the hall-
mark of Kayabi adulthood, particularly male adulthood. Much as elsewhere in
Amazonia (and in preliterate Native North America) these examples suggest
that there is a preference for narrating adult deeds (Brumble 1988; Hendricks
1993).

For Kayabi, only adults have the capacity to "understand" (-kwaap) in full. Once this faculty has been developed it leads to periods in which one interacts intensively with "others" of various sorts—other ethnicities, other spirits, and even other families into which one marries. [2] Through these interactions, which usually take place through travel, adults augment their understanding even further. Knowledge grows by identifying with these "others" enough to assume some of their attributes, such as their names, ways of speaking, emotional states, or bodily comportments—different parts of the assemblage that in Amazonia constitute a "habitus" (Viveiros de Castro 1998, 478).

Based on an examination of cosmology, Viveiros de Castros has argued that, for Amazonian peoples in general (2001) and Tupi-speaking peoples in particular (1992), full personhood involves "an Other-becoming." In the Tupian Arawete case, for example, the person is only complete after dying, having been eaten and revived by the immortal gods—a process that ultimately transforms a person into one of these immortal beings (1992, 1). [3] I argue that, for the Kayabi, human development also takes place through a process of other-becoming. Rather than the after-death fate of persons, however, here I am more concerned with shorter-term identifications that take place over the course of life, especially those that take place during adulthood, as it is these that are often the subject of Kayabi autobiographical narratives.

While both male and female adulthood are marked by travel and interaction with "others," men's travel is recognized as both more frequent and more extensive. Men are supposed to interact more intensively with non-Kayabi people and beings. Because of this difference, the kind of knowledge and understanding they acquire is considered more "distinctive." Adult female knowledge, on the contrary, is framed as "impersonal" or "suprapersonal," the inverse of how it is understood in Western societies, where women are associated with the private and the personal. [4] Kayabi women have the kind of knowledge that is supposed to be passed down in unchanged form and is shared from household to household, what some called "our law" in Portuguese. As a result, the narration of distinctive or "personal" experiences is less appropriate for Kayabi women than it is for men (see Swann and Krupat 1987, xii, for a similar point with respect to Native North America). Even when I approached women outside of ritual settings, they were in general uninterested in narrating "their experiences."

The narrators I focused on in this study—those who delivered oratory, sung Maraka, or sung Jawosi—are, by and large, recognized to have developed a high degree of this distinctive, masculine sort of understanding. Monkey-Leg's narrative is the most extensive as a result of his dream voyages to various domains in the cosmos. Elder headmen such as Leg-Bone and Amapá as well as young chiefs such as João are knowledgeable as a result of having traveled extensively in everyday waking reality. Others describe them as having "traveled all over," "confronted many people," and "seen many things." As one women said of Chief João, "He understands a lot. He is always traveling, going around places, he almost doesn't stop."

In keeping with this emphasis on adult travel, interaction, and identification with those beyond the local group, men's narratives of adulthood self-consciously include the perspectives and quoted speech of various "others." While all utterances have "dialogic overtones"—that is, they incorporate to some extent the words and utterances of others who have spoken previously (Bakhtin 1986, 92), Kayabi ritual genres emphasize and draw attention to this dialogic quality. Many of the accounts, for example, are understood by Kayabi audiences to have been uttered first by persons other than the narrator—to be either in part or in their entirety made up of quoted speech and song (while simultaneously referring to the narrator's experiences). In this chapter I explore the nature of adult male understanding by contrasting it with prior stages and with adult female understanding in order to more fully appreciate and understand the dialogic nature of the men's narratives presented in part 2.

The Development of Understanding

Much as Ellen Basso has observed for the Kalapalo, traveling for the Kayabi is "characterized by experiences of creative, transformative power" (1995, 37). Not everyone who travels, however, is in a position to be affected by this activity. Though children may travel extensively with their parents, for example, they do not gain the same benefits, because during childhood the more general capacity that allows one to understand and know is still developing. Travel beyond the local group leads to knowledge only after adulthood is reached. Prior to this time understanding and knowledge are fostered instead through alternating periods of intense identification and focus upon relatives and periods of exploration close to home. These identifications and movements close to home form the foundation upon which later travels and interactions with others can lead to the further augmentation of understanding. Much as elsewhere in Amazonia there is a "micro-oscillation between alterity and identity that constitutes the lifecycle" (Viveiros de Castro 2001, 35; see also Gow 1997).

This development of understanding begins in infancy, when a new Kayabi baby becomes connected or identified with his or her parents. The unborn soul (i'ang) of a Kayabi baby is brought from the home of either one of the Masters of the Game or one of the spirits, called Mait. Usually they are brought in dream by a shaman, though many young men say they can bring the souls of babies to women without any assistance. After birth, babies' souls are only delicately attached to this world and can be easily captured back by beings from other cosmological domains. To ensure that this does not happen, parents should emphasize the connection and identity they have with their newborns. New parents, for example, should observe food taboos so that the spirits of animals and their masters do not harm or take their babies. They also should not travel far from home directly after a birth to prevent the baby's soul from wandering off to look for them. In general, parents should eat and behave only in ways that are appropriate for a newborn. If a parent's activity is not suitable for a baby's stamina, the child can become tired and sick. If a newborn is to live, it must become identified with his or her parents. This initial identification between baby and parents may account for people's recollection of birth as a time they did not experience firsthand. To describe this period they used the tense and evidential marker *rakue*, which is otherwise used for unwitnessed events in the distant past.

After this initial identification, a child begins to become distinct from his or her parents over the course of the period between birth and the point at which the baby is said to "become firm." A young baby is considered to be soft, not yet fully ripe, much like early produce such as green corn. When a child begins to develop teeth, to eat solid food, and to gain weight, they become "harder" (*ipiratã*). Most babies obtain their first name over the course of this period of "becoming hard." Usually a child's first name is given by the parents or other members of the child's household. Many first names have to do with the appearance of a child at birth or with the birthing process itself. As a baby firms up and becomes its own person, with his or her own name, fewer food and activity taboos are observed by the parents.

Once children "firm up," their growth is marked in terms of their ability to support and move their bodies. Mothers characterize their little children (*kunumi'i*) as being able to "sit up on their own" and then to "stand up on foot" and eventually as "really being able to move around." This ability to move leads to self-directed exploration close to home, which in turn leads to understanding. Bird explained early childhood as a point in the life cycle when children are like mice: they go through all the things that are stored away in a household and "ferret" or discover things by rummaging around. In regard to his own childhood he said, "When I discovered things over and over I was understanding."

Later childhood is a time for letting a child expand relationships beyond parents and the household but within the sphere of relatives. Children between the ages of approximately four and eight (*kunumi*) are extremely gregarious and spend much of their time with children from other households. They form groups that play together and seem to unabashedly enter any house in the village (see also Grünberg n.d. [1970], 123). Parents encourage young children's independence despite parents' claims that they don't understand much yet. It is perfectly reasonable, for example, for a five-year-old to make the decision to stay with her grandparents rather than accompany her parents to another local group for a year-long stay (see also Grünberg n.d. [1970], 135).

Children are not, however, supposed to interact with strangers. While young children do frequently travel away from their local group with their parents, they are not supposed to confront strangers in the way that adults do. Instead, parents condition their children to maintain fear and distance from the non-Kayabi they meet while traveling or who come to visit. During the first several months of my stay, for example, adults would tell their littlest children, who came running out to greet me as I approached their house, that I would stick them with a needle. After several such encounters, I finally asked one man why he continued to warn his children of my dangerousness. He answered that, though he trusted me, he did not want his children to trust other whites or enemies (*tapy'ỹi*) and that the warning was similar to one a child would receive about approaching a dangerous animal such as a jaguar.

During late childhood, after years of movement and local exploration, children are said to "really begin to understand." They begin to hear in the sense of understanding what is said to them and to make connections between experiences. When I asked people to give examples of children in this stage, they pointed to children who were from approximately eight to twelve years old. Usually these children are still called *kunumi*, though girls are often called *kũjãmuku'i* (little young women). At this age children are recognized as knowing how to speak in appropriate ways. They are described as knowing the proper responses to greetings and the proper forms of address (see also Grünberg n.d. [1970], 135). Children at this age are also conceptualized as beginning to have a memory. When Jacaré told me about his life during a more formal interview, for example, he pointed to his approximately eight-year-old grandson and explained that he would begin his story at the point when he was the same age as his grandson because this was when he first began remembering his experiences.

When a child begins to understand and to remember, his or her identity with specific living elders becomes emphasized. In late childhood boys and some girls are given a new name by an elder relative—a parent, uncle, aunt, or,

147

most usually, grandparent. Bird said that even when one changes one's name later in life, "it is hard for people to stop using this second name." Children receive this name from the elder relative they resemble most with respect to skills, behavior, or physical characteristics. The new name may or may not be the name giver's own. If name givers do give away their own name, they revert to using one of their prior names. After such a name exchange there is often some confusion in conversation regarding to whom the inherited name refers. This confusion leads to an explanation about the change of names and provides another opportunity to explicitly talk about the identification the child has with his or her name giver.

In late childhood, children's elders begin to augment their understanding. Rather than obtaining knowledge by exploring on their own, they are frequently given advice about how to act by their parents, grandparents, or, in a group, the village chief. Prior to this age, elders explain and comment very little to children about their actions because, prior to the development of a child's ability to understand, explanations are seen as futile. As with experiences of travel, children do not have the necessary faculties to benefit from such explanations.[5]

The development of understanding and ability through self-directed exploration and casual instruction is followed by a period of intensive parental education. For both boys and girls this period after late childhood is viewed as the time when they finally reach full adult understanding. Individuals at this age are described as having become women or men who can perceive, understand, and do things. Traditionally both boys and girls have encouraged this transition to adulthood by undergoing seclusion in their homes. Boys, however, have not undergone seclusion for several generations. In contrast, girls' seclusion has become even more lengthy and elaborate since the Kayabis' move to the Xingu Park.

Seclusion involves an extremely intense identification with same-sex senior relatives. During seclusion a girl ideally returns to an almost total identification with her mother, characteristic of infancy. This identification is, however, produced largely through the actions of the girl rather than her mother. After a girl begins to menstruate, her body becomes "soft" and "without force," like an infant's. Menstruation is conceptualized as a change of blood, with swelling being the tangible sign of the new blood. At this point the girl enters seclusion within her home. While I was in Kapinu'a different girls observed seclusions of varying lengths. The average amount of time for an acceptable seclusion was one month, though some said they stayed for five months.[6]

During the first few days of seclusion the girl lies in her hammock motionless and naked after having had all her clothes and beads taken away by her mother. She is supposed to communicate only with her mother and to speak only in a whisper. For the duration of seclusion, the girl should stay within her house; most do so to such an extent that their skin becomes very light. During this time mothers tell their daughters what they can and cannot do with respect to the most mundane activities, and girls follow their mothers' orders very closely, particularly with respect to food taboos.

Mothers mold a girl's behavior during seclusion in a manner that is appropriate for an adult woman. Girls who act inappropriately during seclusion are not supposed to be able to change later in life. In light of these beliefs, mothers teach their secluded daughters the skills and etiquette necessary to fully participate in a household as an adult. During seclusion girls intently copy their mothers and other senior female relatives in order to perfect their spinning, weaving, and food preparation skills. Mothers also instruct their daughters on the appropriate way to interact with people. Kayabi consider all of this knowledge and etiquette gained from senior female relatives to be distinctively Kayabi and to have been passed down through generations in an unchanged form.

After seclusion a girl becomes a kūjãmuku and is considered to have transformed into an adult who "understands." There are several tangible signs that indicate a girl's status as a knowing adult. One is a new name. While some girls receive their second name prior to seclusion, most do not receive this name until after they emerge. Another sign of adulthood is body modifications. In the past girls had their faces tattooed during seclusion. Currently face tattooing does not occur, but I did notice that some girls had tattoos on their arms that correspond to their names. One of the most important signs that a girl has become an adult is her ability to produce woven hammocks and baby slings.[7]

In the past boys also underwent seclusion. When a group of boys reached late childhood, the stage of kunumi'uu, an initiation was held. First, all the households in one area gathered together to sing and dance in Jawosi style (Grünberg n.d. [1970] 128). One or several of the adult men would bring a bone or skull of an enemy that had been saved for such an occasion. During this ritual the boys who were undergoing initiation at the time hit and broke the enemy bones, an act that caused their bodies to make new blood and to become soft and malleable, much like girls' bodies in seclusion. For a period of about a month after touching the enemy bones during the Jawosi, boys were sequestered in their own homes, where they too underwent a period of dietary and activity restrictions very similar to those observed by menstruating girls.

During their seclusion boys had a relationship with their fathers that was similar to the ones girls have with their mothers. Like girls, boys followed dietary restrictions and were trained in adult skills and etiquette by their fathers.[8] Fathers explained how to save seeds from one crop to the next, how to hunt, how to weave baskets, and how to make turtle-shell spindles for their future wives and mothers-in-law. Fathers also instructed their sons in good manners. Boys were shown, for example, how to hold their faces without smiling while speaking and were encouraged to be generous to visitors. Boys in seclusion were supposed to concentrate on their fathers' teachings, and to emphasize their faculty of hearing they wore earrings of cutia teeth.[9]

After coming out of seclusion boys were called mya'u and were considered to "understand" sufficiently to marry and join another household as a son-in-law. Signs of their adulthood were much like those for girls: a new name, body modifications, and the ability to produce handicrafts. Previously boys also received their second name only after seclusion. In the past boys also received a facial tattoo while in seclusion.[10] (While only one man in Kapinu'a has a facial tattoo, several elderly men have tattoos on parts of their bodies that correspond to their adult names. Chest, for example, has two bars tattooed on his chest. Others with the name "Leg" have tattoos on parts of their legs.) A mya'u's ability to make complicated handicrafts, such as baskets with intricate woven patterns and spindles, was also a sign that he was knowledgeable enough to become a son-in-law and to produce children of his own.

Men who have grown up in approximately the last forty years have not undergone seclusion. Yet they still speak about having learned from their fathers as youths and describe this process as a mark of adulthood. Fire-of-the-Gods described his own transition to adulthood as a process of learning "how his own father lived" and "how he spoke to people in groups." He explained that when he "learned how his father treated people" he was no longer a boy but a man. Presently, even without the traditional period of seclusion, a similar but less institutionalized type of identification of a boy with his father still takes place.

Augmenting Adult Knowledge

After seclusion for women and after the less-defined time of learning from one's father for men, knowledge is gained through exploration beyond the home. At this age, however, exploration involves travel beyond the local group, and non-Kayabi become particularly important points of orientation and identification. For women this stage is quite short, lasting only until marriage.

For men it lasts indefinitely, into old age. During this stage of life, men and women become interested in assuming some of the qualities of the others with whom they interact. As Carlos Fausto has observed, among many Amazonian peoples, "the constitution of complete persons depends on the acquisition, always renewed, of qualities from the outside" (1999, 937; see also 2001). A person's knowledge during this period is again signaled by new names and to some extent by body modifications—both of which can be understood as signs of identification with others.

Women experience the most freedom of movement in the female life cycle during the period after seclusion. When I asked one elderly woman about her life right after seclusion she said, "Just like you are traveling now, I too traveled, girl." Women's traveling and visiting with other groups are most fully recognized at this stage. Although girls and women often accompany their parents or their husbands on excursions before and after the kũjãmuku stage, they are not recognized as having confronted strangers in the same way as women who have just come out of seclusion. This may be due in part to the fact that women's travel after seclusion is explicitly connected to finding a marriage partner and therefore involves actively engaging with others. While the vast majority of Kayabi women have married Kayabi men, several women have in fact married non-Kayabi they met while traveling right after seclusion.

Regardless of the extent of the actual interaction with non-Kayabi, such affinity being perhaps more of a "generic value" (Viveiros de Castro 2001, 22), women who have just come out of seclusion are more oriented to non-Kayabi lifestyles than other women. This is particularly the case with respect to their beauty treatments and dress. In self-conscious imitation of Upper Xinguan women, Kayabi women currently cut their hair in bangs upon emerging from seclusion. Traditionally Kayabi women have left their hair uncut for the entire lifecycle. Kayabi girls in the Xingu who have just come out of seclusion also now use a dogfish tooth scraper on their body to encourage the production of new blood and a full body. Again this is done in self-conscious imitation of the Upper Xinguans. In the past the Kayabi used a scraper made out of a single cutia tooth and made fewer scratches down the girls' (and boys') bodies. Now an Upper Xinguan–style scraper with several dogfish teeth is used to make a series of scratches. Thorn explained that they changed to the dogfish tooth scraper because they could see that it had superior effects. According to her, one only had to look at the Upper Xinguans to see that their bodies were made much fuller and more beautiful because of the dogfish teeth. Thick hanks of European glass beads that have been popular in the Upper Xingu for decades and are currently associated with the Upper Xinguans by the Kayabi are also popular among young women just out of seclusion.

Women's recognized travel ends when they get married and begin to have children or, in Kayabi, become a ta'yma'e. Marriage itself, however, is a sort of excursion into foreign territory, especially when a woman goes to live with her in-laws (see Viveiros de Castro 2001). One of the last new names a woman receives is often given to her by her sisters-in-law. Indeed, several women remarked that they had been given a name by the women in her husband's household. A few said that they gained a new name from their in-laws when they had their first child.

Once a woman has in-laws, a husband, and children, her acquisition of knowledge is generally seen as complete. One of the terms for a woman who has parents-in-law (and a husband) is, in fact, ekwaapma'e ("one who knows"). Later when she becomes a grandmother or an emiariruma'e, a woman is respected for what she knows as an old person, but she is not spoken about as having accumulated knowledge over her adult life in the same way as a man. Rather, older women's knowledge is framed as "impersonal." They are respected for having a firm understanding of tradition—the way things have always been done and the way people always should live. Consequently they are frequently asked by both men and women for advice on the correct way to behave in various situations. Their knowledge is, however, rarely spoken about as being based on their own distinctive achievements.

In contrast, men—from the time they are a kunumi'uu on into adulthood and later as a grandfather (emyminuma'e)—amass more recognized travel experiences and, as a consequence, more understanding and more names. Men say they understand more than women do because they confront and interact with more types of people. Ultimately, late in life after extensive travel, a man becomes an aerete ("great person"). Some elderly women are on occasion called aerete, but, as Bird explained, this title is more appropriate for men. According to Bird an aerete is someone who is "very well known, has many friends, is a person who everybody likes. It is more for a man. He confronts more, is familiar with more. A woman stays more in the house. She almost doesn't have a name."

A man ultimately becomes an aerete by interacting with people in distant locations over the course of his adult life. These interactions begin to be recognized as such at the kunumi'uu stage. Several men explained that they intentionally went to live with non-Kayabi for a period of time during this phase of life. Stone-Arm, for example, said that he left his uncle's house and went to live with whites at this age. Waist also recalled living with whites as well as Bororo Indians as a kunumi'uu. Bird worked for a trader, traveling up and down rivers on a boat filled with merchandise. He said that he "went in search of whites" during this period. Several elderly men recounted how they went to live and work at pacification posts set up in Kayabi areas when they emerged from seclusion. Currently kunumi'uu take every opportunity to travel to nearby towns, park posts, and ranches to interact with other sorts of peoples.

Currently boys in the kunumi'uu stage are extremely interested in learning such skills as speaking Portuguese and using money and as a consequence are avid participants in the classes held in Kapinu'a. When the opportunity presents itself, they also try to spend extended periods of time studying away from the village. While working for the mayor of São José do Xingu, for example, João invited some of the village boys to live with him at a park post located close to town, where he had arranged for a teacher to give classes.

When young men marry and have young children they tend to travel less. Newly married men commented repeatedly that their wives did not want them to travel. Most seemed to take their wives' opinions very seriously, and I saw more than one young man cancel a trip as a direct result. Men with young babies also stay close to home, as traveling can harm a newborn. A father's travel is likewise restricted by a sick child. Men frequently described the pressure by parents and in-laws to stay home for the benefit of their new baby or sick child. Adult men who do not have a newborn and whose children are all healthy resume shorter-term travel and interaction with non-Kayabi.

Travel is an opportunity for obtaining new names, and changing names is in turn a sign of mobility and knowledge. The Kayabi's move to the Xingu, for example, spurred several names changes (see also Travassos 1984, 78). Jacaré—which means "alligator" in English—said he gave himself this Portuguese name when he arrived in the Xingu because he thought the animal was interesting. Men also took new names after they participated in FUNAI attraction missions, which were organized to contact more remote indigenous people living outside the park in the 1960s and 1970s (77–78). Kayabi men along with others in the Xingu were employed as translators, navigators, rowers, and porters in the team that first contacted the Panará. After returning home, one man took the name "Scar" as a result of the scars the Panará wear on their bodies. Another took the name "Wax" as a result of the red wax the Panará use in their hair, and yet another took the name "Little-Stick" because he repeatedly cut himself on little sticks on the jungle paths during the trip (77–78). When I arrived in Kapinu'a, Jacaré's son told me that he had recently changed his name to "All-Bound-Up" after meeting a policeman in a town outside the park. He said he named himself after the policeman or, more specifically, after the policeman's constraining uniform. At one point in his life, Stone-Arm took the additional name Tururi (which is the onomatopoetic name for a species of songbird) after seeing this sort of bird outside the FUNAI offices in São Paulo. He said about this name: "I discovered it myself." Because of their extensive travel in the dream world, great shamans have some of the largest repertoires of names. Stone-Arm said he had at least five other adult names in addition to Tururi.

Many of the dramatic interactions with non-Kayabi that bring about a name change involve identification with the name giver. For example, one means for an adult man to obtain a new name, recalling sixteenth-century Tupinambá practices (Carneiro da Cunha and Viveiros de Castro 1985), is to kill an enemy (Grünberg n.d. [1970], 137). Kayabi speak about this act as a means of "taking" the victim's name. When a warrior kills an enemy, the enemy's blood also fills the warrior's stomach, a situation that can lead to death if proper precautions are not taken. The name, therefore, comes with a certain amount of corporeal substance. Even less dramatic interactions with other ethnicities can be moments of identification and can be used as a source for new names. One man recounted how he had made friends with a Brazilian who came to visit Diauarum Post and had, after talking with him for several days, traded names with him. He took the man's name and gave him his own. As he explained it, his previous name was "carried away."

Taking on new names in this way not only is a sign that a man has been able to travel but also shows that he has a certain amount of ability to influence others. Unlike men's earlier names and women's names, adult male names are not given by others (such as parents, grandparents, aunts, uncles, or in-laws) but are instead bestowed by the man himself. Only the most powerful and well-respected men, however, are able to make their name changes widely accepted. During my stay in Kapinu'a several young men tried to change their names, but only a few succeeded. Sometimes these new names were adopted by residents of one village but not by those in another, such that a few men had several names in active use at one time. Successful self-naming, therefore, involves the ability to convince others to use the new name—a particularly difficult task in light of the fact that Kayabi men and women shy away from uttering their own names. As Stone-Arm warned me when he gave me my Kayabi name, "Your name should not be spoken by yourself, it is only for others to use."

Narrative Representations of Adult Male Knowledge

The narratives embedded in political oratory, Maraka cures, and Jawosi songs are all travel accounts of one sort or another. The narrators are featured not only as interacting with non-Kayabi but also as taking on some of the attributes of these others, a part of the habitus of each of these beings. As such they demonstrate the extent to which the narrator "is knowledgeable" or "understands" in an adult manner. The oratorical addresses, for example, are about movement both into and out of the park. Amapá describes how, prior to moving to the Xingu, he assumed nonindigenous ways, such as washing with soap and using ammunition, thread, and other store-bought merchandise. Chief João's story about his trip out of the Xingu to participate in the Earth Summit similarly concludes with his mastery of the city of Rio de Janeiro and the practices of its inhabitants.

Monkey-Leg's Maraka music, like all great shamans' songs, is an account of an especially dramatic kind of travel and assumption of others' behavior. Shamans travel to very faraway places as they dream—deep underwater, to the horizon, or into the sky. The "others" with whom shamans meet and identify are perhaps the most radically different sort of beings. As a great shaman sings about the nonhuman spirits he meets in his dream travels during Maraka, he portrays himself as taking on their attributes, often a whole cluster of them. For example, when Monkey-Leg sang about the Master of Eagles (Kwanũ Futat) in his cure for Jacaré, he described this spirit as standing in his doorway, itching from a rash. A few lines later Monkey-Leg described himself (and his mentor) as standing in the eagle spirit's doorway, itching from the same rash. Stone-Arm, in a different Maraka performance, sang about seeing the Master of Sloths smile and yell as he traveled with a human soul that he had taken. Next he described how the spirit laid down and spoke in a low, gruff voice. Stone-Arm then sang about himself in the sloth spirit's village, doing the very same things: laying down, speaking in a low, gruff voice, and finally smiling and yelling as he traveled back to the human community with his patient's soul.

Many Maraka songs also describe parallel emotional states between the shaman and the spirits. These can include feelings of fear, estrangement, or happiness. In Monkey-Leg's Maraka songs sung at Diauarum for Jacaré, he described the spirits as sitting on top of the house, feeling jubilantly happy. Later in his song Monkey-Leg described himself in the same emotional state. In addition to taking on the habitus of a spirit during Maraka songs, shamans also establish a more long-term identification with the spirits: after many dream meetings with a shaman, spirits often exchange their names with the shaman. Names that shamans use in waking reality, such as Monkey-Leg or Stone-Arm, are often the same names that particular spirits once used themselves.

Jawosi songs are likewise accounts of travel into enemy territory. Some describe a warrior's encounters in the forest of another ethnic group such as the Kayapó, Apiaca, or Mundurucú. Others are less specific and describe travel "upriver" or "downriver," where the warrior meets a "tall," "short," "red," or "white" enemy. Many describe the singer's identification with or understanding of his enemy's perspective. The Kayabi warrior in many of these songs, such as those of Leg-Bone or Chest, comes to see his encounter from the enemy's point of view, describing his enemy's feelings of fright, hunger, distress, or eagerness to make peace with the Kayabi warrior. As the warrior sings these songs, he is also painted with designs that call to mind the appearance of the enemy. As in shamanic travels, warriors also assume enemy names to use themselves after the encounter.

The Dialogic Nature of the Narratives

Not only do narrators describe how they move and feel like the "others" they meet, but significant parts of their stories are also told through the quoted speech and song of these people and beings. The words and songs of each of these others are an important part of the habitus that an adult man assumes when he confronts each of them. In this way these genres are very much like Kalapalo historical narratives, which, as Basso points out, consist of extensive conversations of quoted speech (1995, 295). Portions of Maraka performances, Jawosi songs, and even political addresses are understood by Kayabi to have been first produced by people other than the narrator. The Maraka songs that recount shamans' dreams, for example, are first sung by the spirits and only reproduced by shamans. Likewise, Jawosi songs about warriors' battle encounter's emanate "from the bones of enemies." They are heard by the Kayabi warriors rather than created by them. João's and Amapá's oratories are the only examples presented here in which the narrators are the authors in any sense that is equivalent to Western literary traditions. Even these, however, make liberal use of quoted conversations. We learn what Amapá was like as a younger man largely from what Cláudio and Orlando Villas Boas say about him. Similarly, João describes Rio in part by describing a conversation he had with an elderly Kayabi while he was there. His joke about events at the Earth Summit might have also been a version of one or several jokes he heard while at this gathering in Rio. I remember thinking to myself, as I listened to his story, that it did not seem as "Kayabi" as other parts of his address, especially given that it was delivered in Portuguese. As Jane Hill (1995) has discussed, languages encoding different ideologies or perspectives can be used just as much as reported speech to represent a distinctive "voice" in autobiographical narratives. Though I will never know for sure whether João creatively retold something he had heard before, the fact that it gave this impression, at least to me, is significant. Much like Jawosi and Maraka songs, part of the interest in this song for Kayabi listeners may also have been in how it orchestrated various radically different voices or perspectives.

In political oratory, Maraka, and Jawosi, narrators are keen to demonstrate that they have incorporated others' words and perspectives into their self-representations. They do not shy away from creating this dialogic effect. As Basso has observed with respect to Kalapalo biography, "understanding and experiencing anew, in other words, are far from solitary activities in these stories" (1995, 296). Western autobiographic writing, on the contrary, "presupposes a writer intent upon reflection on . . . [the] inward realm of experience" (Weintraub 1974, 823), a realm that is necessarily private according to modern Western notions of the person.

The formal aspects of many of these ritual genres encourage further dialogism. Maraka and Jawosi, for example, involve singing in choral counterpoint. Choral repetition of the songs in a Maraka is yet one more way in which the words and experiences of one person are circulated and assumed by others. People singing in the chorus, repeating the shaman's first-person narrative, begin to feel as though they have also seen and interacted with spirits. They take on the experiences of the shaman as their own. In Jawosi, though the women in the chorus do not feel as though they have been where the soloists have traveled, their repeating choral refrains often frame each of the soloist's lines as quoted speech. This kind of choral framing gives the sense that the soloist's lines are a repetition of the words produced first by someone else, even perhaps a whole series of previous speakers. In one song, for example, after each of the soloist's lines the chorus sang the refrain, "He says to him, Eheeja. He says to him. He says to him. He says to him. Eheeja. He says to him."

The Oscillation between Identity and Difference

The identification with various "others" that narrators describe and enact is not permanent. Amapá, for example, tells about his return to Kayabi ways after his youthful infatuation with whites. Shamans point out that, while one must follow the spirits and imitate their music and behavior, one must never lose one's own perspective. As Stone-Arm's son, Marcos, explained, his spirit familiars will lead him through the cosmos and show him the way to various spirits' homes because they ultimately want to trap him. They want to lose him in the dream world. A dreaming shaman must, therefore, always keep track of which path he took and where he turned so that he can find his way back to the living human community by himself. Shamans, in other words, need to beware of total identification. Similarly, at the end of a Maraka, a shaman always returns to the waking community, leaving the grunting, the yelling, and the postures of the spirits behind. Shamans who follow their spirit guides in an unthinking manner never come back to the living. Likewise, men who sing Jawosi do not want to permanently become the enemy. They call the enemies back into the present only for the duration of their song. Those who become identified with enemies for too long die. Warriors who become full of the enemy's blood as a result of taking his life must undergo seclusion and dietary restrictions to change their blood if they are to avoid this fate. Much as among the Tupian Arawete, who are devoured in the afterlife, completely becoming "the other" is synonymous with death (Viveiros de Castro 1992).

The choral repetition by the male chorus in Maraka and by the female chorus in Jawosi may in fact work as a tether, keeping the narrators tied to the living Kayabi community and guarding against too much identification with these others (see Cormier 2003, 102, for a similar observation about Guajá women's nightly singing). The same repetition that in Maraka allows participants to feel as though they are traveling around with the shaman, for example, may from the shaman's point of view keep him aware of the living Kayabi community. The narrators become suspended between their own community and that of the "others" during these performances.

Undergirding adult men's temporary identifications with human and non-human others, is, however, a more permanent identification with Kayabi elders. A result of child rearing and education during puberty, this identification more profoundly anchors adult men and keeps them tied to the living. In his address Amapá stressed that it is the singing of the elders' songs and the speaking of the Kayabi language that continue to make Kayabi people strong, not their facility with Portuguese, Brazilian-style dancing, or machinery. Shamans, likewise, reach the spirit world only after they have identified with and come to share the dreams of their elder teachers. In the spirit world the spirits of these deceased former shamans will also help a lost shaman and guide him back to the living. In the same way, inherited Jawosi songs come to contemporary singers through the mediation of their elder relatives. Because singing an inherited Jawosi song involves an assumption of the template provided by the song and the application of it to one's own experiences, the lives of previous Kayabi men are assumed in a silent, generic way along with the enemy's perspective.

Adulthood is a period in which, at least for men, there is a constant back-and-forth movement between identifying with non-Kayabi and distancing oneself from them, eventually coming back to an identity with Kayabi persons. One afternoon when Jacaré told me about his life experiences, using the phrase "where I traveled," he described an encounter that captures this process in a particularly concrete and visual way. As part of a much longer narrative, he recounted a trip he took when he was young man (approximately in 1955). He and his younger brother went with an Austrian Ancieta missionary who had long worked in Kayabi areas, Father Dornstauder, to contact remote villages along the Teles Pires River. As a result of working at one of the Kayabi posts as well as at nearby ranches, he and his brother were wearing eyeglasses and clothing. As they approached one remote Kayabi village, people shouted when they saw them, "The enemy is coming." Only when he arrived could Jacaré explain who he was: "I went up to the old one who knew my language and I talked to him. I came up to him, 'No we are not whites. It's me that is coming back again. I am returning from the whites again. It is not a white that I am bringing. It's us, it's us. This is Jupopinima, my younger brother.' . . . Then he came and embraced me. I was so happy. He got my shirt all dirty with his red body paint. He came to receive me. He put lots of red paint on my head with his hand. He got my head all red." In this moment of homecoming, the habitus of the enemy was replaced, covered over with the Kayabi way of life, language and dress.

Self as Other

All the narrative performances discussed in this study celebrate this masculine, adult movement between one's own and the "other." Each gives a sense for how to effect this movement in the most empowering way in the present. In keeping with this oscillation between identity and difference, all the narratives have a dialogic quality. Autobiographical narrative in these rituals is about the mature invocation and management of these various voices. The ideal mature male narrator is therefore represented as composed of many voices; many "others" speak through him—enemies, spirits, and ancestors. To tell about his experiences requires that he quote and orchestrate the voices of these others.

Much as in Kalapalo biography, the representation of interactive relations and conversation in these Kayabi narrative genres diminishes the "autonomy or 'thingness' of personhood" (Basso 1995, 298).[11] Rather, "the Self is initially a figure of the Other" (Viveiros de Castro 2001, 27). The adult male self is presented as a delicate balance of others' ways of behaving, moving, and talking. Individual persons are therefore not perfectly identical to themselves; instead they are "dividuals," a term that has been borrowed from Indian and Melanesian ethnographies to describe the notion of personhood operative in several Amazonian societies (Taylor 2001, 49; 1996; Viveiros de Castro 2001,

25, 33).[12] "Dividual," coined by McKim Marriott (1976) in the Indian context, has been used elsewhere to describe the composite nature of or the generalized sociality within subjects (Strathern 1988, 13). According to Anne-Christine Taylor (2001), for the Amerindian Jivaro, personhood is " 'dividual' in the sense that it is based on an internalized relation to a figure of alterity. . . . Men's subjecthood is predicated on the introjection of an antagonistic, unstable face-to-face relation to an affinal 'enemy' . . . women's identity is based on an intimate, constitutive sibling relation to game animals" (49).[13]

Given this suggestion that the person has a composite or "dividual" nature in some Amerindian groups, autobiographical and biographical narratives may emphasize dialogism elsewhere in Amazonia. Janet Hendrick's detailed transcription of a life history she elicited from a Shuar man contains a "key episode" in which the narrator becomes the respected warrior he is known as for the rest of his life (1993, 245). This episode, in keeping with the Jivaroan notions of personhood outlined by Taylor (2001), interestingly includes the quoted speech of his enemies. Likewise, as mentioned previously, Basso observes that warrior biographies among the Kalapalo are filled with quoted conversations (1995, 295). Laura Graham (1995) has also described how (through a shift in pronominal reference) a Xavante elder, when narrating him dreams, loses the perspective of his individual self and instead merges his self with the self of mythic creators.

In other groups there is evidence that the subject is conceptualized more generally, even beyond moments of self-representation, as being composed of the speech of others. The Muinane of Colombia, for example, understand the "moral self to be constituted by the aggregated speeches of ritual substances such as tobacco and coca. . . . The thoughts which people experience as love for kin, their judgments when they correctly distinguish between good and evil behavior . . . are examples of the speech of some of these substances sounding inside the body" (Londoño-Sulkin 2000, 173). Immoral thoughts are the speeches of animals that sound through a person (173). In societies that conceptualize the self in such a manner, one might expect narrative self-representation to be similar to that found in the ritual genres among the Kayabi—to be largely the representation and orchestration of the speech of others.

THE COSMIC MANAGEMENT OF VOICES

One crisp morning in the dry season as I lay in my hammock under my mosquito net, with a wool blanket covering me from chin to feet, I thought about the effect that Kayabi ritual performances have upon those involved. Thanks to the Kayabi education monitors who tutored me almost daily during my stay, I had started to better understand these events. Rather than worry so much about my place in them, I started to think more about which spirit beings might be present, where the shaman was traveling, or what sort of encounter a Jawosi song was describing. To be sure, I did still worry about myself, hoping that my choral Jawosi singing was not ruining my tape recordings or wondering if it would be rude to ask someone to step out of the action for a moment to ask them a question. Nevertheless, as my understanding grew, I started to get ever so slightly closer to comprehending the experiences of Kayabi participants.

Many classic works on ritual in anthropology have viewed rituals as transformative, drawing attention to the fact that they are able to restructure participants' emotions, perceptions, or interpretations of reality (see, for example, Geertz 1973; Ortner 1978; Turner 1969, [1967] 1982). Kayabi rituals also work to shift participants' consciousness, particularly their sense of how they are situated within the cosmos, that is, how the present moment they are experiencing fits with other times and how those presently living relate to others, both human and "other-than-human persons" (Hallowell 1955) who also inhabit the cosmos. The autobiographic portions of the performances are crucial in this process, as it is the quoted speech and distinct points of view invoked in autobiographical accounts that bring ritual participants into subjective alignment with these other times and beings.[1]

Bringing participants into subjective alignment with these others is not a simple task. In Kayabi cosmology the present is plagued by the most heightened form of "perspectivism" (Viveiros de Castro 1998). Unlike past epochs, at present animals, humans, and spirits all have very different bodily forms, behaviors, foods, and ways of speaking. Much as elsewhere in the Amazon, these differences cause them to perceive reality from very distinct points of view

(Viveiros de Castro 1998). As a result the present is plagued by disharmony, predation, and war.

All three of the Kayabi ritual genres presented in this study attempt to transcend this current state of fragmentation. As in other Amazonian cosmologies, "the whole is not (the) given . . . [t]he whole is, rather, the constructed, that which humans strive to bring forth" (Viveiros de Castro 2001, 28). That autobiographical narratives are about how one person—the leader standing before his audience—has managed to take on the position of various others over the course of his life and to orchestrate these other voices into some sort of whole makes the visible body of the narrator a very powerful symbol of this perspectival unification.

Each ritual, however, attempts to transcend contemporary cosmological fragmentation by aligning and distinguishing very different sets of subjective positions. The vision of the cosmos and the place of contemporary life within it that each ritual suggests are, therefore, not identical to each other. I have characterized the different visions each ritual offers as the "progressive," "degenerative," and "presentist" positions. To understand the different ways these rituals situate participants and restructure their consciousness, I begin by explaining the spaces and times that make up the Kayabi cosmos.

The Nature of the Present

According to Kayabi cosmology there were two earths (awa) prior to the present one. The first was destroyed by a flood. It now exists where these floodwaters still persist, "down below" on the river bottom. The second one arose when the water receded and ended when the sky was formed, creating that which is "above." We currently live in the third mode of existence, between the river bottoms and the sky. A fourth mode of existence will come about when the sky eventually falls back down to earth, reunifying earth and sky but crushing all those below.

Echoing many other South American cosmologies (Whitten 1976, 48; Wright 1998, 64), according to Kayabi cosmology beings from previous epochs have disappeared but they do not cease to exist. As Bird explained to me, once something is made—a person, animal, plant, or object—even though it is destroyed and disappears from sight, its soul ('ang) exists permanently, somewhere. These former beings, however, inhabit a different type of reality than presently living humans. Shamans, because they travel in dream all over the cosmos, know where they reside and can tell about their current existence.

Myths or ancestors' stories describe what these creatures were like in former times, when they were still alive. According to many of these stories, in the time before the earth and sky were distinct levels, humans, animals, objects, and spirits were also not yet distinct from each other. For example, many of the beings who lived on the second earth (called, as a group, the Aejewu'jap) were simultaneously objects and people or simultaneously animals and people, an image of earlier times that is widespread in the Amazon (Hill 1993, 57–61; Viveiros de Castro 1998, 471).

In relating shamans' dream accounts to ancestors' stories, the Masters of the Game are one contemporary vestige of this population.[2] In keeping with their previous manifestation when they were alive, the Masters of the Game are still described as being simultaneously animals and people. Accounts of them often shift, such that at one moment they are described as looking like a particular animal and at another moment as having human features (see also Travassos 1984, 11). At present these vestiges of the second earth live hidden from sight, at the horizon, inside mountains, or deep in the forest.

During the second epoch the earth was also simultaneously populated by superpowerful shamanic beings, called the Mait, and human persons. Among the Mait were personages who could come back to life after being shot full of arrows or who could make a full meal out of just one bean. In keeping with the notion that objects and people where not distinct entities during this epoch, the Mait also had many magical implements that were more like subjects than objects—an arrow that would return after being shot and garden tools that worked by themselves to clear fields and plant crops. The human persons living alongside these empowered Mait were the ancestors of the contemporary Kayabi.

The mode of existence characteristic of this prior earth, in which all sorts of beings were merged or lived in harmony with each other, came to an end when these beings started to perceive that they were different from each other. According to Kayabi ancestors' stories, it was near the end of the second earth when animals and humans divaricated and began to live separately. The story about the origin of deer, for example, describes how a character called Deer, a person-animal who spent his days farming the forest, had his body turned into the shape of a deer's body. A certain Mait did this by tricking Deer: he blew dirt into his eye, and when Deer asked the Mait to help him take it out, Deer stretched his eyes wide, like deer's eyes are today; he pulled his neck out long, like deer's necks are today; and so forth. After being so transformed he ran away into the forest. Since this time deer have acted more like animals than like humans. This Mait continued to play similar tricks until all the contemporary animals were formed into their present shape.

It was shortly after this moment that the character Tujarare went looking for a wife and finally married one of the People-without-Understanding. One of the important things he taught his in-laws was how to see animals as animals, not as people, such as how to kill them without war rituals and how to eat their meat. Prior to this time the People-without-Understanding would only eat fish and treated animals as if they were human. When Tujarare brought the gift of meat eating, he definitively split the perspectives of humans and animals.

Tujarare brought a fragmentation of perspectives among human people as well. Discovering that his new wife among the People-without-Understanding was unfaithful, Tujarare killed her. Not seeing Tujarare's jealousy as a just cause for homicide, her brothers set out to avenge her death. To serve as his warriors, Tujarare created the first Kayabi from various sorts of objects and animals, such as muddy water, manioc porridge, necklaces, twine, toucans, foxes, and jaguars. A war between the People-without-Understanding and the Kayabi ensued in which the Kayabi were victorious. Currently, in our present earth different ethnicities are now always potentially at war with one another. Despite the fact that other ethnic groups are more similar to Kayabi than to animals, these groups are also understood to have slightly different ways of being and slightly different kinds of bodies. (Ethnicity is frequently understood to reside in a person's flesh and muscle.)

The end of the second epoch was also marked by a lack of common perspective among the superpowerful Mait, particularly between the younger and elder Mait. As a result of this fragmentation, the power of the Mait has become lost to humans. Several of the ancestors' stories explain that it was a young Mait called Moon (Jay) who began the process of diminishing humanity's access to the Mait's powers. Moon repeatedly disobeyed his father's and elder brother's directions on how to use their magical tools. As a result, after many mishaps he ultimately destroyed all of their tools (Grünberg n.d. [1970], 194; Ribeiro 1979, 215; Travassos 1984, 313). One man explained the story of Moon in the following way: "Moon ruined everything because never again did knives and axes work by themselves. The rascal son ruined everything. Now when we want to make a garden, we have to work, knock down all the trees because the knives and axes don't do anything alone any more."

According to the ancestors' stories, the actual separation of the sky from the earth was also a result of Moon's disobedience to his elders. Prior to this moment, all was one unified domain. Because the sun shone all the time, Moon's elder brother had been making a basket for shade. When it was done, Moon asked if he could hang it in the sky. His brother gave him the basket but warned him not to travel too far. Moon could not resist the temptation, however, and as a consequence he and the basket became stuck in the far distance, creating the sky.

Once the sky became a separate domain, all the Mait moved up to this level to get away from the Kayabi. As Kayabi say, now the Mait are "things from above." This separation occurred as a result of yet another kind of interpersonal rift, this time on the part of Kayabi women and two Mait brothers. Because these two brothers were making an incessant amount of noise, Kayabi women started to complain and gossip about them. The brothers, not wanting to live with people who spoke poorly of them, convinced all the other Mait to move to the newly created sky. Their departure left humanity alone on the earth's surface. Since this point in time, human access to the powers of the Mait has become limited and only grows more tenuous with each passing generation.

The present mode of existence is, therefore, characterized by disharmony and division. There is day and night rather than a continually shining sun. There is a sky, an earth, and a river bottom rather than one unified domain. Animal spirits take human people's souls for their food or to keep as pets. The Kayabi eat animals and battle other kinds of people. Humans, animals, and spirits no longer share one single mode of existence, one kind of body, or one vision of reality.

This disharmony and division will end in the future when a fourth epoch is realized. The present way of life will come to an end when the sky falls down and the Mait come again to live on earth. This will happen when the giant tree that is currently holding up the sky falls. Much like human society, the Mait who live in the sky continue to fragment and split off into different groups. Currently there are two groups of Mait, one that is hostile toward humans below and one that is friendly toward them and considers themselves to be the "grandparents" of the Kayabi. Those Mait who are hostile to the Kayabi are scheming to chop down the celestial tree and occasionally manage to begin work on this project. Each time they do, however, the Mait who are humanity's allies prop the tree back up and save those living below.

Though the collapse of the sky will crush those on earth, it will potentially also bring about a reunification of perspectives. The Mait will again live on the level of "this earth." Much as in other Tupian and South American cosmologies (Civrieux 1980; Gallois 1988, 159; Wright 1998, 288), there is a cosmic cycle that may reach closure. The distant past and the distant future are related in a manner similar to the way Benjamin Lee Whorf has described the Hopi universe: in the "inconceivable distance from the observer—from all observers—there is an encircling end and beginning of things" (1979, 63).

In the Kayabi cosmos the future is also found in the domains of the past in a slightly more prosaic manner. The souls of Kayabi babies come to earth from the distant domains where creatures of the past now reside (see Cormier 2003, 109, for a similar belief among the Tupian Guajá). The souls of newborns are found in the sky, living with the Mait, or in the homes of the Masters of the Game. Therefore, while in certain respects these domains are repositories of the past, they are more accurately repositories of distant times that are also continually unfolding in the present, a characteristic similar to that observed with respect to the Dreaming of aboriginal Australia (Myers 1986).[3]

Mending the Present Fragmentation

Of all Kayabi rituals, shamanic cures attempt to align the widest number of distinct perspectives. They link up perspectives from several time periods and levels of the cosmos. Following what I have been calling the "degenerative perspective"—the idea that ability and power were greatest among creatures living at the beginning of the cosmos—Maraka rituals align the present with beings from distant pasts. Through their Maraka songs, shamans like Monkey-Leg inhabit the perspective of many of the ancient Masters of the Game, such as Master of Eagles and the Master of Tapirs. Often they take on the perspective of some of the Mait as well and quote songs from these beings.

Shamans' spoken autobiographical accounts in Maraka suggest that healers can only have access to the perspective of these spirits by first inhabiting the subjective space of their elder mentors. Monkey-Leg, for example, dreamed along with his mentor the first time he traveled to the Eagle Spirit. As if to reverse the disobedience of the young Moon, whose disobedience caused much of the present cosmological fragmentation, Monkey-Leg suggests that obedience to elders (a form of taking their perspective as one's own) is the way to reconnect with the power of earlier times. Even the scheduling of Maraka performances—which take place at dusk and, on the final night, last from dusk to dawn—suggests an earlier cosmological time, before the rhythms of night and day were distinct. As such they create a kind of "liminal" time (Turner 1969).

Connecting the living with previous generations of Kayabi and with ancient nonhuman beings also has implications for connecting the living with future generations. As well as singing about the souls of their patients during Maraka, shamans also sing about those yet to be born, those souls still living with the Mait or the Masters of the Game who will animate future Kayabi babies. Many of the songs a shaman sings during the final morning of a Maraka cure are about the unborn children he has brought or will soon bring to women, describing what their life is like in their prebirth spirit homes. Through their Maraka songs, shamans can bring these souls into the community of the living. At Maraka the unborn souls are drawn by Maraka music and congregate in the pot of sweet tapioca drink made for the occasion. Women can become impregnated simply by taking a drink. In Maraka this regenerative power is accessed by taking on the perspective or subjectivity of elders such as contemporary great shamans, great shamans of past generations, and ancient power beings.

In contrast to Maraka, political oratory is a genre more singularly oriented toward linking the present with the time that is just about to unfold. Leaders who speak in this mode are much less likely to stress identification with past generations and the power of the previous epochs. Rather, following the "progressive trajectory," they stress how the generations have surpassed each other and interpret the present as the beginning of a time in which the Kayabi will be more in control of their destiny. This genre presents the passage of time in a more positive light than does Maraka ritual. Rather than keeping them more distant from power, the passage of time brings the Kayabi closer to regaining the power they lost in earlier epochs. For example, when Fire-of-the-Gods became the assistant to the chief, he often compared the tractors and power saws found at park posts to the magical tools that Moon ruined in the past. Likewise, he saw literacy as an important skill that would allow the Kayabi and other indigenous people to regain some of the power and control that had been lost in the third earth. With the ability to read and write and the associated technology, he believed that they could both influence NGOs as well as enter government positions to improve their living conditions significantly.

Fire-of-the-Gods was not alone in interpreting technologies and skills associated with non-Indians as similar to the power of the Mait (see also Travassos 1984). His father, Leg-Bone, once told a large gathering at Chief João's house about the whites' first appearance among the Kayabi. Demonstrating that history and myth are not separate modes of consciousness (Turner 1988a, 1988b), he told this story in the style of a Kayabi ancestor's story. Beginning with a well-known tale, he first told about how the Mait left the surface of the earth and went to live in the sky. To build their homes in the sky, he said, they used power tools to dig holes for their house posts. Turning to me he commented, "Just like your people." In the sky they took videos of many of their activities, including their attempt to fell the celestial tree.[4] Finally a group of Mait visited the Kayabi on earth after being called back by a Kayabi shaman. They descended upon a house in which a woman and her children were alone, the man having gone hunting. Playing with the listener's sense of dread about what might happen next, he described how slowly the hunter walked home. Then with his characteristic wit in describing the ways of "my people," he told how, upon entering the woman's house, the Mait each pulled out paper and pencil and began to write down Kayabi words for various objects. Finally, the Mait took the woman and her daughter to a faraway city, leaving knives and pots tied to their hammock strings in exchange.

Whether Leg-Bone's story was intended or received as a factual account, a humorous parody, or a bit of both, I cannot say with certainty. It nevertheless linked non-Kayabi skills such as literacy and the influx of "white" objects such as knives and pots with the breakup of the Kayabi family. In this story these new technologies and skills are harbingers of the end of a viable life rather than innovations that will allow the Kayabi to regain lost abilities. For many elders "white" influences are more associated with the cataclysm that will bring about the fourth earth than with the renewal of powers during the fourth earth. The degenerative position articulated so clearly in shamanic rituals with respect to health therefore resonates for them in a wider variety of contexts than it does for younger men like Fire-of-the-Gods.

While the autobiographical narratives embedded in political oratory are more monologic than those embedded in Maraka, political addresses such as those by Chief João or Amapá still make liberal use of quoted speech. In political addresses it is the speaking styles and language (Portuguese) of the ethnic group that currently wields the most power (nonindigenous Brazilians) that is evoked rather than the music of the spirits. In the two examples of this genre included in this book, the voices of whites are not quoted to show inappropriate or harmful behavior, in the way Leg-Bone, for example, describes the Mait and whites in his story (see also Basso 1979 on Apache joking). Rather, aspects of the whites' perspective come to be inhabited with less of an overt message that this perspective is dangerous or ridiculous. Amapá, for example, merges his voice with that of the whites and concludes that this point of view is simply "the way it is." João too describes himself as acting like an urbanite in Rio in a more flattering than ridiculous light. In short, the autobiographical narratives embedded in political oratory attempt to align narrators with powerful contemporary ethnic others and to communicate for those listening that the narrator, because of this alignment, is a bridge between the present and a more empowered future existence.

Finally, Jawosi rituals set about to unite perspectives among different sorts of Kayabi living in the present and to give them a sense of their position within the larger cosmological circulation of life. As they do this they also differentiate the living from the dead. Curiously, they do this by summoning the perspectives or voices of dead enemies. The dead enemy becomes a medium for welding various contemporary Kayabi points of view together, perceiving how the living fit into a larger cycle, and distancing dead relatives.

The Jawosi genre is a mechanism for bringing many living Kayabi into alignment. When a full Jawosi is performed, including visitors from other local groups, the enemy's perspective becomes a way to metaphorically transpose the battle experiences of the visiting adult men onto the young messengers who were sent out to invite them. Not only are different generations of living Kayabi linked, but residents of different local groups and households are also united. Residents of other local groups, while not necessarily hostile to each other, are viewed as people with whom relations are slightly problematic. As one Kayabi man phrased it, "If people get along with each other, they live together." When messengers from a hosting group are sent out to shadow their guests, and when the guests sing about their assassin-messengers, these distinctions in ways of life and disagreements are momentarily overshadowed.

Repetition by the women's chorus of the enemies' songs in counterpoint to the male soloists' lines adds an important element not heard in other rituals. By repeating the enemies' songs owned by each patriline, the women's chorus becomes the collective group that stands for the totality of Kayabi tradition. Over the course of a Jawosi ritual, the women's singing is a vehicle for singing all the songs of distinctive enemies and distinctive patrilines.

While over the course of a Jawosi ritual different factions are merged, first through different enemies' songs and then through the women's chorus, there is a hint throughout the ritual that the linchpin in all of this—the perspective of the enemy—is perceived in a contradictory way. It is simultaneously inhabited with intimacy and held at arm's length. For example, in addition to unmooring these accounts from a specific time period, the lack of tense and evidential markers in these songs suggests a particularly strong sense of shared experience between the warrior and the enemy. With respect to the narrative tradition of the Kalapalo, Ellen Basso has observed that the most elaborate use of evidentials occurs in story contexts where there is an outright denial of shared experience or point of view. They show up in "situations of doubt, potential discord, and of actual disputes, and especially in situations of dialogue where persuasion and resistance to persuasion take place" (1995, 39). If this observation can be extended to the Kayabi, the unusually low use of evidentials in Jawosi songs would suggest the opposite—that these are stories in which there is harmony and effective persuasion. In fact, many Jawosi songs, such as that of Leg-Bone, describe how the warrior and enemy know each other's thoughts.

The stories that Jawosi songs recount, however, are not ultimately about a harmonious blending of perspectives. Rather, they tell how enemies try to persuade Kayabi warriors on the validity of their point of view, but fail. Moreover, many Jawosi songs make use of disturbing imagery involving metaphors of trees, animals, or food. Enemy bodies are, for example, chopped, shot, or boiled. The effect is a powerful, almost dizzying, alternation of perspectives over the course of a series of these songs. In one the enemy is human, with a subjectivity identical to that of a Kayabi warrior; in the next the enemy is an animal or plant, an object to be preyed upon or harvested. The alternation between the enemy portrayed as self and as other is evocative of the larger cycling of substances and souls in the cosmos, according to which death for one kind of entity means new life for another. These rituals encourage participants to see the play between alternative perspectives and nudge them toward taking the perspective that a deceased love one, if properly forgotten, ultimately implies new life.

The Importance of the Body

Leaders' autobiographical narratives become important in aligning the fragmentary perspectives of the present because in these stories different perspectives come together in the experience of one person's body. Several have pointed out the importance of the body in Amazonian thought (Conklin 2001, xx; Overing and Passes 2000; Seeger, da Matta, and Viveiros de Castro 1979; Viveiros de Castro 1998, 479). Viveiros de Castro has even observed that "the Amerindian Bildung happens in the body more than in the spirit, there is no 'spiritual' change which is not a bodily transformation, a redefinition of its effects and capacities" (1998, 481).

In the ritual contexts I have discussed, each narrator's body is a locus and animator of a variety of perspectives or voices. As such, each body provides a powerful image of how these perspectives can be brought into alignment. Though shamans leave their bodies during dream to travel to spirit villages, they bear the marks of their dream adventures on their physical bodies. Stone-Arm, in his cures, shows the scars on his thigh gained from the sloth spirit as well as the scars on his arms inflicted by other spirit beings. Monkey-Leg, during his Maraka cure for Jacaré, directed attention to how his hand was the seat of various spirits coming to earth. Likewise, the bodies of Jawosi singers are painted like the bodies of the enemies they have encountered. Similarly, men who assume the position of chief or assistant to the chief are often known to wear full sets of Western clothing. While at a practical level the Western outfits simply enable these mediators to engage more effectively beyond Kayabi communities, they are not completely unlike the enemy body paint worn by Jawosi singers. The tangible body of the narrator, in conjunction with his narratives about where he has been and with whom he has identified, becomes the vehicle for imagining the alignment of various fragmented perspectives. The bodies of these men in ritual context serve "as the paradigm . . . of the limits of individuality," just as they serve as the paradigm of individuality for many in the West (Turner 1995a, 145).

CONCLUSION

The more comfortable I became with my Kayabi hosts, the more inadvertently I began to converse with friends such as Fire-of-the-Gods and Bird in the style I was accustomed to talking with my friends and family back in Chicago. More than once I remember being deep in conversation (in Portuguese) and commenting that so-and-so was a "nice person" or "a trustworthy person" or alternately that so-and-so was "not confidant" or was a "jealous person." Each time I made such a statement I had the sense of a small "start," perhaps a bit of "culture shock," on the part of my interlocutor. Never once were comments like this directly confirmed or challenged, as interlocutors back home would have done.

After returning from Brazil I read a comment in Ellen Basso's book *The Last Cannibals* to the effect that Kalapalo storytellers prefer not to label people's emotions, motives, or distinctive character (1995, 295). Rather, these aspects of persons are represented through their quoted speech as functions of conversations with others. Thinking back on my stay in Kapinu'a, I believe Kayabi also describe people more in terms of their interpersonal relations, reproducing how a person acted or spoke with others at particular moments rather than labeling someone as a "type of person." This mode of description is consistent with Amazonian conceptualizations of self and person in which subjective experience and action are not conceptualized as properties of individual subjects but rather as properties of relationships (Pollock 1996; Basso 1995).

In writing this book I have self-consciously tried to offer a similar representation of individual people as well as the community of Kapinu'a. Rather than setting out to "tell one person's story," as so many life histories do, I have attempted to give a sense of several Kayabi people as they interact with each other, particularly in ritual events. I hope that this mode of portraiture, if I can even call it that, is more in keeping with indigenous ideas about selves and persons.

The general picture of the mature Kayabi man that results is one in which the subject is intentionally multiple or "dividual." Years of travel and identification with various sorts of others are understood to produce a subject who manages and orchestrates voices rather than one who is uniformly identical to himself. These men are intimately interconnected with a variety of others—ancestors, spirits, and enemies—who speak through them. As a result, their autobiographical narratives are highly dialogic, and they are more akin to symphony conductors than to introspective writers of autobiographies in Western traditions.

By approaching autobiographical narratives as they are situated in ritual, they can be understood as social phenomena. In this tradition, ritual genres of autobiography are a medium through which experiences can circulate between people. They often describe as shared what in most Western traditions would be considered private. Dreams of spirits or thoughts during war, for example, are not understood as the property of only one subject or even as originating "within" a single subject.

Likewise, while autobiography or life history research often focuses on how the creation of these types of narratives is psychologically meaningful or does certain kinds of subjective work—that is, transforms the narrator in particular ways (see Langness and Frank 1981; Watson and Watson-Franke 1985)—I have emphasized instead how the performances of these kinds of narratives have the potential to transform others. Through their autobiographic narratives, Kayabi leaders encourage others to approach contemporary problems in specific ways, and as they do so they also encourage larger transformations of how to think, at a very subjective level, about the way the present fits into the cosmos.

These ritual performances suggest that, by establishing connections and identifications between certain sorts of subjects from other times and places, one can confront and overcome the specific problems of the present. Each type of ritual performance, however, calls for the alignment of a different set of subjective positions. In Maraka cures, shamans stress that current generations should have an identification with past generations, both living and dead, in order to achieve health and strength in the present. In Jawosi songs, family headmen encourage an intergenerational identification among the living but a distance between the living and the dead in order to achieve well-being in the face of debilitating sadness. In political oratory, men differentiate themselves from past generations in order to give guidance on the most empowering way to engage with the national society. They associate their own past behavior with that of wayward followers and tell about how they have changed, giving their listeners a path to follow. In each of these events, agency follows from a connection or identification between subjects and is not a product or capability of an isolated individual.

The perspectives offered in each of these ritual events are "ideologies" in the sense that they are "practical understanding[s]" more than the conscious management of ideas (Comaroff 1985, 4; see also Basso 1995, 394; Voloshinov 1987). These perspectives or ideologies are not therefore represented as a set of abstract principles; rather, they take shape through a type of engagement with a narrator and with a ritual form. The resulting picture of life in a village such as Kapinu'a is one in which several different competing perspectives or ideologies are presented over the course of several different rituals. These ideologies are in dialogue with each other, each inviting argument from the other (see Comaroff and Comaroff 1992). Given that this relatively remote Amazon village is composed of only a few hundred people, one would expect to find the opposite—a high degree of homogeneity and uniformity in perspective.

Ideological fomentation in the Amazon, however, has been linked to its invasion and occupation by nonindigenous peoples, including the formation of new kinds of societies out of refugee groups, even where these national populations are not present in great numbers (Basso 1995, 302). The Kayabi families in the Xingu are composed people who relocated precisely because of the pressure of the frontier. Certainly the development of new-style villages and "chiefly" leadership is a likely cause of some of these ideological splits. It is very possible that in earlier times the three ritual genres discussed here might have presented more homogeneous perspectives on how to have strength and well-being. Perhaps Jawosi songs, for example, resembled Maraka and made more mention of past generations, referring more to cycles of violence like some of Stone-Arm's songs and the songs of the sixteenth-century Tupinambá (Carneiro da Cunha and Viveiros de Castro 1985). If, according to Kayabi cosmology, the unification of perspectives is only to be achieved in some distant time yet to unfold or in the mythic past, perhaps these rituals have been, to a certain degree, inviting argument from each other for a very long time.

NOTES

Introduction

1. While the presence of researchers, Brazilian as well as foreign, is relatively common in the Xingu Park reservation, Kayabi villages have had far fewer than other communities. Most Kayabi villages in the Xingu have hosted researchers only for a few days, if at all. However, the anthropologist Georg Grünberg spent several months in the Xingu with Kayabi in 1966, as did Elizabeth Travassos in 1981 and 1982 (Grünberg n.d. [1970]; Travassos 1984). In the 1980s the SIL linguist Helga Weiss spent an extended period in Kapinu'a, the village I discuss in this book. In addition, Mariana Kawall Leal Ferreira carried out anthropological research with Kayabi individuals while living and teaching at the northern park post in the 1980s. Outside the park, Kayabi in the Rio dos Peixes hosted Georg Grünberg for most of 1966 (Grünberg n.d. [1970]) and Elizabeth Travassos for a few months in 1980 (Travassos 1984). Since the 1990s, the Brazilian anthropologist Lea Tomass has also spent extended field stays in Xinguan Kayabi villages.

2. I make no claim, following Geertz (1973, 360–64), that I gain access to the actual experience of "a self." Rather, I am looking at Kayabi narrative representations of experiences and in part asking what these events can tell us about the Kayabi understandings that overlap with modern Euro-Western notions of the self.

3. Here I am more in line with what James Peacock and Dorothy Holland (1993) call "psychosocial approaches," works that study self-narrative as events in social as opposed to psychological processes; see also Cain 1991; Peacock 1978.

4. Following Sherry Ortner's definition, I understand agency to be "that dimension of power that is located in the actor's subjective sense of authorization, control, [and] effectiveness in the world," as well as the more meaning-oriented "active projection of the self toward some desired end" (1999, 147).

5. I understand ritual dimensions to be those that set certain behavior apart from the daily routine, as relatively stylized or formalized behavior that encourages an unusually attentive state of mind and that can therefore effect a transformation or reorganize social arrangements as well as mirror them (see Geertz 1973; Moore and Myerhoff 1977; Tambiah 1985).

6. On ritualization see Blommaert 2001; Silverstein 2001; Toren 2001.

7. In other publications—Oakdale 2001, 2002, and 2004—I have spelled the name of this ritual as "Jowosi."

8. I do not, however, focus specifically on the musical dimensions of the autobiographical texts.

9. For examples of other similar "pragmatic" approaches to ritual among indigenous South Americans, see Graham 1995 and Urban 1991. Jonathan Hill (1993) provides a detailed account of how Wakuénai specialists understand their speech in ritual to be powerful.

10. Here I follow a growing body of recent works on ritual, such as Comaroff 1985; Dussart 2000; Foster 1995; Piot 1999; and Rodríguez 1996.

11. See, for example, Herdt [1981] 1994; Nabokov 2000; Obeyesekere 1990.

12. The distinction between the narrating or speech event and the narrated event is found in Jakobsen 1971 and is developed in Bauman 1986 and Silverstein 1993, 1996, 1999, among others.

13. I am drawing on Donald Brenneis's (1999) discussion that connects Burke's "identification" with an explicit concern with the relationship between the event of narration and the narrated event.

14. I am explicitly not looking at identity in the sense described by Erik Erikson (1968) (see Fogelson 1998). Others who have recently focused upon the shifting, fragmentary nature of identity or the deployment of different identities in different contexts include Fischer (1986), Kondo (1990), and Tsing (1993, 254).

15. See Abu-Lughod 1991, 1993; Kondo 1990; Ortner 1996; and Tsing 1993 with respect to this point. See Brightman 1995 for a discussion and critique of some of these aforementioned authors, as well as for a discussion of Drummond 1980 and Rosaldo 1989 with respect to this general topic.

16. Following Allport (1942) and Watson and Watson-Franke (1985), I define "personal documents" as "any expressive production of the individual that can be used to throw light on his view of himself, his life situation, or the state of the world as he understands it, at some particular point in time or over the passage of time" (Watson and Watson-Franke 1985, 2).

17. For overviews on how they have been used in anthropology, see Crapanzano 1984; Langness and Frank 1981; Peacock and Holland 1993; Watson and Watson-Franke 1985.

18. As Vincent Crapanzano has pointed out, behind the notion that a narrator is a typical member of his or her culture lies a distorted view of culture as homogeneous (1984, 954).

19. Similarly, Comaroff and Comaroff point out that to treat biography as a neutral window on history projects the logic of rational individualism. They call instead for situating being and action, comparatively, within their diverse cultural contexts (1992, 26).

20. See Brumble 1988 and Wong 1992 for North American examples and Hendricks 1993 for a South American example.

21. With respect to discourse-centered approaches, I am drawing on Bauman 1986; Bauman and Briggs 1990; Bauman and Sherzer 1974; Sherzer 1983; Silverstein and Urban 1996; and Urban 1991.

22. Specifically with respect to genre, see Bakhtin 1986; Briggs and Bauman 1992; Crapanzano 1996; Hanks 1987; Silverstein 1996, 1999. Jane Hill (1985) has also used Bakhtinian insights in developing the concept of a "voice system" in autobiographical narrative.

23. On these topics see Miller et al. 1990; Miller and Moore 1989; Wortham 1994; Ochs, Smith, and Taylor 1989.

24. As such, this work is more in line with the approaches of Erving Goffman (1959, 1981), G. H. Mead ([1934] 1977), and Milton Singer (1984) than with traditional life history research. Within life history research Oscar Lewis's *The Children of Sanchez* (1961) is remarkable for juxtaposing the life histories of five family members. This allows the reader to see some of the structures of identification (and differentiation) at work—for example, which family members have similar points of view or styles of narration.

1. The Perils of Living in the Xingu Indigenous Park

1. This community includes other Tupi-speaking peoples as well as Arawak-, Carib-, and Trumai-speaking groups (Agostinho 1974, 15; Basso 1973, 3). Despite the fact that they speak several different languages, these peoples share common dietary restrictions, rituals, and myths as well as a common set of values, the most important of which are generosity and peaceful behavior (Agostinho 1974; Basso 1973, 1995).

2. Both newcomers and long-time residents in the north of the park are outsiders with respect to the Upper Xinguan community. The Suyá and Kayapó were, for example, historically the enemies of the Upper Xinguans (Schwartzman 1988, 335). At present the Lower Xinguans take part in Upper Xinguan rituals only to a very limited degree.

3. The Villas Boas brothers persuaded several peoples who lived in heavily colonized areas to move inside the park for protection. Relocation was necessary for these peoples only because the government of the state of Mato Grosso cut by 75 percent the original 1952 plan for the park's boundaries—to its present size of thirty thousand square kilometers (Schwartzman 1988, 338, 326). Since the 1990s, the Kayapó and Panará, however, have moved back to their areas outside the park.

4. This figure is from an Escola Paulista 1992 census. I estimated the Xinguan Kayabi population to have been approximately 560 in August 1993. Other Kayabi continue to live outside the park as well (see also Hemming 2003, 142–46).

5. Some were reported to have been living in the park as early as 1950 (Grünberg n.d. [1970], 52). Later, in 1955, forty more people were reported to have come from the Teles Pires (52). Many of these Kayabi came from the tributaries of the Teles Pires, the main ones being the Verde and Paranatinga Rivers.

6. According to Georg Grünberg, in 1966 thirteen people came from Pará (n.d. [1970], 53). Some Kayabi told me that they came in 1971 and 1973. One three-person family now living in Kapinu'a came from Pará in the early 1990s (see also Hemming 2003, 142–46).

7. The Kayabi in this area are reported to have first attacked the post. In 1924, after two workers were killed, the post closed down (Grünberg n.d. [1970], 45). It was established again in 1925, 180 kilometers above the mouth of the Verde along the Paratinga (45). Only in 1926 did friendly groups come to visit the post (45). In 1929, after the Kayabi killed the sixth post employee, the post was transferred again, this time 10 kilometers south, where it was renamed José Bezerra (47).

8. Kayabi did seek out more formal education from missionaries. Father Dornstauder, the missionary from the Catholic (Anchieta) mission at Utiariti (located outside of Kayabi territories), visited the Teles Pires in 1953, 1954, and 1955 and took several Kayabi, who wanted to go, back to the Utiariti mission for instruction in literacy, crafts such as sewing, and Catholic doctrine (Grünberg n.d. [1970]; Schultz 1964, 222).

9. The Roncador-Xingu expedition was constructing airstrips between Manaus and the south of Brazil (Davis 1980, 48; Hemming 2003, 81). The strip constructed in the Upper Xingu is now closed.

10. This same NGO, formerly the Rain Forest Foundation, now a part of Instituto Socioambiental (ISA), stopped this use of the ferry.

11. Despite the cost, a very few individuals do manage to make these trips. In 1992 four people from Pará visited Kapinu'a. One man came to visit his father for a few days, and another couple came with their baby to visit the man's parents. This particular man met his wife on a visit to Pará from the Xingu years earlier.

12. One of the most frequent complaints I heard from park residents in the early 1990s was the lack of availability of adequate instruction in these subjects (see also Ferreira 1992).

13. For a full discussion of the noble and ignoble facets of Indian identity within Brazil, see Ramos 1998.

14. The image of the park as a place without history is parallel to the utopian denial of history, which, according to James Holston (1989), guided the plans for the capital city of Brasília, conceived and built in approximately the same era as the park.

15. In the June 17, 1992, issue of *Veja* magazine, Mario Juruna was pictured standing in front of a large jaguar skin with a T-shirt stretched tight over his substantial stomach. The caption reads, "Juruna: '[what] animals are good for is barbecuing'" ("Cacique Amigo da Onça" 1992). The reader's eye is drawn from the spots on the jaguar skin behind Mario Juruna's head directly to the spots on a "jaguar skin" purse that Bianca Jagger is wearing around her trim waist in the photo directly above him. This jaguar skin, the reader finds out, is the appropriate sort for the occasion: fake.

16. This is changing to some extent because of Sting's visits to the Kayapó and ISA's involvement in the Lower Xingu, though the feeling is still that the Kayapó, with their elaborate rituals, receive the most outside aid.

17. The Kayapó are also skillful manipulators of the "savage" side of Brazilian Indian identity. Schwartzman (1988) and Turner (1991) have pointed out that the Kayapó have consistently and successfully used the "wild" facet of "Indian" identity vis-à-vis the national society to their favor.

2. The Perils of New-Style Villages

1. While food was shared regularly among households in Kapinu'a, as a foreign researcher I was in a somewhat unique position. The village as a whole, not just João and Pretty, felt it was their duty to feed me throughout my stay.

2. Several people credited doctors from the Escola Paulista who run the medical program in the Xingu with "having ordered" people to build their households together in one location.

3. Waud Kracke has characterized the Kagwahiv in this way as well (personal communication).

4. In the past, when a man and woman were married, the marriage ritual consisted of rolling them in a hammock for a day and having the bride's father present them with smoked game. These gifts of meat very likely both represented the productive power of the father-in-law and entailed a series of return gifts of (uncooked) meat on the part of the son-in-law.

5. Kayabi do not consider the oval shape to be traditional but, rather, a style taken from Brazilian settlers. Unlike many Brazilian houses in the interior, Kayabi houses are not raised off the ground.

6. Late in life Jacaré cultivated a very dear friendship with Helga Weiss of SIL and aided her in the production of written language materials.

7. Even in 1993, however, one young man in Kapinu'a had married a very young girl and was living with her family.

8. A few do get around this problem by collecting consumer goods from the chief and then redistributing these items at the household level.

9. Similar comments were never made about girls. This is very likely because female initiation is still practiced in full and even exaggerated form at present in the Xingu.

10. For others, particularly the young monitors and village chiefs, the village school is understood as encouraging a certain amount of Kayabi control over their own adolescents rather than entrusting their education to other ethnic groups. Kayabi teachers, rather than nonindigenous Brazilians, teach others how to write and speak Portuguese. Moreover, if Kayabi adolescents were to work outside the park rather than attend school, nonindigenous Brazilians would be directing their labor and their on-the-job learning. Even within the park other indigenous people are frequently in control of posts where Kayabi work.

3. The Self-Conscious "Indian"

1. The Shavante, for example, have an evening men's council in the plaza during which elder men speak in *ihi mrémé* (elder's speech) style (Graham 1993, 733). Graham describes this style as "music like," "formally distinct from conversational Xavante," and "characterized by extensive repetition and parallelism, a unique voice quality and special intonation pattern," giving it a "distinct acoustic shape" (733). Elders also use phonetic variation, some phrases and words, and imploded lateral clicks that are not part of everyday speech (733). According to Seeger, the Suyá *me mbai hwa kapérni* ("everybody listens speech") used to exhort the community to behave correctly is highly structured and has long cadences and phrases that are more regular than everyday speech (1986, 62). This is especially true when the thumping of a club or the slapping of an arm against a trunk is used as an accompaniment (66).

2. My own tape recordings of these events are few because I felt people would not want me to record the issues discussed, such as disputes or admonitions. Also, by the time a dispute was brought to the chief, tempers were usually at their limit.

3. This talk was unfortunately not tape-recorded but rather reconstructed from field notes and memory.

4. Attention to pauses (Tedlock 1983) or the construction of verse format (Hymes 1981), while useful for many arguments, does not advance the points I make here.

5. I am indebted to an anonymous reviewer for *American Ethnologist* for this insight.

6. *Caraiba* is, however, used to refer to whites among the Kayabi as well as other Xinguans.

7. João never made me feel subservient outside of these public gatherings, however. When he was not worried about the opinions of other villagers, he was much less authoritarian. On the contrary, he was someone who seemed as though he really was trying to understand my unusual position in his home and in his village.

4. The Healing Power of Shamanic Career Narration

1. In Kapinu'a six other individuals were recognized as being *ipájé*, including one woman. One other woman had previously been *ipájé* but had lost her powers. *Pájéretes* (great shamans), however, are always male.

2. Charles Wagley reports a Tapirape version of this story (1977, 180), in which the monster (*anchunga-aiuma*) dances around a pot of boiling water rather than a pit. In both the Tapirape and Kayabi versions these two brothers are also ultimately connected to the creation of nonindigenous Brazilians.

3. The two Maraka I attended took place over the course of four and three nights. Maraka can also take place for just two nights or one night as well (see Travassos 1984, 118, 142).

4. Stone-Arm said that women used to sing along with the men but no longer do. De Léry also describes witnessing a Tupinambá ritual in the sixteenth century that centered around the prophets or shamans he calls *caraibes*, in which men, while

dancing in a circle, sang a refrain very similar to that of the Kayabi Maraka. De Léry describes how each of the caraibes' verses was followed by the men's chorus and then again by a chorus of women and children, who were secluded in a separate house (1990, 142). Travassos writes that she received a tape recording of a Maraka held in the early 1980s at Diauarum Post during which women did in fact sing along with the men's chorus (1984, 143). In the two Marakas that I attended and the others that Travassos describes, however, the women did not sing.

5. In Kamayura and Asurini Maraka, a group of shamans gather to cure together, and the cure has more to do with their collective work (Bastos 1984–85; Müller 1990, 144; n.d.). In Arawete or Tapirapé cures, the shaman's wife plays a much more prominent role than she does in Kayabi Maraka (Viveiros de Castro 1992; Wagley 1977, 201). Kayabi shamans' wives do occasionally fill their husbands' pipes and straighten their hammocks during Maraka performances.

6. Spirits do come to earth and speak through the voice of the shaman in the Mairok ceremony—a shamanic cure similar to the "shaking tent" of indigenous North America.

7. Nonempowered individuals do, however, see spirits when they take on the form of common animals, but this is a sort of disguise and not their true "spirit appearance."

8. These differences may also have been the result of the men's greater fluency in Portuguese and my deficiencies in speaking Kayabi with the women. At the time, unfortunately, I did not ask the women if they too felt as though they were traveling to these other cosmological realms.

9. See Pollock 1996, 333, for a similar observation on the incidental role of the Kulina patient.

10. Travassos writes that Monkey-Leg also told her about how he first became empowered in the early 1980s (1984, 66). Although it is a paraphrased Portuguese translation, many of the episodes and much of the quoted speech are remarkably similar to those in his 1992 account.

11. Monkey-Leg also seems to imply that younger people are not destined to become empowered in the same way as he is. He refers to the "frog singing in the port" as "my frog" (je kutawa). This spirit frog would very likely have been dangerous for a nonempowered person. People are known to be pulled underwater to their deaths by these spirits when they happen upon them.

5. Headmen's Songs and the End of Mourning

1. With respect to the origin of this ritual, Kayabi people say that it came from Tujarare, the empowered figure of a previous epoch who created the Kayabi. He was the one who first taught his in-laws, the People-without-Understanding, how to hold a proper Jawosi.

2. The ritual during which these songs are sung resembles the war ceremonies of other Tupian peoples, such as the Arawete "strong beer festival," the Kagwahiv

"head-trophy dance," the Parakanã "Tobacco Festival," and the sixteenth-century Tumpinambá verbal dueling and execution of enemies (Fausto 1999; Kracke 1978, 45; Grünberg n.d. [1970], 127; Viveiros de Castro 1992, 133, 291).

3. See Jamieson 2000, 84, and Kracke 1978 for other Amazonian cases in which emotions have a similar corporeal seat.

4. Travassos also comments on the bias of audience members to interpret Jawosi subjectively (1993, 473).

5. Kayabi string teeth and wrap them with cotton to make thick necklaces that are worn during Jawosi.

6. When his uncle sang this song it may have referred to the Apiacá. According to many of the older men, songs about white animals refer to the Apiacá because they did not wear red annatto body paint like other peoples. The Kayabi also raised Apiacá children in the past. On the other hand, Waist's uncle may have inherited the song. In this case the "white oropendulas" may have referred to a different people of earlier import who could also be construed as "white" and who also lived in a mountainous region with another people who used red annatto body paint.

7. For the Tupian Arawete, dead enemies are also the origin of songs called *awi maraka*. The deceased enemy is called the "song teacher" (*marakã memo'o hã*) (Viveiros de Castro 1992, 240–43). Similarly among the Tupian Parakanã, songs are gifts from enemies appearing in dreams (Fausto 2001, 940).

8. See also Fausto 2001 for an example of how the performers of similar types of songs among the Parakanã are both killer and victim.

9. Because Kayabi take the name of enemies they have killed, uttering the "name of the victim" may also, in some cases, be uttering the name of the Kayabi killer.

10. When a full Jawosi is held, complete with a doll made of palm fiber that is shot with arrows on the last day, the owner of the Jawosi is given all of the arrows that were used. This was not part of Fire-of-the-Gods's Jawosi, and he did not, to my knowledge, receive any payment for organizing the event.

11. In the event of a baby's death, such a collective expression of mourning does not usually take place.

12. Affines in Jacaré's household were the first to begin the necessary daily activities, taking care of their even more grief-stricken relatives.

13. For the Arawete the victim is supposed to "feather the killer's head . . . and make him deranged" (Viveiros de Castro 1992, 245).

14. Viveiros de Castro has pointed out the connection between sharing a perspective and sharing bodily substances in the Amazon (1998).

15. This particular Jawosi song was unusual in that all agreed that it referred to an incident that happened long ago and was almost like an ancestor's story. Unlike the other songs, it used the tense or evidential *rakue*, meaning that the event took place in the distant past and was unexperienced by the speaker, much like the events of myth.

16. Viveiros de Castro has pointed out that in the Arawete "strong beer festival" the warrior-singer also "unifies and promotes non-differentiation" (1992, 117).

17. This song contains reported speech that employs the tense and evidential marker *ikue*, indicating that the events spoken about were in the experienced but distant past.

18. Descola (1996) has since modified this mode to include a third mode of understanding the social and ecological system, "protectionism."

19. Shamans do not share this fate: they go to reside with the Mait in the sky and live much as they did while on earth.

20. I am unsure to what extent nonparticipation in the first few Jawosi is considered to be standard etiquette for a mourner.

6. The Kayabi Life Cycle and Development of a Dialogic Self

1. In this way these Kayabi autobiographical narratives are very much like Kalapalo biographies (Basso 1995).

2. As Viveiros de Castro has commented, "The other is first and foremost an affine" (2001, 23).

3. Taking this argument further and synthesizing ethnographic material from throughout the Amazon, Viveiros de Castro (2001) argues that there is a more general Amazonian structure according to which affinity or alterity is the dominant principle over consanguinity or identity.

4. See also Viveiros de Castro 1992, 141, for a similar association among the Arawete.

5. Children who were at this stage of beginning to understand also began attending classes in Portuguese at the village school. In keeping with the emphasis on the child as a self-motivated agent, attendance was entirely optional and left up to the children themselves. Girls of this age were not prohibited from attending, but most of the younger students were boys.

6. Grünberg was told that upon first menstruation a girl would sit naked on a large rock that had been brought into her long house for one day. Then she would bathe and lie in her hammock for three more days (n.d. [1970], 136).

7. In the past, I was told, girls used to sing in solo upon receiving their new name. Currently, a girl's emergence is much less dramatic and passes without any public ceremony.

8. They too ate a diet of corn for the first few days of seclusion, but boys, unlike girls, ate black corn (*awasiũn*). Later they could not eat meat, fish, peanuts, beans, or manioc.

9. In the past, girls also wore earrings of toucan feathers. I saw only one girl with earrings during seclusion in 1992–93.

10. According to Grünberg, boys' mouths were tattooed with black at the beginning of seclusion, after a shaman sung for them and after they received a second name from their father. The last time tattooing occurred among people from the Peixes River area was well before 1964 (n.d. [1970], 136).

11. See also Londoño-Sulkin 2000, 172.

12. See Marriott 1976, 1990; Marriott and Inden 1977; and Lamb 2000 for the development of this notion in an Indian context. See Strathern 1988 for a discussion of this concept in a Melanesian context.

13. For the Tupian Guajá, the "self" similarly has a plural dimension, as they "believe in the simultaneous existence of multiple past versions of themselves . . . which lead independent existences in the *iwa*, their celestial home" (Cormier 2003, 90). The self or selves existing in the iwa, or sky domain, are the images of a person as represented in dreams, memories, and photos.

7. The Cosmic Management of Voices

1. The transformative nature of autobiography has been commented on by many (see Langness and Frank 1981, 93). While most stress how it can transform the narrator's own consciousness, here I emphasize how it transforms audience members.

2. The Masters of the Fish, the Karuat, are remnants of the first earth, which is now covered by water.

3. For a comparison of the Dreaming with another Tupian cosmology, that of the Guajá, see Cormier 2003, 190.

4. Leg-Bone said that he had seen footage from this film at a park post, though his son thought he must have been mistaken, as he did not think that the Mait possessed video cameras.

REFERENCES

Abu-Lughod, Lila. 1991. Writing against Culture. In *Recapturing Anthropology: Working in the Present*, ed. R. Fox, 137–62. Santa Fe: School of American Research Press.
———. 1993. *Writing Women's Worlds*. Berkeley: University of California Press.
Agostinho, Pedro. 1974. *Kwarip: Mito e Ritual no Alto Xingu*. São Paulo: EDUSP.
Albert, Bruce. 2000. O Ouro Canibal e a Queda do Céu. In *Pacificando o Branco*, ed. B. Albert and A. R. Ramos, 239–74. São Paulo: Editora UNESP.
Alès, Catherine. 2000. Anger as a Marker of Love: The Ethic of Conviviality among the Yanomami. In *The Anthropology of Love and Anger*, ed. J. Overing and A. Passes, 133–51. New York: Routledge.
Allport, Gordon. 1942. *The Use of Personal Documents in Psychological Science*. Social Science Research Council Bulletin 49. New York: The Council.
Bakhtin, M. M. 1986. *Speech Genres and Other Late Essays*. Austin: University of Texas Press.
———. 1993. *Problems with Dostoevsky's Poetics*. Trans. C. Emerson and M. Holquist. Austin: University of Texas Press.
Bakhtin, M. M., and P. N. Medvedev. 1978. *The Formal Method in Literary Scholarship*. Trans. A. J. Wehrle. Baltimore: Johns Hopkins University Press.
Basso, Ellen. 1973. *The Kalapalo Indians of Central Brazil*. New York: Holt, Rinehart, and Winston.
———. 1985. *A Musical View of the Universe*. Philadelphia: University of Pennsylvania Press.
———. 1995. *The Last Cannibals*. Austin: University of Texas Press.
———. 2001. Comments on "Ritual Communication and Linguistic Ideology" by Joel Robbins. *Current Anthropology* 42 (5): 600–601.
Basso, Keith. 1979. *Portraits of "The Whiteman."* Cambridge: Cambridge University Press.
Bastos, Rafael J. de M. 1984–85. O "Payemeramaraka" Kamayurá—uma Contribuição à Etnografia de Xamanismo do Alto Xingu. *Revista de Antropologia* 27–28: 139–77.
Bauman, Richard. 1986. *Story, Performance, and Event*. Cambridge: Cambridge University Press.
———. 1992. Contextualization, Tradition, and the Dialogic of Genres: Icelandic Legends of the Kraftaskáld. In *Rethinking Context*, ed. C. Goodwin and A. Duranti, 125–45. Cambridge: Cambridge University Press.

Bauman, Richard, and Charles Briggs. 1990. Poetics and Performance as Critical Perspectives on Language and Social Life. *Annual Review of Anthropology* 19: 59–88.

Bauman, Richard, and Joel Sherzer, eds. 1974. *Explorations in the Ethnography of Speaking.* Cambridge: Cambridge University Press.

Blommaert, Jan. 2001. Comments on "Ritual Communication and Linguistic Ideology" by Joel Robbins. *Current Anthropology* 42 (5): 601–2.

Bourdieu, Pierre. 1987. The Biographical Illusion. Working Papers and Proceedings of the Center for Psychosocial Studies 14, ed. R. Parmentier and G. Urban, 1–7. Chicago: Center for Psychosocial Studies.

Braudel, Fernand. 1972. *The Mediterranean.* Trans. S. Reynolds. New York: Harper and Row.

Brenneis, Donald. 1999. Identifying Practice: Comments on the Pragmatic Turn in Psychological Anthropology. *Ethos* 27: 530–35.

Briggs, Charles. 1993. Personal Sentiments and Polyphonic Voices in Warao Women's Ritual Wailing: Music and Poetics in a Critical and Collective Discourse. *American Anthropology* 95 (4): 929–57.

Briggs, Charles. 1996. The Politics of Discursive Authority in Research on the "Invention of Tradition." *Cultural Anthropology* 11 (4): 435–69.

Briggs, Charles, and Richard Bauman. 1992. Genre, Intertextuality, and Social Power. *Journal of Linguistic Anthropology* 2 (2): 131–72.

Brightman, Robert. 1995. Forget Culture: Replacement, Transcendence, Relexification. *Cultural Anthropologist* 10 (4): 509–46.

Brown, Michael. 1993. Facing the State, Facing the World: Amazonia's Native Leaders and the New Politics of Identity. *L'Homme* 33 (2–4): 311–30.

Brumble, H. David, III. 1988. *American Indian Autobiography.* Berkeley: University of California Press.

Burke, Kenneth. 1953. *A Rhetoric of Motives.* New York: Prentice-Hall.

Cain, Carole. 1991. Personal Stories: Identity Acquisition and Self-Understanding in Alcoholics Anonymous. *Ethos* 19: 210–53.

Carneiro da Cunha, Manuela, and Eduardo Viveiros de Castro. 1985. Vingança e Temporalidade: Os Tupinambá. *Journal de la Société des Américanistes* 71: 191–208.

Chagnon, Napoleon. 1997. *Yanomamö.* Fort Worth: Harcourt Brace College.

Civrieux, Marc de. 1980. Watuna: An Orinoco Creation Cycle. Ed. and trans. D. M. Guss. Berkeley: North Point.

Clastres, Pierre. [1972] 1998. *Chronicle of the Guayaki Indians.* New York: Zone.

——. [1974] 1987. *Society against the State.* New York: Zone Books.

Comaroff, Jean. 1985. *Body of Power, Spirit of Resistance.* Chicago: University of Chicago Press.

Comaroff, Jean, and John Comaroff. 1992. *Ethnography and the Historical Imagination.* Chicago: University of Chicago Press.

Conklin, Beth A. 1997. Body Paint, Feathers, and VCRs: Aesthetics and Authenticity in Amazonian Activism. *American Ethnologist* 24: 711–37.

———. 2001. *Consuming Grief*. Austin: University of Texas Press.

———. 2002. Shamans versus Pirates in the Amazonian Treasure Chest. *American Anthropologist* 104 (4): 1050–61.

Conklin, Beth A., and Laura Graham. 1995. The Shifting Middle Ground: Amazonian Indians and Eco-Politics. *American Anthropologist* 97 (4): 695–710.

Cormier, Loretta. 2003. *Kinship with Monkeys: The Guajá Foragers of Eastern Amazonia*. New York: Columbia University Press.

Cowell, Adrian. 1974. *The Tribe That Hides from Man*. New York: Stein and Day.

Crapanzano, Vincent. 1980. *Tuhami*. Chicago: University of Chicago Press.

———. 1984. Life-Histories. *American Anthropologist* 86 (4): 953–59.

———. 1996. "Self"-Centering Narratives. In *Natural Histories of Discourse*, ed. M. Silverstein and G. Urban, 106–27. Chicago: University of Chicago Press.

Davis, Shelton H. 1980. *Victims of the Miracle*. Cambridge: Cambridge University Press.

Descola, Philippe. 1992. Societies of Nature and the Nature of Society. In *Conceptualizing Society*, ed. A. Kuper, 107–26. London: Routledge.

———. 1996. Constructing Natures: Symbolic Ecology and Social Practice. In *Nature and Society*, ed. P. Descola and G. Pálsson, 82–102. New York: Routledge.

Dobson, Rose. 1988. *Gramática Práctica com Exercícios de Língua Kayabí*. Cuiabá, Mato Grosso, Brazil: Summer Institute of Linguistics.

Dollard, John. 1935. *Criteria for the Life History*. New Haven: Yale University Press.

Drummond, Lee. 1980. The Cultural Continuum: A Theory of Intersystems. *Man* (n.s.) 15 (2): 352–74.

DuBois, Cora. 1944. *The People of Alor: The Social-Psychological Study of an East Indian Island*. New York: Harcourt, Brace.

Dussart, Françoise. 2000. *The Politics of Ritual in an Aboriginal Settlement*. Washington DC: Smithsonian Institution Press.

Dyk, Walter. 1938. *Son of Old Man Hat: A Navaho Autobiography*. New York: Harcourt, Brace.

Erikson, Erik. 1968. Identity, Psychosocial. In *International Encyclopedia of the Social Sciences*, ed. D. L. Sills, 7:61–65. New York: Macmillan and Free Press.

Fausto, Carlos. 1999. Of Enemies and Pets: Warfare and Shamanism in Amazônia. *American Ethnologist* 26 (4): 933–56.

———. 2001. *Inimigos Fiéis: História, Guerra e Xamanismo na Amazônia*. São Paulo: Editora da Universidade de São Paulo.

Ferreira, Mariana Kawall Leal. 1992. Da Origem dos Homens a Conquista da Escrita: Um Estudo Sobre Povos Indígenas e Educação Escolar no Brasil. MA thesis, University of São Paulo.

———. 1997. When 1 + 1 = 2: Making Mathematics in Central Brazil. *American Ethnologist* 24 (1): 132–47.

Ferreira, Manoel Rodrigues. 1983. *Aspectos do Alto Xingu e a Vera Cruz*. São Paulo: Nobel Secretaria de Estado da Cultura.

Fischer, Michael. 1986. Ethnicity and the Post-Modern Arts of Memory. In *Writing Cul-*

ture, ed. J. Clifford and G. E. Marcus, 194–233. Berkeley: University of California Press.

Fisher, William H. 1994. Megadevelopment, Environmentalism, and Resistance: The Institutional Context of Kayapó Indigenous Politics in Central Brazil. *Human Organization* 53 (3): 220–32.

———. 2000. *Rain Forest Exchanges*. Washington DC: Smithsonian Institution Press.

Fogelson, Raymond. 1989. The Ethnohistory of Events and Nonevents. *Ethnohistory* 36 (2): 133–47.

———. 1998. Perspectives on Native American Identity. In *Studying Native America*, ed. R. Thornton, 40–59. Madison: University of Wisconsin Press.

Foster, Robert. 1995. *Social Reproduction and History in Melanesia*. Cambridge: Cambridge University Press.

Gallois, Dominique Tilkin. 1988. O Movimento na Cosmologia Waiàpi: Criação, Expansão e Transformação do Universo. PhD diss., University of São Paulo.

Geertz, Clifford. 1973. *The Interpretation of Cultures*. New York: Basic Books.

Goffman, Erving. 1959. *The Presentation of Self in Everyday Life*. New York: Doubleday Anchor Books.

———. 1981. *Forms of Talk*. Philadelphia: University of Pennsylvania Press.

Gow, David. 1997. O Parentesco como Conciência Humana: O Caso dos Piro. *Mana* 3 (2): 39–65.

———. 2000. Helpless—The Affective Preconditions of Piro Social Life. In *The Anthropology of Love and Anger*, ed. J. Overing and A. Passes, 46–63. New York: Routledge.

Gow, David, and Joanne Rappaport. 2002. The Indigenous Public Voice. In *Indigenous Movements, Self-Representation, and the State in Latin America*, ed. K. B. Warren and J. E. Jackson, 47–80. Austin: University of Texas Press.

Graham, Laura. 1986. Three Modes of Shavante Vocal Expression: Wailing, Collective Singing, and Political Oratory. In *Native South American Discourse*, ed. J. Sherzer and G. Urban, 83–118. New York: Mouton de Gruyter.

———. 1993. A Public Sphere in Amazonia? The Depersonalized Collaborative Construction of Discourse in Xavante. *American Ethnologist* 20 (4): 717–41.

———. 1995. *Performing Dreams*. Austin: University of Texas Press.

———. 2002. How Should an Indian Speak? Amazonian Indians and the Symbolic Politics of Language in the Global Public Sphere. In *Indigenous Movements, Self-Representation, and the State in Latin America*, ed. K. B. Warren and J. E. Jackson, 181–228. Austin: University of Texas Press.

Grünberg, Georg. n.d. [1970]. Contribuições para a Etnologia dos Kayabi do Brasil Central. Trans. E. Wenzel. São Paulo: Centro Ecumênico de Documentação e Informação. Manuscript. (Originally published as Beiträge zur ethnographie der Kayabí zentralbrasiliens, *Archiv für Völkerkunde* 24: 21–186.)

Hallowell, A. I. 1955. *Culture and Experience*. Philadelphia: University of Pennsylvania Press.

Hanbury-Tenison, Robin. 1973. *A Question of Survival for the Indians of Brazil*. New York: Angus and Robertson.

Hanks, William. 1987. Discourse Genres in a Theory of Practice. *American Ethnologist* 14 (4): 668–92.

———. 1996. Exorcism and the Description of Participant Roles. In *Natural Histories of Discourse*, ed. M. Silverstein and G. Urban, 160–200. Chicago: University of Chicago Press.

Harris, Grace. 1989. Concepts of Individual, Self, and Person in Description and Analysis. *American Anthropologist* 91 (3): 599–612.

Hemming, John. 2003. *Die If You Must: Brazilian Indians in the Twentieth Century*. Oxford: Macmillan.

Hendricks, Janet Wall. 1992. Symbolic Counterhegemony among the Ecuadorian Shuar. In *Nation-States and Indians in Latin America*, ed. G. Urban and J. Sherzer, 53–71. Austin: University of Texas Press.

———. 1993. *To Drink of Death: The Narrative of a Shuar Warrior*. Tucson: University of Arizona Press.

Herdt, Gilbert. [1981] 1994. *Guardians of the Flutes*. Chicago: University of Chicago Press.

Hill, Jane. 1995. The Voices of Don Gabriel: Responsibility and Self in a Modern Mexicano Narrative. In *The Dialogic Emergence of Culture*, ed. D. Tedlock and B. Mannheim, 97–147. Urbana: University of Illinois Press.

Hill, Jonathan. 1993. *Keepers of the Sacred Chants*. Tucson: University of Arizona Press.

Holston, James. 1989. *The Modernist City*. Chicago: University of Chicago Press.

Hugh-Jones, Stephen. 1979. *The Palm and the Pleiades*. Cambridge: Cambridge University Press.

Hymes, Dell. 1981. *"In Vain I Tried to Tell You": Essays in Native American Ethnopoetics*. Philadelphia: University of Pennsylvania Press.

Jackson, Jean. 1989. Is There a Way to Talk about Making Culture without Making Enemies? *Dialectical Anthropology* 14 (20): 127–43.

———. 1991. Being and Becoming an Indian in the Vaupés. In *Nation-States and Indians in Latin America*, ed. G. Urban and J. Sherzer, 131–55. Austin: University of Texas Press.

———. 1995a. Culture, Genuine and Spurious: The Politics of Indianness in the Vaupés, Colombia. *American Ethnologist* 22 (1): 3–27.

———. 1995b. Preserving Indian Culture: Shaman Schools and Ethno-Education in the Vaupés, Colombia. *Cultural Anthropology* 10 (3): 302–29.

Jakobsen, Roman. 1971. *Selected Writings*. The Hague: Mouton.

Jamieson, Mark. 2000. Compassion, Anger, and Broken Hearts: Ontology and the Role of Language in the Miskitu Lament. In *The Anthropology of Love and Anger*, ed. J. Overing and A. Passes, 82–96. New York: Routledge.

Kelly, John D., and Martha Kaplan. 1990. History, Structure, and Ritual. *Annual Review of Anthropology* 19: 119–50.

Kluckhohn, Clyde. 1939. Theoretical Basis for an Empirical Method for Studying the Acquisition of Culture by Individuals. *Man* 39: 98–103.

———. 1945. The Personal Document in Anthropological Science. In *The Use of Personal Documents in History, Anthropology, and Sociology*, ed. L. Gottschalk et al., 78–173. Social Science Research Council Bulletin 53. New York: The Council.

———. 1949. Needed Refinements in the Biographical Approach. In *Culture and Personality*, ed. S. Sargent and M. Smith, 75–92. New York: Viking Fund.

Kondo, Dorinne K. 1990. *Crafting Selves: Power, Gender, and Discourses of Identity in a Japanese Workplace*. Chicago: University of Chicago Press.

Kracke, Waud. 1978. *Force and Persuasion*. Chicago: University of Chicago Press.

———. 1981a. Kagwahiv Mourning I: Dreams of a Bereaved Father. *Ethos* 9 (4): 258–75.

———. 1981b. Don't Let the Piranha Bite Your Liver. In *Working Papers on South American Indians*, ed. K. Kensinger, 92–142. Bennington VT: Bennington College.

———. 1987. Myths in Dreams, Thought in Images: An Amazonian Contribution to the Psychoanalytic Theory of Primary Process. In *Dreaming: Anthropological and Psychological Interpretations*, ed. B. Tedlock, 31–54. New York: Cambridge University Press.

Krupat, Arnold. 1985. *For Those Who Come After: A Study of Native American Autobiography*. Berkeley: University of California Press.

———. 1992. *Ethnocriticism: Ethnography, History, Literature*. Berkeley: University of California Press.

———. 1994. *Native American Autobiography*. Madison: University of Wisconsin Press.

Lamb, Sarah. 2000. *White Saris and Sweet Mangoes*. Berkeley: University of California Press.

Lan, David. 1985. *Guns and Rain*. Berkeley: University of California Press.

Langness, L. L., and Gelya Frank. 1981. *Lives: An Anthropological Approach to Biography*. Novato CA: Chandler and Sharp.

Las Casas, Roberto Décio. 1964. Indios e Brasileiros no Vale do Rio Tapajós. *Boletim do Museu Paraense Emílio Goeldi* 23: 1–31.

Léry, Jean de. 1990. *History of a Voyage to the Land of Brazil*. Trans. J. Whatley. Berkeley: University of California Press.

Lévi-Strauss, Claude. [1955] 1975. *Tristes Tropiques*. Trans. J. and D. Weightman. New York: Atheneum.

———. 1967. The Social and Psychological Aspects of Chieftainship in a Primitive Tribe: The Nambikuara of Northwestern Mato Grosso. In *Comparative Political Systems*, ed. R. Cohen and J. Middleton, 45–62. Garden City NY: Natural History Press.

Lewis, Oscar. 1961. *The Children of Sanchez*. New York: Random House.

Lizot, Jacques. 1991. *Tales of the Yanomami*. Cambridge: Cambridge University Press.

Londoño-Sulkin, Carlos David. 2000. "Though It Comes as Evil, I Embrace It as Good": Social Sensibilities and the Transformation of Malignant Agency among the

Muinane. In *The Anthropology of Love and Anger*, ed. J. Overing and A. Passes, 170–86. New York: Routledge.

Lorrain, Claire. 2000. Cosmic Reproduction: Economics and Politics among the Kulina of Southwest Amazonia. *Journal of the Royal Anthropological Institute* 6:293–310.

Lutz, Catherine, and Geoffrey White. 1986. The Anthropology of Emotions. *Annual Review of Anthropology* 15: 405–36.

Manchete. 1992a. Earth Summit '92. Special Issue, May, 32–35.

Manchete. 1992b. Heading toward the Third Millennium. Special Issue, May, 84–89.

Marriott, McKim. 1976. Hindu Transactions: Diversity without Dualism. In *Transaction and Meaning: Directions in the Anthropology of Exchange and Symbolic Behavior*, ed. B. Kapferer, 109–42. Philadelphia: Institute for the Study of Human Issues.

———. 1990. Constructing an Indian Ethnopsychology. In *India through Hingu Categories*, ed. M. Marriott, 1–39. New Delhi: Sage.

Marriott, McKim, and Ronald Inden. 1977. Toward an Ethnosociology of South Asian Caste Systems. In *The New Wind: Changing Identities in South Asia*, ed. K. David, 227–38. The Hague: Mouton.

Maybury-Lewis, David. 1988. *The Savage and the Innocent*. Boston: Beacon Press.

———. 1991. Becoming Indian in Lowland South America. In *Nation-States and Indians in Latin America*, ed. G. Urban and J. Sherzer, 207–35. Austin: University of Texas Press.

Mead, George Herbert. [1934] 1977. *On Social Psychology*. Ed. Anselm Strauss. Chicago: University of Chicago Press.

Merlan, Francesca, and Alan Rumsey. 1991. *Ku Waru*. Cambridge: Cambridge University Press.

Miller, Peggy, and Barbara Byhouwer Moore. 1989. Narrative Conjunctions of Caregiver and Child. *Ethos* 17 (4): 43–64.

Miller, Peggy, Randolph Potts, Heidi Fung, Lisa Hoogstra, and Judy Mintz. 1990. Narrative Practices and the Social Construction of Self in Childhood. *American Ethnologist* 17 (2): 292–311.

Mintz, Sidney. 1960. *Workers in the Cane: A Puerto Rican Life History*. Yale Caribbean Series, vol. 2. New Haven: Yale University Press.

Moore, Robert. 1993. Performance Form and the Voices of Five Characters in Five Versions of the Wasco Coyote Cycle. In *Reflexive Language: Reported Speech and Metapragmatics*, ed. J. A. Lucy, 213–40. Cambridge: Cambridge University Press.

Moore, Sally F., and Barbara G. Myerhoff. 1977. *Secular Ritual*. Amsterdam: Van Gorcum, Assen.

Müller, Regina. N.d. Maraká, Ritual Xamanístico dos Asuriní do Xingu. Manuscript.

———. 1990. *Os Asuriní do Xingu*. Campinas: Editora Unicamp.

Murphy, Robert. 1978. *Headhunter's Heritage*. New York: Octagon Books.

Myers, Fred. 1986. *Pintupi Country, Pintupi Self*. Washington DC: Smithsonian Institution Press.

Nabokov, Isabelle. 2000. *Religion against the Self*. Oxford: Oxford University Press.

Nimuendajú, Curt. 1948. The Cayabi, Tapanyuna, and Apiaca. In *Handbook of South American Indians*, ed. J. Steward, 307–20. Washington DC: U.S. Government Printing Office.

Oakdale, Suzanne. 1996. The Power of Experience: Agency and Identity in Kayabi Healing and Political Process in the Xingu Indigenous Park. PhD diss., University of Chicago.

————. 2001. History and Forgetting in an Indigenous Community. *Ethnohistory* 48 (3): 381–401.

————. 2002. Creating a Continuity between Self and Other: First-Person Narration in an Amazonian Context. *Ethos* 30 (1–2): 158–75.

————. 2004. The Culture-Conscious Brazilian Indian: Representing and Reworking Indianness in Kayabi Political Discourse. *American Ethnologist* 31 (1): 60–76.

Obeyesekere, Gananath. 1990. *The Work of Culture*. Chicago: University of Chicago Press.

Ochs, E., R. Smith, and C. Taylor. 1989. Dinner Narratives as Detective Stories. *Cultural Dynamics* 2: 238–57.

Ortner, Sherry. 1978. *Sherpas through Their Rituals*. Cambridge: Cambridge University Press.

————. 1996. *Making Gender: The Politics and Erotics of Culture*. Boston: Beacon.

————. 1999. Thick Resistance: Death and the Cultural Construction of Agency in Himalayan Mountaineering. In *The Fate of "Culture": Geertz and Beyond*, ed. S. Ortner, 136–63. Berkeley: University of California Press.

Overing, Joanna, and Alan Passes. 2000. Introduction: Conviviality and the Opening Up of Amazonian Anthropology. In *The Anthropology of Love and Anger*, 1–30. New York: Routledge.

Peacock, James L. 1978. *Muslim Puritans: The Reformist Psychology in Southeast Asian Islam*. Berkeley: University of California Press.

Peacock, James L., and Dorothy C. Holland. 1993. The Narrated Self: Life Stories in Process. *Ethos* 21 (4): 367–83.

Piot, Charles. 1999. *Remotely Global*. Chicago: University of Chicago Press.

Pollock, Donald. 1992. Culina Shamanism. In *Portals of Power: Shamanism in South America*, ed. E. J. Langdon and G. Bear, 25–40. Albuquerque: University of New Mexico Press.

————. 1993. Death and the Afterdeath among the Kulina. *Latin American Anthropology Review* 5 (2): 61–64.

————. 1996. Personhood and Illness among the Kulina. *Medical Anthropological Quarterly* 10 (3): 319–41.

Price, David. 1981. Nabiquara Leadership. *American Anthropologist* 8: 686–708.

Pyrineus de Sousa, Antonio. 1916. *Exploração do Rio Paranatinga*. Publicação 34. Rio de Janeiro: Commissão de Linhas Telegraphicas Estrategicas de Matto-Grosso ao Amazonas.

Radin, Paul. 1920. *The Autobiography of a Winnebago Indian*. Berkeley: University of California Press.

Ramos, Alcida R. 1984. Frontier Expansion and Indian Peoples in the Brazilian Amazon. In *Frontier Expansion in Amazonia*, ed. M. Schmink and C. H. Wood, 83–104. Gainesville: University of Florida Press.

———. 1988. Indian Voices: Contact Experienced and Expressed. In *Rethinking History and Myth*, ed. J. Hill, 214–34. Urbana: University of Illinois Press.

———. 1998. *Indigenism: Ethnic Politics in Brazil*. Madison: University of Wisconsin Press.

Ribeiro, Berta. 1979. *Diário do Xingu*. Rio de Janeiro: Paz e Terra.

Ribeiro, Darcy. 1970. *Os Índios e a Civilização*. São Paulo: Edições Loyola.

Rodríguez, Sylvia. 1996. *The Matachines Dance*. Albuquerque: University of New Mexico Press.

Rosaldo, Renato. 1989. *Culture and Truth: The Remaking of Social Analysis*. Boston: Beacon.

Rosengren, Dan. 1987. *In the Eyes of the Beholder: Leadership and the Social Construction of Power and Dominance among the Matsigenka of the Peruvian Amazon*. Göteborg: Göteborgs Etnografiska Museum.

Rubenstein, Steven. 2002. *Alejandro Tsakimp: A Shuar Healer in the Margins of History*. Lincoln: University of Nebraska Press.

Sammons, Kay, and Joel Sherzer. 2000. *Translating Native Latin American Verbal Art*. Washington DC: Smithsonian Institution Press.

Santos Granero, Fernando. 1986. Power, Ideology, and the Ritual of Production in Lowland South America. Man 21: 657–79.

———. 1993. From Prisioner of the Group to Darling of the Gods. L'Homme 33: 213–30.

Schmidt, Max. 1942a. Resultados da minha Expedição Bienal a Mato-Grosso. Boletin do Museu Nacional 16–17: 241–85.

———. 1942b. Los Kayabís en Mato-Grosso (Brasil). Revista de la Sociedad Scientifica del Paraguay 5 (6): 1–34.

Schwartzman, Stephan. 1988. The Panara of the Xingu National Park: The Transformation of a Society. PhD diss., University of Chicago.

Seeger, Anthony. 1986. Oratory Is Spoken, Myth Is Told, and Song Is Sung, but They Are All Music to My Ears. In *Native South American Discourse*, ed. J. Sherzer and G. Urban, 59–82. New York: Mouton de Gruyter.

Seeger, Anthony, Roberto da Matta, and E. B. Viveiros de Castro. 1979. A Constução da Pessoa nas Sociedades Indígenas Brasileiras. Boletim do Museu Nacional 32: 2–19.

Serra, Olympio. 1979. The Xingu Park as It Is. Cultural Survival, Special Report—Brazil, 1: 59–68.

Sherzer, Joel. 1983. *Kuna Ways of Speaking*. Austin: University of Texas Press.

Shostak, Marjorie. 1981. *Nisa: The Life and Words of a !Kung Woman*. Cambridge: Harvard University Press.

SIL. 1991. Arquivo de Textos Indígenas. Brasília D.F.: SIL.

Silverstein, Michael. 1993. Metapragmatic Discourse and Metapragmatic Function. In *Reflexive Language*, ed. J. A. Lucy, 33–58. Cambridge: Cambridge University Press.

————. 1996. The Secret Life of Texts. In *The Natural History of Discourse*, ed. M. Silverstein and G. Urban, 81–105. Chicago: University of Chicago Press.

————. 1999. NIMBY Goes Linguistic: Conflicted "Voicings" from the Culture of Local Language Communities. Paper presented at the Department of English/Discourse Studies, Texas A&M University, March 12.

————. 2001. Comments on "Ritual Communication and Linguistic Ideology" by Joel Robbins. *Current Anthropology* 42 (5): 606–8.

Silverstein, Michael, and Greg Urban, eds. 1996. *The Natural History of Discourse.* Chicago: University of Chicago Press.

Simões, Mario. 1963. Os "Txikão" e Outros Tribos Marginais do Alto Xingu. *Revista do Museu Paulista* 19: 76–104.

Singer, Milton. 1984. *Man's Glassy Essence: Explorations in Semiotic Anthropology.* Bloomington: Indiana University Press.

Souza Lima, Antonio de. 1992. On Indigenism and Nationality in Brazil. In *Nation-States and Indians in Latin America*, ed. G. Urban and J. Sherzer, 236–58. Austin: University of Texas Press.

Sting, and Jean-Pierre Dutilleux. 1989. *Jungle Stories: The Fight for the Amazon.* London: Barrie and Jenkins.

Strathern, Marilyn. 1988. *The Gender of the Gift.* Berkeley: University of California Press.

Swann, Brian, and Arnold Krupat. 1987. Introduction. In *I Tell You Now*, ed. B. Swann and A. Krupat, ix–xv. Lincoln: University of Nebraska Press.

Tambiah, Stanley J. 1985. *Culture, Thought, and Social Action.* Cambridge: Harvard University Press.

Taussig, Michael. 1980. *Shamanism, Colonialism, and the Wildman: A Study in Terror and Healing.* Chicago: University of Chicago Press.

Taylor, Anne-Christine. 1993. Remembering to Forget: Identity, Mourning, and Memory among the Jivaro. *Man* 28 (4): 653–78.

————. 1996. The Soul's Body and Its States: An Amazonian Perspective on the Nature of Being Human. *Journal of the Royal Anthropological Institute* 2 (2): 201–15.

————. 2001. Wives, Pets, and Affines: Marriage among the Jivaro. In *Beyond the Visible and the Material*, ed. L. Rival and N. Whitehead, 45–56. Oxford: Oxford University Press.

Tedlock, Dennis. 1983. *The Spoken Word and the Work of Interpretation.* Philadelphia: University of Pennsylvania Press.

Toren, Christina. 2001. Comments on "Ritual Communication and Linguistic Ideology" by Joel Robbins. *Current Anthropology* 42 (5): 608–9.

Travassos, Elizabeth. 1984. Xamanism e Música entre os Kayabi. MA thesis, Universidade Federal do Rio de Janeiro.

————. 1993. A Tradiçaõ Guerreira nas Narrativas e nos Cantos Caiabis. In *Karl Von den Steinen: Um Século de Antropologia no Xingu*, ed. V. Penteado Coelho, 447–84. São Paulo: Editora da Universidade de São Paulo.

Tsing, Anna Lowenhaupt. 1993. *In the Realm of the Diamond Queen.* Princeton: Princeton University Press.

Turner, Terence. 1988a. History, Myth, and Social Consciousness among the Kayapó of Central Brazil. In *Rethinking History and Myth,* ed. J. D. Hill, 195–213. Urbana: University of Illinois Press.

———. 1988b. Commentary: Ethno-Ethnohistory: Myth and History in Native South American Representations of Contact with Western Society. In *Rethinking History and Myth,* ed. J. D. Hill, 235–81. Urbana: University of Illinois Press.

———. 1991. Representing, Resisting, Rethinking: Historical Transformations of Kayapo Culture and Anthropological Consciousness. In *Colonial Situations,* ed. G. Stocking, 285–313. Madison: University of Wisconsin Press.

———. 1992. Defiant Images: The Kayapo Appropriation of Video. *Anthropology Today* 8 (6): 5–16.

———. 1995a. Social Body and Embodied Subject: Bodiliness, Subjectivity, and Sociality among the Kayapo. *Cultural Anthropology* 10 (2): 143–70.

———. 1995b. An Indigenous People's Struggle for Socially Equitable and Ecologically Sustainable Production. *Journal of Latin American Anthropology* 1 (1): 98–121.

———. 2000. Indigenous Rights, Environmental Protection, and the Struggle over Forest Resources in the Amazon: The Case of the Brazilian Kayapo. In *Earth, Air, Fire, Water: Humanistic Studies of the Environment,* ed. J. Ker Conway, K. Keniston, and L. Marx, 145–69. Amherst: University of Massachusetts Press.

Turner, Victor. [1967] 1982. *The Forest of Symbols.* Ithaca: Cornell University Press.

———. 1969. *The Ritual Process.* New York: Aldine de Gruyter.

Urban, Greg. 1989. The "I" of Discourse. In *Semiotics, Self, and Society,* ed. B. Lee and G. Urban, 27–51. Berlin: Mouton de Gruyter.

———. 1991. *A Discourse-Centered Approach to Culture.* Austin: University of Texas Press.

———. 1992. The Semiotics of State-Indian Linguistic Relationships: Peru, Paraguay, and Brazil. In *Nation-States and Indians in Latin America,* ed. G. Urban and J. Sherzer, 307–30. Austin: University of Texas Press.

Urban, Greg, and Joel Sherzer, eds. 1992. *Nation-States and Indians in Latin America.* Austin: University of Texas Press.

Veja. 1992. Cacique Amigo da Onça. June 17.

Villas Boas, Orlando, and Cláudio Villas Boas. 1973. *Xingu: The Indians, Their Myths.* New York: Farrar, Straus, and Giroux.

Viveiros de Castro, Eduardo. 1979. When the Mask Is Removed, What Is the Truth about the Xingu National Park? *Cultural Survival,* Special Report—Brazil, 1:56–59.

———. 1992. *From the Enemy's Point of View.* Chicago: University of Chicago Press.

———. 1998. Cosmological Deixis and Amerindian Perspectivism. *Journal of the Royal Anthropological Institute* 4 (3): 469–88.

———. 2001. GUT Feelings about Amazonia: Potential Affinity and the Construction of Sociality. In *Beyond the Visible and the Material,* ed. L. Rival and N. Whitehead, 19–44. Oxford: Oxford University Press.

Voloshinov, V. N. 1987. *Freudianism: A Critical Sketch.* Trans. I. R. Titunik. Ed. I. R. Titunik and N. H. Bruss. Bloomington: University of Indiana Press.

von den Steinen, Karl. 1942. *O Brasil Central.* Trans. C. B. Cannabrava. São Paulo: Companhia Editora Nacional.

Wagley, Charles. 1977 [1983]. *Welcome of Tears.* Prospect Heights IL: Waveland.

Watson, Lawrence, and Maria-Barbara Watson-Franke. 1985. *Interpreting Life Histories: An Anthropological Inquiry.* New Brunswick: Rutgers University Press.

Weintraub, Karl. 1974. Autobiography and Historical Consciousness. *Critical Inquiry* 1 (1): 821–48.

Whitehead, Neil. 2003. *Histories and Historicities in Amazonia.* Lincoln: University of Nebraska Press.

Whitten, Norman. 1976. *Sacha Runa: Ethnicity and Adaptation of Ecuadorian Jungle Quicha.* Urbana: University of Illinois Press.

———. 1981. *Cultural Transformations and Ethnicity in Modern Ecuador.* Urbana: University of Illinois Press.

Whorf, Benjamin Lee. 1979. *Language, Thought, and Reality.* Ed. J. B. Caroll. Cambridge: MIT Press.

Wong, Hertha Dawn. 1992. *Sending My Heart Back across the Years: Tradition and Innovation in Native American Autobiography.* New York: Oxford University Press.

Wortham, Stanton. 1994. *Acting Out Participant Examples in the Classroom.* Amsterdam: John Benjamins.

Wright, Robin. 1998. *Cosmos, Self, and History in Baniwa Religion.* Austin: University of Texas Press.

SOURCE ACKNOWLEDGMENTS

Portions of the introduction, chapter 1, and chapter 6 previously appeared as "Creating a Continuity between Self and Other: First-Person Narration in an Amazonian Ritual Context," in *Ethos* 30, no. 1–2 (March 2002): 158–75, reprinted by permission.

Portions of chapters 2 and 4 are reprinted from "The Culture-Conscious Brazilian Indian: Representing and Reworking Indianness in Kayabi Political Discourse," in *American Ethnologist* 31, no. 1 (2004): 60–75, with permission of the American Anthropological Association. © 2004 American Anthropological Association.

Portions of chapter 6 previously appeared as "History and Forgetting in an Indigenous Amazonian Community," in *Ethnohistory* 48, no. 3 (Summer 2001): 381–402. Reprinted by permission.

INDEX